Practical Suggestions:

- Invite your catechumen or candidate, along with your companion's family, to sit with you during the liturgy.

- Introduce your family and your friends to your companion.

- When you see your catechumen or candidate, smile and acknowledge his or her presence.

- Call your companion by name!

- Go through the parish bulletin with your companion and explain what the various activities listed are about.

- Introduce your companion to some of the people whose names are in the bulletin.

- Take your companion on a walk around the parish grounds or plant. Familiarize your companion with where things are and what activities take place there.

- Actively respond to questions your companion asks about the Church or parish life.

Can my children be baptized (or received) into the Church when I am baptized (or received) into the Church?

The Catholic Church prepares school-age children for Baptism, Confirmation, and Eucharist in a process similar to the one adults take part in. Children have a sponsor and participate in the same stages and celebrations that adults participate in. In most parishes, special age-appropriate sessions are available for children. Children who have not yet reached school age may be baptized; or, if already baptized, they may be received into the Church along with their parents without the need for a special process.

I (or my spouse) have been married before. Does that present a problem to my becoming a Catholic?

Ordinarily the Catholic Church assumes that a person's first marriage is a valid marriage. If you (or your spouse or your fiancee) have been previously married, it is important to talk your situation over with someone who is informed of particular marriage laws of the Church. Every marriage situation is different.

Sometimes an annulment may be necessary. The annulment is a formal procedure of the Catholic Church. It looks for evidence that some essential dimension of a valid Christian marriage was missing from the beginning. It does not say that a civil marriage never occurred, or the children born of that marriage are illegitimate. Because the annulment process takes some time to complete, begin talking with a pastoral minister as soon as you sense you are truly drawn to the Catholic Church.

? I am engaged to a Catholic. Can I become Catholic in time for our wedding?

Maybe yes, and maybe no. The journey to baptism or full membership in the Catholic Church takes time. The timeline of a faith journey does not always coincide with that of a wedding.

If you are engaged, the deepening of your relationship with your fiancee and the preparation for your wedding takes time. The deepening of your relationship with the Church community and the preparation for your baptism or full membership in that community also takes time. The faith journey to become Catholic takes time and energy. It may or may not be possible for both journeys to arrive at a particular calendar date at the same time.

For example, the Catholic Church suggests that a person spend a year in the Catechumenate to prepare for baptism or full initiation into the Church. The sacramental celebration of this initiation occurs once yearly at the Easter Vigil. Even if you begin inquiring about the Catholic faith a year before your marriage, your baptism may not occur before the date of your wedding. The Church wants to work with you. But sometimes working such a conflict out is beyond the Church's control—and not what is ultimately best for you. At times it is helpful to wait until after marriage to begin your inquiry into becoming Catholic to be sure this desire is out of your personal conviction. Becoming Catholic should not come from the pressure of an impending wedding.

SECOND READING

1 Thessalonians 4:13–18 or 4:13–14

A reading from the first Letter of Saint Paul to the Thessalonians

(Include bracketed text for Long Form)

We do not want you to be unaware, brothers and sisters, about those who have fallen asleep, so that you may not grieve like the rest, who have no hope. For if we believe that Jesus died and rose, so too will God, through Jesus, bring with him those who have fallen asleep. [Indeed, we tell you this, on the word of the Lord, that we who are alive, who are left until the coming of the Lord, will surely not precede those who have fallen asleep. For the Lord himself, with a word of command, with the voice of an archangel and with the trumpet of God, will come down from heaven, and the dead in Christ will rise first. Then we who are alive, who are left, will be caught up together with them in the clouds to meet the Lord in the air. Thus we shall always be with the Lord. Therefore, console one another with these words.]

The word of the Lord. **Thanks be to God.**

STAND

GOSPEL ACCLAMATION

Matthew 24:42a, 44

(R&A 141)

(Omit if not sung)

℟. Al - le - lu - ia! Al - le - lu - ia! Al - le - lu - ia!

▸ Stay awake and be ready!
For you do not know on what day your Lord will come. ℟.

GOSPEL READING

Matthew 25:1–13

The Lord be with you.
And also with you.
A reading from the holy Gospel according to Matthew
Glory to you, Lord.

Jesus told his disciples this parable: "The kingdom of heaven will be like ten virgins who took their lamps and went out to meet the bridegroom. Five of them were foolish and five were wise. The foolish ones, when taking their lamps, brought no oil with them, but the wise brought flasks of oil with their lamps. Since the bridegroom was long delayed, they all became drowsy and fell asleep. At midnight, there was a cry, 'Behold, the bridegroom! Come out to meet him!' Then all those virgins got up and trimmed their lamps. The foolish ones said to the wise, 'Give

NOVEMBER 7
32ND SUNDAY IN ORDINARY TIME

FIRST READING

Wisdom 6:12-

A reading from the Book of Wisdom

Resplendent and unfading is wisdom,
and she is readily perceived by those who love her,
and found by those who seek her.
She hastens to make herself known in anticipation of their desire;
whoever watches for her at dawn shall not be disappointed,
for he shall find her sitting by his gate.

For taking thought of wisdom
perfection of prudence
and whoever for her sake k·
vigil
shall quickly be free from c·
because she makes her ow
rounds, seeking those of her,
and graciously appears to
the ways,
and meets them with all so

The word of the Lord. **Thanks be to God.**

RESPONSORIAL PSALM

Psalm 63:2, 3–4,

(R&A 140)

℟. My soul is thirst-ing for you, O Lord my ___ G

▶ O God, you are my God whom I seek;
for you my flesh pines and my soul thirsts
like the earth, parched, lifeless and without water. ℟.

▶ Thus have I gazed toward you in the sanctuary
to see your power and your glory,
for your kindness is a greater good than life;
my lips shall glorify you. ℟.

▶ Thus will I bless you while I live;
lifting up my hands, I will call upon your name.
As with the riches of a banquet shall my soul be satisfied,
and with exultant lips my mouth shall praise you. ℟.

▶ I will remember you upon my couch,
and through the night-watches I will meditate on you:
you are my help,
and in the shadow of your wings I shout for joy. ℟.

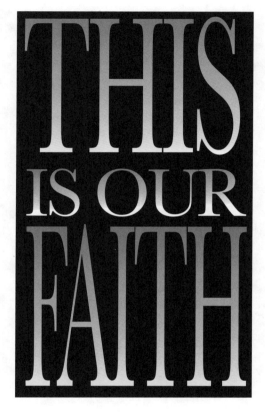

A Catholic Catechism for Adults

Revised Edition

Correlated and Referenced to the Catechism of the Catholic Church

A Catholic Catechism for Adults

Michael Francis Pennock

AVE MARIA PRESS   Notre Dame, Indiana 46556

Nihil Obstat: The Reverend Peter M. Mihalic, S.T.D., M.Div.
    Censor Deputatas
Imprimatur: The Most Reverend Anthony M. Pilla, D.D., M.A.
    Bishop of Cleveland
    Given at Cleveland, OH on 9 February 1998
© 1998 by Ave Maria Press, Inc.

International Standard Book Number: 0-87793-653-6
Cover and text design by Brian Conley
Printed and bound in the United States of America.

Library of Congress Cataloging-in-Publication Data
Pennock, Michael.
    This is our faith : a Catholic catechism for adults / Michael Francis Pennock. — Rev. ed.
    p.   cm.
    "Now correlated and referenced to the Catechism of the Catholic Church."
    Includes bibliographical references and index.
    ISBN 0-87793-653-6
    1. Catholic Church—Catechisms—English. 2. Catholic Church. Catechismus Ecclesiae Catholicae. English. I. Title.
BX1961.P45   1998
238'.2—dc21   98-4077
                                                            CIP

To my loving wife Carol and our children Scott, Jennifer, Amy, and Christopher.

Acknowledgments

I wish to thank my editor, Mike Amodei, for his help on this edition of *This Is Our Faith* and for my former editor, Joan Marie Laflamme, who made wonderful contributions to the first edition. The Lord has blessed me with outstanding editors over the years. I also wish to thank my publisher Frank Cunningham of Ave Maria Press for his encouragement to write this book. His friendship, support, and many kindnesses have greatly enriched my writing ministry.

Many other people deserve my gratitude: my parents Frank and Louise Pennock (RIP) for sharing their love of the Catholic faith with me; the many dedicated, good Sisters of the Incarnate Word who demonstrated to me when I was a youngster that the Catholic church is a loving mother; my high school and college Jesuit teachers who showed through their lives that our efforts should be directed to God's greater honor and glory; my colleagues in religious education at St. Ignatius High School—their friendship has shown me the meaning of Christian community; the countless number of students over the years whose response to my teaching has made sharing the Catholic faith with them a real joy—it is truly good news to know that my students are my brothers and sisters in the Lord; the many outstanding priests who have inspired my ministry over the years, especially Fr. Paul Hritz and Fr. Mark DiNardo and Bishop Anthony Pilla, whose pastoral leadership and personal example of compassion and holiness inspire every Catholic in the diocese of Cleveland; and the many friends whose support and love have sustained me in my ministry.

Above all else, though, I wish to thank the Lord Jesus for all these wonderful people, for the gift of his salvation and love, and for the privilege of working as a catechist. May his name be praised forever.

Contents

Introduction

*Leave your country, your kindred and your father's house for a
country which I shall show you; and I shall make you a great
nation, I shall bless you and make your name famous; you are
to be a blessing!*

— Genesis 12:1-2

A spiritual classic entitled *The Way of a Pilgrim* speaks to the
hearts of contemporary searchers. Its anonymous author lived in
nineteenth-century Russia. He tells of his lifelong pilgrimage, a
search for a way to get closer to God through prayer. The book begins humbly:

By the grace of God I am a Christian, by my deeds a great sinner,
and by my calling a homeless wanderer of humblest origin,
roaming from place to place. My possessions consist of a knapsack with dry crusts of bread on my back and in my bosom the
Holy Bible. This is all![1]

The Russian monk reminds all seekers of God that we are pilgrims in a foreign land. Someday we will have to leave it, forsaking
our possessions. For the anonymous pilgrim a knapsack and dried
bread were sufficient for his physical needs; the Bible provided
nourishment for his spiritual needs. By traveling simply he unclut-
tered his life for the journey.

In our more complex and sophisticated world we could hardly
get by with the simple supplies of a nineteenth-century wanderer.
Nonetheless, we are "strangers in a strange land" who are on a lifelong journey. This journey has as its ultimate destination union with
the God who made us and sustains us.

Insight, Determination, Support

The Christian life is a journey which requires insight, determination, and support to keep going. There is always a danger that we
will get so distracted by the sights along the way that we will forget
about our final destination. Thus, the Christian pilgrimage requires
clear vision to discern correctly the direction indicators along the

way. The Bible provided vision for the Russian pilgrim; it is still a major source of insight for the Christian journey.

Determination is also needed because the way is not easy. The ancient Israelites were led by God for forty years through a dangerous desert. God's Chosen People could never have sustained their journey on their own. Many times they wished to turn back. They seemed to prefer slavery to the freedom Yahweh promised them. They persevered in their quest because Yahweh himself stayed with them in a powerful way; his presence helped them attain their goal. Christians today are assured of one thing: If we stay close to God in his Son Jesus, the power of the Holy Spirit will sustain us to the end. St. Paul writes:

> And let us never slacken in doing good; for if we do not give up, we shall have our harvest in due time (Gal 6:9).

Today's Christian pilgrims also need support. No one can survive without other people. The nineteenth-century wanderer begged food from others and received spiritual encouragement from many holy people. Today's spiritual pilgrims also need others to support and nourish them on their life's journey. The good news of the Christian life is that those who follow the way of Jesus become members of his body. United to the Lord they derive strength and power from him and their fellow travelers. The inspiration of his life and sacrifice on the cross, his ongoing friendship, his presence to us through other people—these make the journey bearable and even adventurous.

An Invitation

I offer this book to those who want to know more about how the Catholic community journeys to the Father. This book is for Catholics who wish to get a simple, but thorough overview of their faith. This second edition of *This Is Our Faith* has been revised in light of the *Catechism of the Catholic Church* (CCC), the first universal catechism since the Council of Trent in the sixteenth century. I have arranged it to conform to the four pillars as presented in the *Catechism*, namely, the Profession of Faith (creed), the Celebration of the Christian Mystery (sacraments), Life in Christ (Catholic morality and commandments), and Christian Prayer (especially the Our Father). *This Is Our Faith* is organized as a series of questions. Next to each question is one or more reference numbers for the *Catechism of the Catholic Church*. These have been provided for readers who would like to plunge deeper and see a fuller development of the questions and responses as presented in the *Catechism*.

I also offer this book for those who are approaching the Catholic community for the first time, for example, catechumens who are engaged in an initiation process in preparation for receiving the sacraments. The book can be read alone and reflected on individually or it can be adapted for group use. Especially if it is used as part of the adult initiation process, it would be good for participants to exchange their insights, witness to their faith, and share and discuss their questions.

As a catechist and religious educator for more than thirty years, I have been privileged to share my own faith journey and that of the Catholic community with thousands of young people and adults in many settings. I have found that understanding typically follows the presentation of good, solid, basic knowledge. The goal of understanding the Catholic faith should be above all else the love and appreciation for the Lord who lives in and guides the faith community.

I invite you, the reader of this book, on a journey of understanding, of faith sharing, of prayer, and of reflection on the Catholic faith. My own prayer for all of us is that we come to love our Lord Jesus Christ even more. He has accomplished great things in us and for us. He continues to shower his love on us, and he calls us to an eternal destiny of joy. Let us never forget that teaching about the church has one major purpose: to draw us to Jesus. Remember his promise:

> "I shall see you again, and your hearts will be full of joy, and that joy no one shall take from you . . . . "Father, I want those you have given me to be with me where I am, so that they may always see my glory" (Jn 16:22; 17:24).

Organization of the Book

1. *The Profession of Faith* The first eleven chapters of the book take up the major articles of the Nicene Creed, a major profession of faith of all Christians. These topics include God the Father; Jesus; the Holy Spirit; the doctrine of the Blessed Trinity; the church; ecumenism; the communion of saints; Mary, the Mother of God; and human destiny.

2. *The Celebration of the Christian Mystery* Chapters 12 through 16 treat the important topics of Christian worship and the sacraments, the ongoing signs of the Lord's presence, friendship, and love to us. Sacraments are vital ways to live the Christian life in the Catholic community.

3. *Life in Christ* Chapters 17 through 21 discuss how Christians should live and interact with others on their faith journey. Topics include the foundations of Christian moral life, Jesus' command to love, and the Ten Commandments.

4. *Christian Prayer* Chapter 22 introduces the basics of Christian prayer, a key means to traveling a path of holiness. Furthermore, it discusses the petitions of the Lord's Prayer, which has been called "the gospel in miniature."

Appendix The appendix provides a summary of Catholic identity, describes the organization of the church, and discusses traditional religious vocations. It also supplies the texts of some traditional and important Catholic prayers. Finally, a glossary of key terms important to Catholics is included. Terms in **boldface** in the book are listed and defined in this glossary.

You may wish to read the book sequentially from beginning to end or choose to read the sections in random order. I do recommend that you read together all the chapters in a given section before moving to another. Feel free to skip around from topic to topic, treating the book as a resource book. Refer to the table of contents, glossary, and index for listings of individual topics and terms.

Chapter Features

Each chapter has a similar format. Each begins with a relevant scripture passage, a citation to the Nicene Creed, or another suitable quotation. After a brief introduction, usually involving a short anecdote, the main ideas are presented as responses to questions. This traditional catechism format also helps to organize and reference key teachings, and allows readers to digest the material in manageable portions.

The concluding remarks typically summarize the key idea of the chapter and attempt to apply it to daily living.

Prayer plays a central role in the life of the Christian. The book recognizes this by providing a prayer reflection after each chapter. Exposure to different kinds and ways of prayer should help to enrich the reading and application of the book to the Christian faith journey.

Discussion/reflection questions are provided to help the reader interact with the material and to apply it to daily life. I encourage you to discuss the questions and share your faith life with others. The Lord clearly speaks to us through our conversations with our Christian brothers and sisters.

Finally, each chapter concludes with a reference for further reading. The references provided are to the Bible, God's word which speaks to our hearts. In addition, throughout the text itself are woven numerous scripture passages to show the intimate relationship between Catholic doctrine and the word of God.

Prayer Reflection

Do not be afraid, for I have redeemed you; I have called you by your name, you are mine. Should you pass through the waters, I shall be with you; or through rivers, they will not swallow you up. Should you walk through fire, you will not suffer, and the flame will not burn you. For I am Yahweh, your God, the Holy One of Israel, your Savior (Is 43:1-3).

Part 1:

The Profession of Faith

The simple declarative sentence, "Jesus is Lord," is a miniature creed, that is, a statement or profession of one's beliefs. The church has issued some official creeds, most notably the Apostles' Creed and the Nicene Creed, both of which expressed the faith of the early Christian communities. *Their* faith remains *our* faith today.

The word *creed* comes from the Latin *Credo*, which means "I believe." But what Christians really proclaim is, "We believe." We do not invent our own faith; we receive it from God through the church. As the Hippocratic oath binds doctors into a community of healers, so our recitation of the creed unites us to our brothers and sisters in the faith.

For centuries, Catholics have been professing their faith in the Triune God by proclaiming the Nicene Creed. This creed clearly formulates essential Christian doctrines about God the Father, Son, and Holy Spirit, the church, salvation, and human destiny. It resulted after decades of controversy begun by a learned Egyptian priest, Arius, who denied that Jesus, the Son, always existed with the Father. In effect, Arius denied Jesus' divinity.

The raging Arian controversy caused extreme dissension in the church. As a result, the Emperor Constantine convoked the first general or ecumenical council at Nicaea in 325. It was the first of twenty-one such councils in the church's rich history. A major achievement of this council was to declare clearly the divinity of Jesus by issuing the Nicene Creed. The second ecumenical council, the Council of Constantinople (381), endorsed and expanded this creed. It has served well as a summary of Catholic faith ever since.

This section will examine the individual articles of the Nicene Creed as our profession of faith.

Chapter One

The Existence of God

Now we see only reflections in a mirror, mere riddles, but then we shall be seeing face to face. Now, I can know only imperfectly; but then I shall know just as fully as I am myself known.
—1 Corinthians 13:12

Every thinking, feeling human being at some time or other has an awesome experience, one that shakes the very ground he or she walks on. It is at such times that most of us tend to turn to God, to wonder about that hidden presence which we have somehow sensed. These experiences force us to ask questions about the meaning of life . . . and death. Why am I here? Why is there suffering? Why do my loved ones and I have to die? What is the meaning of love?

Our Catholic faith provides us with tremendous hope when reflecting on questions like these. It teaches us that an infinitely loving God created us to share in his own life, calling us to seek, to know, and to love him. God is always drawing close to us, inviting us into the unity of his family, the church.

To accomplish this, when the fullness of time had come, God sent his Son as Redeemer and Savior. In his Son and through him, he invites all people to become, in the Holy Spirit, his adopted children and thus heirs of his blessed life (CCC 1).

This chapter takes up two issues: questions of God's existence and how God has communicated with humanity.

Is It Normal to Believe in God? [CCC 27-30; 44-45]

The heavy questions that strike us as we travel through life often force us to face the issue of God's existence. Most people conclude that God exists, even though no one can see God. They are like the little boy who flew a kite so high that it soared into some low-flying clouds. A passerby asked the boy how he knew the kite was still up in the sky. The boy told the inquisitor to put his hand on the string and feel the pull of the unseen kite. God's existence and presence are like this. We may not see God face-to-face, but we can feel God's tug on our hearts. This tug reveals that we are religious beings by nature; we seek God and we allow God to seek us.

Not everyone in our world agrees, however. For example, atheists, for various reasons, deny God's existence. Some, who trust only in material reality, claim God cannot be experienced with the senses; hence, for them, God does not exist. Others hold that belief in God downgrades what it means to be human; for them, humanity is the only god. Still others reject the notion of God because they find the suffering and evil in the world incompatible with the existence of a supreme and loving Being. And, in truth, some are atheists because they do not want a religion and its God telling them how to behave, perhaps urging them to change an irresponsible, selfish, or immoral lifestyle.

Between the believers and the atheists are the agnostics who claim that we cannot know for certain if there is a God or not. Hence, they decide not to decide. The question of the existence of God makes little practical difference in their lives.

Atheists and agnostics—and also self-named believers who are in fact indifferent to spiritual realities—challenge believers to reflect more deeply on their own faith and why they believe in God.

Does God Exist? *[CCC 31-32; 34-35; 47]*

In his letter to the Romans, St. Paul teaches that we can discover God's existence by reflecting on the things God has made (Rom 1:18-21). The Catholic church also teaches that human reason can know with certainty the existence of God from creation.

St. Paul and church teaching do not claim that each and every person can and does come to a knowledge of God's existence through reason. Rather, they assert that humans are rationally able to discover the hidden God because "ever since the creation of the world, the invisible existence of God and his everlasting power have been clearly seen by the mind's understanding of created things" (Rom 1:20). Belief in God is not unreasonable or foolish as some non-believers claim.

Some of the arguments for the existence of God include personal experience, common human experience, human history, and demonstrations based on reason.

What Does Personal Experience Tell Us About God? *[CCC 27-30; 33; 46]*

Our own experience can guide us to God. Our feelings of dependency, our sense of wonder and awe and joy, our feelings of being invited and called to do greater things than we are doing right now—all of these may speak of a God who has made us to discover him. When we reflect on ourselves as something very special in creation, we are given some strong insights that help us conclude there is a Creator who brought us into existence. The following are traditional arguments for the existence of God. One of them may strike a response with you.

An unquenchable thirst for happiness. We all want to be happy. We spend a lot of our time and energy trying to do things and acquire things that we think will make us happy. Yet our happiness fades and we soon find ourselves desiring something else. Are we creatures doomed to be ultimately frustrated? We want happiness, but the more we pursue it, the more it seems to slip away.

Can it be that a Creator made us with a hunger for happiness which nothing in this world can completely satisfy? Might it be that God implanted in us a kind of homing device which causes us to be restless until we find him? This restlessness for *total* happiness points to a Supreme Being who made us this way, with a keen desire for God implanted in our hearts. God made us for himself and always attracts us to him. In the words of St. Augustine, "You are great, Lord, . . . because you have made us for yourself and our heart is restless until it finds its rest in you" (*Confessions*, 1.1.1).

Sense of justice. Have you ever felt that the evil people of the world will someday be called to task? It seems unfair that cheaters and liars and killers often prosper in this life while some good people suffer and are taken advantage of. We have a fundamental feeling that things will be reversed someday, that there is a Power that will right all wrongs, if not in this life, then in the next.

Love. How can we explain the greatest reality known to us, the sense of being cared for and loved? Love is a spiritual reality that is not explained by the material universe. It must come from somewhere, ultimately from Love itself, the being we call God. (The same can be said for intelligence; it must ultimately come from Intelligence itself, God.)

The human person. Christians believe that the human person is made in God's image and likeness. Our openness to truth and beauty, our sense of moral goodness, our ability to love, even at great personal cost—all these reveal a spiritual depth to humans. They point to the existence of a soul, "the seed of eternity" God implants in us. The capacity for these spiritual activities, rooted in the soul, can have their origin only in a spiritual Being of infinite Goodness, a being we call God who has created humans in his own image and likeness.

What Does Our Common Experience Tell Us About God? [CCC 51-53]

From the earliest times human beings have testified to the existence of God. An overwhelming majority of cultures has believed in some being who is greater than any of its members. There have been atheistic governments which deny God, but many of the people in those countries still held fast to a belief in God.

One can argue that such an observation does not prove that there is a God. Yet it is still very convincing that the common human experience has acknowledged a God who unites, heals, and preserves the human race.

People have not agreed on the exact nature of this superior being or how many of these beings there may be. Some picture a vengeful, spiteful god. Others see a remote figure, like a clock maker who constructs his masterpiece but is then quite content to allow it to run by itself. Still others imagine a capricious god, one who toys with and torments his creatures.

Disagreement on what God is like does not disprove God's existence, however. These differences merely show that, left to our own clouded intellects, we cannot perceive God clearly. We know *someone* is there, but God's true identity is not crystal clear to us using our minds alone. We need God's direct help if we are to know God as God really is.

What Does Reason Tell Us About God? [CCC 31-32; 46]

St. Thomas Aquinas, the great medieval theologian, summed up five so-called proofs for the existence of God. They all come down to affirming that we can discover God by looking at movement, becoming, contingency, order, and beauty in the world (CCC 32). For example, Aquinas points out that everything we know of in existence was caused by something or someone else. There has to be a source which was the first cause—an uncaused cause which logically always existed. This first cause the philosophers call God. The other arguments are similar.

Our own personal reflection on the beauty, immensity, symmetry, and power of creation can give us an awareness of a God who made all things and keeps them in existence. Alfred North Whitehead once said that God is the poet of the world. God's lyricism can be discovered in truth, beauty, and goodness. Our reflections and experiences of awe and wonder point to the existence of God.

Does God Communicate With Us? *[CCC 51]*

Christians believe not only that God exists, but also that God freely, lovingly, and graciously communicated himself to us. As the Second Vatican Council taught:

> In His goodness and wisdom, God chose to reveal Himself and to make known to us the hidden purpose of his will by which through Christ, the Word made flesh, man has access to the Father in the Holy Spirit and comes to share in the divine nature (Dogmatic Constitution on Divine Revelation, 2).

What Is Divine Revelation? *[CCC 50-54]*

Christians believe in divine revelation. What do we mean by this important term? First, we must emphasize that God is primarily a mystery; God's ways are above our ways, and God's thoughts are above our thoughts. God is totally other; no human words, no human thoughts can totally explain who God is. In a certain sense God is hidden behind a veil. As we have seen, though, we can use our minds to figure out that there must be a God who made everything and keeps it in existence. And by studying carefully what God has made, we can say some things about him. For example, when we look at the vastness of the universe, we must conclude that the one who made it is an infinite being, that is, one who is not limited. Or when we reflect on the existence of intelligent life in the universe, we are led to conclude that the Creator himself must be an intelligent being to the *nth* degree, an all-knowing being who is the very source of human intelligence.

Basically, we can conclude that God is a perfect being who is in no way limited like the creatures God has made. God goes beyond all creatures. But we must remember that human reason alone can only give us a veiled or clouded knowledge of God. One conclusion from this is to realize that our images of God are limited and imperfect. We must not confuse our images of God with the incomprehensible, invisible, infinite God.

Yet, Christians believe that God freely chose to communicate himself and his plan for our salvation to his creatures. This free gift of God's self-communication is known as supernatural or divine revelation. Literally, *revelation* means "unveiling." We believe that out of the abundance of his love, God unveiled himself in human history and speaks to us as friends, lives among us, and invites us into fellowship with him. We call this revelation supernatural because we, as God's creatures, do not have a natural right to this intimate friendship with God. God's self-disclosure, God's invitation to a deeper life of love is purely a gift on God's part.

At many moments in the past and by many means, God spoke to our ancestors through the prophets; but in our time, the final days, he has spoken to us in the person of his Son, whom he appointed heir of all things and through whom he made the ages (Heb 1:1-2).

What Is Salvation History? *[CCC 54-67]*

The story of God's self-disclosure, God's saving action in history, is known as **salvation history**. The story of God's generous love began with the creation of our first parents. After their fall God promised to redeem us and gave hope of eternal life to the human race. God's abiding love revealed itself in covenant—loving agreements between God and humans. For example, in the **covenant** with Noah after the Flood, God immediately began to reach out to the divided peoples with the goal of eventually uniting all people in Christ our Lord.

A profound event in God's plan was the covenant with Abraham and the creation of the nation of Israel. Through the patriarchs, the founding fathers of Israel, and Moses, through whom God revealed the divine law, God taught the people of Israel to acknowledge him as the one true God. Through prophets like Isaiah and Jeremiah, God gave Israel hope for salvation: a future Messiah who would write a new covenant in the hearts of all humans. The poor and humble, whose dependence on God was shown beautifully in the life of Mary the Mother of God, bear this hope in a special way.

Salvation history reached its high point in the coming of Jesus Christ, the fullness of God's revelation. Jesus is the Word of God made flesh, the Son, who lived among us, taught us in human words and deeds about his Father, and completed the Father's work of salvation. Jesus is God's final Word; God has no other word to give us. To see Jesus is to see the Father.

How Do We Learn of Salvation History?
[CCC 74-87; 101-114; 121-125; 134-141]

The story of salvation history lives on in sacred scripture (the Bible) and in the sacred **Tradition** of the Christian community. The **Bible** is the written record of revelation and contains the inspired testimony of people like the prophets and apostles about God's marvelous deeds in human history. "Sacred Scripture is the word of God inasmuch as it is consigned to writing under the inspiration of the divine Spirit" (*Constitution on Divine Revelation*, 9). This means that God inspired the human authors of the Bible to use their talents to write what God wanted written, and nothing more.

The Hebrew scriptures (contained in the Old Testament) record God's teaching to the Jewish people and God's interactions in their history. They tell how God called the Chosen People out of Egypt into the Promised Land, how they became a nation and a religious community, and how they grew to know and worship the one true God. An indispensable part of divine revelation, the Old Testament provides significant teaching about God, sound wisdom for living a good life, and a rich legacy of prayer. Further, it contains in a hidden way the mystery of our salvation.

The New Testament chronicles the life and teachings of Jesus Christ and announces the good news of God's plan of salvation for all people everywhere. The gospels are the heart of the Bible because they are the prime source of our knowledge about Jesus' life and teaching.

Tradition hands on God's word, first given to the apostles by the Lord and the Holy Spirit, to the successors of the apostles (the bishops and pope). Enlightened by the Holy Spirit, these successors faithfully preserve, explain, and spread it to the ends of the earth. Through this living Tradition, "the Church, in her teaching, life, and worship perpetuates and hands on to all generations all that she herself is, all that she believes" (*Dogmatic Constitution on Divine Revelation*, 8). Catholics accept and honor equally both Scripture and Tradition as two modes of God's transmission of revelation.

What Is Our Response to God's Communication? *[CCC 26; 91-100; 142-144]*

God's self-communication and plan for us require a response on our part. That response is known as **faith**, a commitment of our whole lives to a loving God and a resounding "yes" to the truths God has shared with us in Christ our Lord. The letter to the Hebrews defines faith as the "assurance of things we hoped for, the conviction of things not seen" (Heb 11:1, *NRSV*).

Where Do We Get Faith? *[CCC 145-171]*

Faith, like revelation, is a free gift of God. Through the action of the Holy Spirit, the gift of faith enables us to submit our wills and intellects to God. Faith is also a virtue that attracts us to God the Father. It binds us to God in a love relationship, giving us conviction, commitment, and trust with regard to realities that we can neither see nor clearly prove.

Faith enables us to accept Jesus as Lord. It equips us to live his life of loving service in the Catholic faith community. It empowers us to believe the truths God has revealed because God revealed them.

And faith in Jesus enables us to share in the life of the Holy Spirit who reveals to us who Jesus is. Thus Christian faith proclaims belief in one God: Father, Son, and Holy Spirit.

Although faith is a gift from God by which the Holy Spirit empowers us to live and believe divine revelation, our response is only human if it is free. Thus, no one can be forced to embrace faith against his or her will. Faith involves a *free* human act where our minds and our hearts cooperate with divine grace.

We can look to Abraham and Mary as two scriptural models of faith. In obedience to God, Abraham left his homeland to become a stranger and pilgrim in a promised land. Through his fidelity God created a people and prepared the way for the Messiah. The Blessed Mother's entire life exhibited a steadfast "yes" to God. Her faithfulness helped fulfill in a sublime way God's work of salvation through her Son, Jesus Christ.

Finally, Catholics recognize that faith is an act of the church. It comes before, gives life to, supports, and nourishes the faith of the individual, God's gift to us. As John's gospel teaches, faith in the Son leads to eternal life; disobedience to his word leads to the wrath of God (Jn 3:36).

Concluding Reflections

We began this chapter with the question of God's existence and we end with faith. St. Anselm of Canterbury had it right: "For I do not seek to understand that I may believe, but I believe in order to understand."

It is reasonable to believe in God. Personal experiences, universal human belief, human history, and rational reflection all point to a Supreme Being who has made our universe and keeps it in existence.

Christian belief does not stop with the fact of God's existence. This is only the beginning. God has revealed himself to us not only through the stamp of a creative touch on those things we can observe, but also by getting involved in human history. God formed a people and through them gave to the human community the Word, the Son, Jesus Christ.

Who is this God for you? How do you perceive God's existence? How does God speak to you through the material world? Have you discovered God through Christian revelation?

Prayer Reflection

"Stop and smell the roses" is common but sound advice. We can never be so preoccupied on our faith journey that we miss seeing God in the beautiful creation he has made.

Reflection on creation moves the believer to adoration and praise. Both Jews and Christians turn to the Psalms for inspiration in addressing the almighty God.

> Yahweh our Lord, how majestic is your name throughout the world! I look up at your heavens, shaped by your fingers, at the moon and the stars you set firm— what are human beings that you spare a thought for them, or the child of Adam that you care for him? Yet you have made him little less than a god, you have crowned him with glory and beauty, made him lord of the works of your hands, put all things under his feet (Ps 8:1, 3-6).

For Discussion

1. What was the most earthshaking experience of your life? How did it speak to you of God?
2. Some people say it is impossible to "prove" one person's love for another; love must be experienced to be believed. Explain how you have experienced another's love for you. Discuss how you have experienced God's love.
3. What proof for God's existence do you find most convincing? How have you seen God acting in your life?
4. How is your faith different since your childhood days? In what ways is it deeper? How has it affected how you live your life? In what ways can your faith grow?
5. What is the most significant question you ask about life? How might the existence of a loving God be an answer to that question?
6. How do you image God? Where did you get those images? Explain how they help or hinder your faith.

Further Reading

Psalms 8, 19, 29, 65, 104

Chapter Two

God: Our Loving Creator

*"Listen, Israel: Yahweh our God is the one, the only Yahweh.
You must love Yahweh your God with all your heart, with all
your soul, with all your strength."*
— Deuteronomy 6:4-5

A little girl in a third-grade religion class was intently drawing
a picture. Her teacher asked her what she was doing. The girl
replied that she was drawing a picture of God. Gently the teacher
told the girl that no one knows what God looks like. Innocently and
confidently the budding artist replied, "They will when I am done."

Perhaps we all have our own private picture of God, one we
confidently own and treasure for ourselves. But the problem is that
no one *owns* God. For ultimately God is a **mystery.** As the great so-
ciologist of religion Rudolph Otto wrote in his classic *The Idea of the
Holy,* "If the human mind could fully explain God, then God would
cease to exist."[1]

We cannot fully explain God, but we believe in God nevertheless, a God who revealed the divine name to Moses as Yahweh, "I
Am" (see Ex 3:4-14 and *CCC* 205-209). A name expresses the essence
of a person. "I Am" means that God is not some abstract force but
an always present spirit who is the very ground of our being and of
all that exists. "I Am" also reveals that God is a sacred mystery before whom Moses took off his shoes and bowed in reverence. God's
omnipotent, eternal, awesome nature is beyond our small minds to
grasp. However, Christians have been given the knowledge of
God's true identity through the Son who revealed God's true nature: love. "We have come to know and to believe in the love God
has for us. God is love, and whoever remains in love remains in God
and God in him" (1 Jn 4:16, NAB).

God revealed to Moses the truth about the divine name, and
through him made a covenant with the people. When Moses came

down from the mountain, he instructed the people to listen to hear the truth about God and how God wanted them to live. Today we must also listen to what is essential. In the Nicene Creed we profess:

> We believe in one God, the Father, the Almighty, maker of heaven and earth, of all that is, seen and unseen.

Ultimately, this Creator God is a God of love who asks for our love in return. Love is the path to union with God and our eternal happiness. This chapter will focus on revelation about God and God's creation, especially from the words of the Hebrew scriptures. Chapters 3 and 4 will turn to the New Testament, examining in more detail about God's ultimate revelation through his Son Jesus Christ.

What Is the Old Testament? *[CCC 105-107; 121-123; 134-138]*

A prime means of listening to God is by reading and reflecting on the Old Testament and New Testament. Christians believe that these writings—the Bible—are God's words in human words. Their message is a word worth listening to. The Hebrew scriptures or Jewish Bible is contained in the Old Testament.

The Bible, which literally means "The Book," is a collection of books which contain different kinds of literature—poetry, history, religious myth (story), prayers, proverbs, and the like. They have one thing in common though: All are *inspired* because God influenced the biblical writers in such a way that they recorded what God wanted. **Inspiration** refers to the guidance of the Holy Spirit in the process of writing the holy scriptures.

Catholics recognize 46 books as the official list (**canon**) of inspired books of the Old Testament. We can divide the Old Testament books into four major categories:

The *Pentateuch* treats God's covenant of love with the Israelites (later called the "Jews") and sets down their response, that is, the Law or Torah. (Five books: Genesis, Exodus, Leviticus, Numbers, Deuteronomy.)

The *Historical Books* recount the story of God's saving activity in the history of the Chosen People. (Sixteen books: Joshua, Judges, Ruth, 1 and 2 Samuel, 1 and 2 Kings, 1 and 2 Chronicles, Ezra, Nehemiah, Tobit, Judith, Esther, 1 and 2 Maccabees.)

The *Wisdom Books* contain prayers, poems and common-sense advice on how to live a faithful, good life. (Seven books: Job, Psalms, Proverbs, Ecclesiastes, Song of Songs, Wisdom, Sirach.)

The *Prophetical Books* repeatedly call the Chosen People to repent and be faithful to God's covenant. (Eighteen books: Isaiah,

Jeremiah, Lamentations, Baruch, Ezekiel, Daniel, Hosea, Joel, Amos, Obadiah, Jonah, Micah, Nahum, Habakkuk, Zephaniah, Haggai, Zechariah, Malachi.)

How Does Faith Speak About "One" God? *[CCC 199-204; 210-211]*

God's revelation to the Israelites (Jews), the Chosen People, shows that God is one and unique. In communicating the divine name, God also reveals that he is a living, faithful God, the God of the Israelites' ancestors, and a God who will always be with the people (Ex 3:13-15).

The one God is merciful and gracious, demonstrated by God's involvement in the history of the Chosen People. This history is one of **covenant.** In general, a covenant is a commitment between two parties to do something for each other. Unlike a contract which is based on legal obligations, God's covenant with the Jews was based on freely given divine love. In covenant God promised to create a nation (covenant with Abraham), to sustain them as a people (covenant with Moses, the Exodus experience), to give them a land (Canaan), to help them establish self-rule, and to send them a Messiah (covenant with David).

In return for God's many and great blessings, the Jews were to obey God's law which is summarized in the Ten Commandments. This law gave the Jews an identity distinct from their neighbors and gave them a special task, a mission to witness to the true God.

The most important aspect of the Israelites' response was to worship Yahweh and to testify to him as the one, true God, the source of all being and the one who keeps everything in existence. All other gods were false and thus powerless; only Yahweh was the true, living, unique God. Old Testament history is full of the sad story of how the Israelites were unfaithful to God, and how they continually fell back to the worship of false gods (for example, rain gods or the gods of worldly power and prestige). But the Old Testament also tells a happy story, the story of God's continual loving faithfulness despite the sinfulness of the Chosen People. This happy story continues with the coming of the Messiah who would offer salvation not only to the Jews, but to all people.

How Does the Old Testament Reveal God as Love and Truth? *[CCC 218-221; 231]*

"God, "He who is," revealed himself to Israel as the one "abounding in steadfast love and faithfulness. . . . In all his works God displays not only his kindness, goodness, grace, and steadfast love, but also his trustworthiness, constancy, faithfulness, and truth" (CCC 214).

These traits exhibit themselves marvelously in the story of salvation history recorded in the Hebrew scriptures. Here is a sample list of some key Old Testament passages that reveal a God of truth and love.

1. *God chooses the Hebrews and makes them a people.*

    Yahweh said to Abram, "Leave your country, your kindred and your father's house for a country which I shall show you; and I shall make you a great nation, I shall bless you and make your name famous; you are to be a blessing!" (Gn 12:1-2).
2. *God frees the Israelites from Egypt.*

    "And I have come down to rescue them from the clutches of the Egyptians and bring them up out of that country, to a country rich and broad, to a country flowing with milk and honey" (Ex 3:8).
3. *God establishes a covenant with the Israelites, making them a holy nation.*

    "So now, if you are really prepared to obey me and keep my covenant, you, out of all peoples, shall be my personal possession, for the whole world is mine. For me you shall be a kingdom of priests, a holy nation" (Ex 19:5-6).
4. *God gives the Israelites a land.*

    "Make provisions ready, for in three days' time you will cross this Jordan and go on to take possession of the land which Yahweh your God is giving you as your own" (Jos 1:11).
5. *God establishes the kingdom of David.*

    (See 2 Sm 7:8-16.)
6. *God sends prophets to guide the Israelites.*

    "Turn from your wicked ways and keep my commandments and my laws in accordance with the entire Law which I laid down for your fathers and delivered to them through my servants the prophets" (2 Kgs 17:13).
7. *God sustains the Chosen People in Babylon and restores them to Israel.*

    "Console my people, console them,"
    says your God.

    "Speak to the heart of Jerusalem
    and cry to her
    that her period of service is ended,
    that her guilt has been atoned for" (Is 40:1-2).

What Are Some Qualities of God? *[CCC 212-217; 268-271]*

The Old Testament figure Job—long in suffering—knew well that the unlimited, almighty God was beyond human comprehension:

> You have told me about great works that I cannot understand, about marvels which are beyond me, of which I know nothing (Jb 42:3).

What Job learned through his trials is that God's divine mercy extends to all. In God's mysterious way, humans are rescued from sin and restored to divine friendship.

Thus, God is revealed as love. But God has many other attributes as well. Here are nine that St. Thomas Aquinas listed as qualities that seem to comprise God's nature. Passages from the Hebrew scriptures reveal each of these qualities.

1. *God is unique.* There is no God like Yahweh.

> For thus says Yahweh, the Creator of the heavens—
> he is God, who shaped the earth and made it,
> who set it firm;
> he did not create it to be chaos,
> he formed it to be lived in:
> I am Yahweh, and there is no other (Is 45:18).

2. *God is infinite and omnipotent.* God is everywhere, unlimited, and all- powerful. God can do everything.

> For I know that Yahweh is great,
> our Lord is above all gods,
> Yahweh does whatever he pleases
> in heaven, on earth,
> in the waters and all the depths (Ps 135:5-6).

3. *God is eternal.* God always was and always will be. God is the one being who cannot not be. God is.

> Did you not know? Had you not heard?
> Yahweh is the everlasting God,
> he created the remotest parts of the earth (Is 40:28).

4. *God is immense.* God is not limited to space.

> "Yet will God really live with human beings on earth? Why, the heavens, the highest of the heavens, cannot contain you. How much less this temple built by me!" (1 Kgs 8:27).

5. *God contains all things.*

> Strongly she [wisdom] reaches from one end of the world to the other and she governs the whole world for its good (Wis 8:1).

6. *God is immutable.* God does not change—ever.

> Long ago you laid the earth's foundations,
> the heavens are the work of your hands.
> They pass away but you remain;
> they all wear out like a garment,

like outworn clothes you change them;
but you never alter, and your years never end (Ps 102:25-27).

7. *God is utterly simple—a pure Spirit.* The opposite of simple is complex, which means divisible into parts. In God there are no parts, no divisions. God is not material and God's image cannot be made.

> You shall not make yourself a carved image or any likeness of anything in heaven above or earth beneath or in the waters under the earth (Ex 20:4).

8. *God is personal.* God is alive (the source of all life), knows all things, and loves and cares beyond limit. The saving God manifested personal love through the compassionate acts in the history of the Israelites and most supremely by sending the Son, Jesus Christ, to all people.

> I have loved you with an everlasting love
> and so I still maintain my faithful love for you (Jer 31:3).

9. *God is supremely holy.* Holiness is a quality of being absolutely other than creation. God's goodness and love are unlimited. We cannot praise the holy God enough.

> Where shall we find sufficient power to glorify him,
> since he is the Great One, above all his works? (Sir 43:28).

What Is the Central Truth Revealed About God?
[CCC 232-237]

The Most Holy **Trinity** is the central mystery of our Christian faith and life, the source of all other mysteries of our faith. Salvation history coincides with the activity of how the one true God—Father, Son, and Holy Spirit—reveals himself and reconciles and unites us to him.

In brief, the doctrine of the Trinity teaches that Jesus is the visible image of the Father, the invisible God; and the Holy Spirit is sent by the Father in the name of the Son.

We know God is a Trinity of persons because God has revealed this awesome truth to us. Jesus teaches that God is Father (for example, see Jn 17:1). The Father teaches that he has a Son (for example, at Jesus' baptism, Lk 3:22). And Jesus reveals that the Father will send the Holy Spirit in his name, a Spirit of truth and love (see Jn 14:16).

We will consider the doctrine of the Trinity more fully in Chapter 6.

Who Is God the Creator? *[CCC 279-308; 315-323; 337-349; 355-373; 380-384]*

The two creation stories (Genesis 1:1–2:4 and Genesis 2:5-25) reveal that God is the Creator who made all things out of nothing. God freely created out of divine love and goodness to show forth and share his glory, beauty, truth, and goodness. God both sustains and rules the ordered world created through his wisdom. **Divine providence**—God's active interest in guiding creation to perfection—is always present to help the world develop according to God's plan. This providence wills the interdependence of all creatures, thus imparting to humans the awesome duty to act responsibly towards other creatures and to be faithful stewards of God's beautiful world.

The New Testament tells us that God created and keeps everything in existence through the eternal Word, God's beloved Son. The church also proclaims the creative activity of the Holy Spirit, "the giver of life" and the "source of every good" (*CCC* 291). Marvelously, we humans are created in God's image. This gives us tremendous dignity for each of us is a *someone*, a person loved by God, not a something.

> God created man in the image of himself, in the image of God he created him, male and female he created them (Gn 1:27).

All that God created was good. Unlike the Babylonian creation stories which hold that there is an evil god along with a good god, and that our human existence is the result of evil, the Hebrew scriptures' picture of God is one of goodness, power, freedom, and generosity.

We humans, the crown of God's creation, are endowed with both a physical body and a spiritual nature. Our spiritual nature enables us to think, to choose between right and wrong, and to love. Though made of a body and soul, humans are a unity. Furthermore, our immortal souls are created immediately by God. We are immortal in the sense that, although we each have a personal beginning, we will never cease to exist. Our vocation is to reproduce in our own lives the image of Jesus Christ, God's Son, "the image of the invisible God." Finally, as social beings who live in community, we must renew the face of the earth and lovingly offer our efforts, in thanksgiving and praise, back to the Father.

> God blessed them, saying to them, "Be fruitful, multiply, fill the earth and subdue it. Be masters of the fish of the sea, the birds of heaven, and all the living creatures that move on earth" (Gn 1:28).

If God Is Good, Why Is There Evil and Suffering in the World? [CCC 272-274; 309-314; 324]

The Old Testament's book of Job wrestled with this same question. Job was a good man who lost all his children and property and contracted a horrible disease. Always trusting God despite his setbacks, Job's sufferings helped him grow as a person. And that is one partial answer to why there is suffering: Good can come from it. As the old saying adapted from the book of Ecclesiastes states, "God writes straight with crooked lines" (7:13-14).

Job's ordeal did give him a further insight on the question of evil and suffering. Toward the end of his trials, Job says to God,

> You have told me about great works that I cannot understand, about marvels which are beyond me, of which I know nothing . . . but now, having seen you with my own eyes, I retract what I have said and repent in dust and ashes (Jb 42:3-6).

Job admits that God's ways are mysterious and that ultimately we cannot fully understand them. It takes humility and trust to admit that we can never understand the mystery of innocent suffering and evil in the world. But divine revelation helps us understand some things about the world's evil. Consider these points.

- *God's created world is on a journey to perfection.* It is *not yet* perfect. The world is in a process of becoming. Nature's constructive and destructive forces exist side-by-side. The more perfect exists alongside the less perfect. "With physical good there also exists *physical evil* as long as creation has not reached perfection" (CCC 310).

As the star athlete must experience pain to hone her skills, so the world undergoes pain to achieve the perfection God has in store. We cannot now appreciate the pain involved in this growth process because innocent people suffer at the hands of nature. But we believe that in God's wisdom this growth is good for individuals and humanity as it journeys to perfection.

- *The source of much moral evil is the result of the misuse of freedom.* Out of divine goodness, God created humans (and angels) as intelligent and *free* creatures. Intelligence and freedom make us beings of tremendous dignity and not mere automatons. But these two gifts require responsibility. We must freely choose to love God and others on our journey toward eternity. When we refuse to love, we sin. And sin brings about incredible evil and suffering.

Christian revelation tells us that when some angels chose to sin, the fallen angels, also known as devils, unleashed evil in the world in opposition to God. This might explain some of the natural evil in the world.

Christian revelation also informs us that our first parents abused their freedom and committed a sin whose consequences infected all their descendants. This sin of Adam and Eve is known as the original sin. Moral evil entered the world through the original sin and has led to all types of human sin like war, abortion, drug abuse, prejudice, greed that causes immense poverty, sexual aberration, etc. God does not *cause* moral evil like this. Humans, by misusing their freedom, are its cause. God *permits* it, however, because God loves and respects the free creatures he has made. And in a way known only to God (a truth that Job eventually admitted), God knows how to derive good out of all evil.

- *Christian faith announces the good news of Jesus Christ, who conquered the forces of evil.* Certainly, the worst moral evil in the world was for humans to put to death the innocent God-man. Like any normal person, Jesus abhorred suffering and even asked his Father to protect him from it. But Jesus freely embraced the sufferings that unjustly came his way by submitting to his Father, "May your will be done." The Father heard Jesus' prayer, not by saving Jesus from death, but by saving him *out* of death. Jesus' suffering, death, *and* resurrection have conquered the worst evil: death and separation from God. If we love as Jesus teaches us to do and join our sufferings to him, we will share forever in the Lord's blissful, superabundant, joy-filled life. And this "good news" helps us cope with the mystery of evil and suffering.

What Is Original Sin? *[CCC 374-379; 386-390; 396-412; 415-421]*

The Old Testament helps explain the origin of some of the world's evil. In the Genesis story (3:1-24), for example, we see that though created in God's image and in a friendship relationship with God, humans had the chance to either accept or reject God's love. Original sin is the unhappy story of Adam and Eve's rejection of God's love, which resulted in humanity's loss of Yahweh's friendship. They abused their freedom by disobeying God, not trusting in God's goodness. Adam and Eve each chose self over God, resulting in the immediate loss of the grace of original holiness.

The sin of our first parents brought about a disunity between God and humans. Genesis also tells us that this fractured relationship resulted in a corresponding disharmony of our human nature and our alienation from one another. Human nature is now weakened in its powers and subject to ignorance, suffering, the inclination to sin, and death. As the Hebrew scriptures so graphically report in stories like Cain's murder of Abel (Gn 4:1-16) and the countless other stories of the Israelites failure to live God's law, after the Fall, sin became a part of the human experience and human history.

The church teaches that all humans are implicated in original sin. Adam and Eve's personal sin affected human nature. Their original sin was transmitted to future generations who inherited a human condition deprived of original justice and holiness (see CCC, 404).

Note that when the church teaches that we inherit original sin, the church is not saying that original sin is an *actual* sin we personally commit. Rather, we are born into a condition where we are inclined to give in to the powers of evil which surround us. We cannot be freed from that condition by our own strength. Only Jesus, God's Son, can liberate us from the power of sin.

> But the Lord Himself came to free and strengthen man, renewing him inwardly and casting out that prince of this world (cf. Jn 12:31) who held him in the bondage of sin (Pastoral Constitution on the Church in the Modern World, No. 13).

The good news of Jesus Christ is that our Lord has won for us greater blessings than those which sin has taken from us.

Does the Old Testament Reveal a Savior? *[CCC 522]*

The Old Testament reveals a saving God, one who wants the friendship of his beloved creatures. Thus, we see that a major theme of salvation history is God's loving faithfulness to unfaithful creatures. For example, the prophet Hosea compares Yahweh to a faithful husband who refuses to abandon his harlot wife, Israel. Or the Song of Songs praises Yahweh as a passionate lover whose love and fidelity to his beloved (Israel) knows no bounds.

The Old Testament continually shows how God's love is manifested through deeds as well as words. God's deeds reflect a saving God, one who rescues Israel from the bondage of slavery in Egypt, one who sustains them in the desert, one who gives them a land and a king, one who keeps them alive in captivity, one who returns them to their land.

The high point of God's loving concern is the promise to send a Messiah, a savior, a comforter who will restore humanity's proper relationship with God.

But you Bethlehem (Ephrathah),
the least of the clans of Judah,
from you will come for me
a future ruler of Israel
whose origins go back to the distant past,
to the days of old (Mi 5:1).

In fulfillment of his promise God sent his only Son, Jesus Christ. The account of his coming is the centerpiece of the New Testament story.

Do Angels Exist? *[CCC 325-336; 350-352]*

The Nicene Creed proclaims that God created all that is seen and unseen. This includes pure spirits known as angels whose existence is attested to in both scripture and Tradition. Angels are spiritual created beings, personal and immortal, who are capable of thinking and loving. We believe that they, like humans, had an opportunity to love and accept their loving Creator or reject him out of prideful self-interest. **Angels** are those invisible spiritual beings who lovingly worship God.

Scripture describes the main functions of angels (a word meaning "messenger") as servants of God. They are mediators between God and humans. The New Testament tells how angels are active during critical times of salvation history: the angel Gabriel is at the annunciation and angels are present at the birth of Jesus. Angels are also present during Jesus' trials in the desert and the garden of Gethsemane, at the resurrection, and at the ascension of Jesus into heaven. In fact, Jesus Christ is the Lord of the angels because they were created *through* and *for* him.

During the liturgical year, the church celebrates two special feasts involving angels. September 29 is the feast of the archangels ("highest angels"), Sts. Michael, Raphael, and Gabriel, the only angels the Bible names. October 2 is the feast of the guardian angels. Traditionally, Catholics and other Christians have believed that each of us has a guardian angel to watch over us. Church tradition strongly supports belief in and devotion to our guardian angels, asking for their spiritual help, especially in times of temptation. In his classic *Introduction to the Devout Life* (16), St. Francis de Sales writes:

Become familiar with the angels and see how they are often present though unseen in your life. Above all, have particular love and reverence . . . for your own guardian angel. Pray often to them.[2]

Does Satan Exist? *[CCC 391-395; 414]*

The church teaches the existence of fallen angels known as demons, devils (from a word meaning "slanderer"), and Satan (deceiver). From the first book of the Bible (Genesis) which speaks of the serpent tempting Adam and Eve, to the last book (Revelation) which reports a symbolic heavenly battle between good and evil angels, scripture assumes and teaches the existence of these "bad angels." Created good by God, Satan (also called the "devil" or "Lucifer") and other demons became evil by their own doing. This fall consisted of a free, radical, and irrevocable rejection of God and God's reign.

In Jesus' ministry, evil spirits appear or are mentioned frequently—at the time of his desert fast, as demons he exorcised in many of his healings, in many of his teachings (for example, when he said the Father's kingdom would prevail over demons), and in his commission to the apostles to expel demons.

Although some references to demons and devils can be explained as figurative language, the Bible has scores of other references to personal, spiritual beings who have chosen evil and are at war against God and God's kingdom. Based on this scriptural testimony, and the consistent teaching of the church through history, the church continues to teach the existence of Satan and other demons. God allows Satan to tempt us, but God will not allow him to harm us. (Although demon possession exists, the church's ritual of exorcism warns against coming to that conclusion too quickly. Many alleged possessions have turned out to be emotional disturbances or the results of fraud.)

Calling on the help of our patron saint, praying to our guardian angel, reading scripture, and in a special way appealing to our Blessed Mother—are all valuable ways to resist the devil's temptations and grow in a grace-filled life. The church cautions us to be aware of the subtle thoughts, lies, and tricks that reduce our freedom and turn us from God's love.

Remember this bedrock truth of our faith: Satan is only a creature. The good news proclaims that the power of Jesus Christ has conquered Satan. The evil one cannot prevent God's reign from growing. We need not fear the devil's influence in our lives if we stay close to Jesus who saved us from sin and the work of the evil one. Evil is a great mystery. But the greater reality is the victory of Jesus, our Lord and Savior, who has triumphed over evil and death!

Concluding Reflections

We have looked at some basic Catholic teachings about God, especially as the Hebrew scriptures reveal him. We have seen that God is one, true, living, a supremely holy, unique, omnipotent, eternal, and immense being who contains all things. God is above human understanding, a pure spirit, and a personal, thinking, absolutely loving being who is intimately concerned with his creation. Most central, God is a Trinity of Persons: Father, Son, and Holy Spirit.

God has created all things out of nothing and keeps them in existence. God has made us in the divine image with a supernatural destiny. God desires our happiness and is faithful to us even when we reject him. God always stands ready to redeem us through his Son, Jesus Christ.

A good question, though: How do these truths affect our lives? Do they make any difference?

Sometimes we are so bombarded with distractions that we don't hear God speaking to us. God can be the farthest thing from our minds. But we should pause periodically and hear what God is saying. God's message can make a difference in our daily lives. Consider:

- *God loves each of us greatly.* God shows this through all creation, especially our own existence. God's goodness and love have many concrete implications. He loves us unconditionally by giving us life and endowing us with unique talents. God sees what he has made—each of us—and declares that what he has made is good, very good. Others may measure us against their expectations and find us wanting. But God loves us for who we are. If we let this knowledge sink into our inner awareness, we will begin to take great joy in all creation—especially our own existence.

- *Life has meaning,* even in the moments we find most confusing. Reality is good, and God cares about us. In turn, God wants us to care for each other and the precious world he gave to us. This will lead to our happiness, something God wills for all of us.

- The Hebrew scriptures reveal that *God is involved in our lives.* God is everywhere, closer to us than we are to ourselves. God endows us with dignity and unites us to all others who are our brothers and sisters. In addition, Yahweh promised the Chosen People that he would never abandon them, and he did not. Through Jesus in the Holy Spirit, God also promises never to abandon us, regardless of how often we sin or turn from his love. God's generous love is always available to us, if we but repent and turn to receive it.

Behind our current concerns, worries, and situation in life is the more fundamental truth of God's great love for us. The Lord asks us: "How do you feel about this? What should you do right now to make my Father's love for you the most important reality in your life? Will you come to know his greatness and majesty? Will you thank God for his goodness? Will you trust in God's providence, that God is guiding *your* life?"

Prayer Reflection

Psalm 23 is the most beloved of all psalms. It epitomizes the closeness of God's love so richly revealed in the Hebrew scriptures. Pray it slowly and meditatively.

> Yahweh is my shepherd, I lack nothing.
> In grassy meadows he lets me lie.
> By tranquil streams he leads me
> to restore my spirit.
> He guides me in paths of saving justice
> as befits his name.
> Even were I to walk in a ravine as dark as death
> I should fear no danger, for you are at my side.
> Your staff and your crook are there to soothe me.
> You prepare a table for me
> under the eyes of my enemies;
> you anoint my head with oil;
> my cup brims over.
> Kindness and faithful love pursue me
> every day of my life.
> I make my home in the house of Yahweh
> for all time to come.

For Discussion

1. The Christian God is a God of covenant. God will always be faithful. What does this say to you about God? What does it require of you?
2. If scripture is God's inspired word, then it should play a central role in Christian life. Prayerfully read and reflect on next Sunday's readings. What do these readings reveal about God? What do they reveal about you?
3. When have you sensed the majesty of God? Describe a personal experience when God seemed especially close to you.
4. What evidences can you give for the existence of original sin in the world? In your life?
5. Do you view the world as basically good or basically evil? Explain.

Further Reading

Genesis 1:1–2:4; 2:5-25 (creation accounts)
Genesis 12 and 15 (God's covenant with Abraham)

Chapter Three

Jesus: Lord and Messiah

For this is how God loved the world:
he gave his only Son,
so that everyone who believes in him may not perish
but may have eternal life.
— John 3:16

We believe in one Lord, Jesus Christ
the only Son of God,
eternally begotten of the Father
God from God, Light from Light,
true God from true God,
begotten, not made, one in Being with the Father.
Through him all things were made.
For us men and for our salvation he came down from heaven:
by the power of the Holy Spirit he was born of the Virgin Mary,
and became man.
— from the Nicene Creed

Who are the inspiring people in your life? Whom do you look up to and admire?

Today's world thrusts upon us varied models of the so-called great. Grocery-store tabloids want us to admire the Hollywood-types, the money-hungry sports figures, those who are clever in the marketplace and various other "beautiful people." They urge us to emulate the lifestyles of the materially successful.

But who is truly great? The dictionary tells us that a great person is superior in quality, noble, excellent. G. K. Chesterton once observed that some so-called greats make everyone else feel small. But the really great person is the one who makes every other person feel great.

For countless people Jesus Christ is the model of greatness. Christians believe that Jesus was born great because he was God's only Son. But Jesus was born in the most humble of circumstances. And he was killed, condemned as a criminal. Jesus' life teaches us that the meaning of greatness does not lie in personal wealth, privileged status, or popular acceptance. Jesus reveals that the way to greatness is to live a life serving others and loving them without condition. His life, death, and resurrection have brought about the greatest achievement of all: our eternal salvation.

Jesus is at the very heart of the Christian faith journey. He is the Father's total revelation. Jesus teaches:

> I am the Way; I am Truth and Life. No one can come to the Father except through me. If you know me, you will know my Father too (Jn 14:6-7).

This chapter will examine what the gospels tell us about Jesus and discuss some beliefs that Christians have about their Lord. As you read, keep in both mind and heart what Jesus means to you.

Did Jesus Really Exist? *[CCC 423]*

Few people today seriously doubt the historical existence of Jesus. Ancient Roman and Jewish writers take his existence for granted. For example, the Roman historian Tacitus placed the blame for the great fire in Rome in AD 64 on Christians. He derived their name from "Christus," taken from the man who was put to death by the Roman governor Pontius Pilate. Also, Pliny the Younger, the Roman governor of Bithnyia, wrote to the emperor Trajan (c. AD 112) telling him about Christians who worshipped Christ as a god. Neither he nor the emperor in his return letter ever questioned Jesus' actual existence.

The famous first-century Jewish historian Josephus mentioned Jesus in two of his writings. The Jewish rabbinical collection of writings known as the Talmud likewise has a record of Jesus. Had Jesus never lived, then it is likely that the Jewish leaders would have tried to disprove the Christian claim about his existence. But to the contrary, they take for granted in their writings that he indeed was once alive.

Most people conclude, therefore, that the Christian religion must be founded on a real person. After all, what did anyone have to gain politically or economically from making up a story about Jesus? As a matter of fact, with the exception of John, all the apostles were put to death for their preaching about Jesus.

Finally, the gospels provide the best argument for Jesus' existence. The words and teachings attributed to Jesus bear the stamp of an individual who taught with unique insight and authority. The parables, for example, are powerful, life-giving, and original. They contain earth-shaking truths like these: God is a loving "Abba-Daddy," whom we can approach with confidence; God's reign is in our midst, so we must repent and believe; God loves everyone, especially the marginalized, and therefore you should also love everyone. These teachings, and others like them, argue quite convincingly for the existence of a memorable teacher behind them.

What Is the Primary Source of Knowledge of Jesus?
[CCC 120, 124-125; 461-463]

The primary source of knowledge about Jesus is the New Testament. Every page of its 27 books proclaims the **Incarnation,** the teaching that God became man in Jesus Christ. Belief in this doctrine is, in fact, the distinctive sign of Christian faith. Like the Hebrew scriptures (contained in the Old Testament), the New Testament is a collection of books which announces the fulfillment of God's promises in his Son, Jesus Christ. It contains the following category of books:

The *Gospels* are faith testimonies proclaiming salvation through Jesus Christ. They contain both facts about the historical Jesus and the faith of early Christians on the meaning of Jesus' life, death, and resurrection. (Four books: Matthew, Mark, Luke, John.)

The *Acts of the Apostles* deals with the early history of the church under the guidance of the Holy Spirit, from Pentecost Sunday to the arrest of Paul in Rome around AD 63. It was written by the author of the gospel of Luke as a sequel to the gospel.

The *Pauline Epistles*, the earliest New Testament writings, take up particular problems faced by the early churches and continually proclaim the centrality of faith in Jesus. (Thirteen books: Modern scholars attribute seven of these to Paul—Romans, 1 and 2 Corinthians, Galatians, Philippians, 1 Thessalonians, and Philemon. The other six were probably written by disciples of Paul— Ephesians, Colossians, 2 Thessalonians, 1 and 2 Timothy, and Titus.)

The *Epistle to the Hebrews* deals with the priesthood of Jesus. Its author is unknown.

The *Seven Catholic Epistles* were written to encourage the universal (catholic) church to keep the true faith and to remind Christians to live Christ-filled lives. (Seven books: James, 1 and 2 Peter, 1, 2 and 3 John, Jude.)

Revelation (The Apocalypse) is a highly symbolic work written to aid Christians under persecution to remain steadfastly loyal to Jesus.

The gospels are our main source of information about the historical Jesus, but above all they are faith testimonials announcing the good news of salvation. Their primary interest is to herald the good news of and about Jesus. The authors, the four evangelists (literally, "proclaimers of the good news"), let their faith in Jesus as

Lord shine forth. They are not primarily interested in all the historical details of Jesus' life on earth, but rather in the good deeds he performed, the words of salvation he taught, and the meaning of his passion, death, resurrection, and glorification.

How Were the Gospels Written? [CCC 126]

Catholics believe that the gospels were written at the end of a three-stage process.

Stage 1: The Life and Teaching of Jesus. This period lasted from the birth of Jesus around 4-6 BC to his death around AD 30 or 33. It includes what Jesus did and taught. Preeminent in each gospel is testimony about Jesus' death and resurrection. The church teaches that the gospels faithfully hand on what the historical Jesus did and taught for our eternal salvation.

Stage 2: Oral Preaching about Jesus. This period lasted from the founding of the church on Pentecost Sunday until the gospels were written. During this time the apostles reflected on the meaning of Jesus and God's work through him. They used hymns, catechetical lessons, prayers, stories, testimonies, and the like to present the words and deeds of Jesus. Some of the traditions about Jesus probably began to take written form during these years.

Stage 3: Written Gospels. The different gospels were written over a period of about 35 years. Mark wrote around AD 65, Luke and Matthew between AD 75 and 85, and John in the last decade of the first century. Each evangelist adapted his materials keeping in mind the circumstances of the particular audience for whom he was writing. Thus, we have four versions of the gospel ("good news") because each of the evangelists was writing for a different community of Christians (for example, Gentiles or Jewish converts) in different circumstances.

What Do We Know About Jesus' Early Life? [CCC 512-534; 561-564]

Matthew and Luke begin Jesus' story with the mystery of his conception. At the annunciation ("announcement" of the birth) to Mary, that faith-filled, obedient daughter of Israel prayed, "Let it be done to me according to your word." Mary freely consented to give birth to "the Son of the Most High." She was not married, and her child would be conceived by the power of the Holy Spirit. Ever-virgin, Mary became the Mother of God and the spiritual mother of all those Jesus came to save. Her openness to God's action in her life serves as a model for Christian discipleship.

Only the gospels of Matthew and Luke give us many details about Jesus' early life. Matthew and Luke both write that Jesus was born of the Virgin Mary in a humble stable in Bethlehem during the reign of Herod the Great. They also tell us of the infancy mysteries which reveal much about Jesus' person and mission. For example, Luke writes of Jesus' circumcision, symbolizing his incorporation into the Chosen People and his humble submission to the Law. The epiphany (Mt 2:1-12), when the magi from the East visit Jesus, reveals that Jesus is not only the Messiah of Israel but God's Son and the Savior of all nations as well. The flight into Egypt and the slaughter of the innocent children clearly indicate how the forces of darkness oppose the Light of the world, and are reminders of the Israelite's experience in Egypt: the slaughter of male babies and the exodus into the desert. The presentation of Jesus in the Temple reveals Jesus' background as a faithful and devoted Jew.

Jesus grew up quietly in the obscure village of Nazareth. Joseph, his foster father, taught him carpentry. Luke records that Jesus accompanied Mary and Joseph to Jerusalem for the great religious feasts of the Jews. Luke also writes that the 12-year-old Jesus astounded the Temple teachers with his intelligence. We hear nothing of Jesus' life after this event other than that he "increased in wisdom, in stature, and in favor with God and with people" (Lk 2:52). These "hidden years" of Jesus' youth reveal a Savior who shared our daily life, humble and out of the limelight. His simple obedience to his mother and foster father and his otherwise ordinary upbringing help us to identify clearly with Jesus. His humble example is our model for how to live, pray, and suffer for our faith.

Did Jesus Have Brothers and Sisters? *[CCC 484-487; 496-501; 510]*

Some people who read the gospels notice that Matthew mentions "brothers" of Jesus and that Mark even names them (Mk 6:3). Thus they conclude that Jesus had siblings, and that Mary had other children.

Catholics have traditionally believed that Jesus did not have blood brothers and sisters and that Mary was always a virgin. For example, the gospels state that Mary was a virgin and that Jesus was conceived miraculously by the power of the Holy Spirit (Mt 1:20 and Lk 1:35), leading to the dogma of the **virgin birth**. The Fathers of the church taught that the virginal conception was God's work, a mystery of salvation. It is a sign of both Jesus' divinity and humanity. The gospels give no indication that Mary had children after the birth of Jesus. Furthermore, church tradition has always taught the perpetual virginity of Mary.

The texts which refer to Jesus' brothers (and sisters) use a word which can also mean *cousin* or even some distant relations of the same generation. Even today people who live in Near Eastern countries and in other tightly knit communities refer to their cousins as brothers and sisters. Further, the gospels also identify two of these so-called brothers of Jesus—James and Joseph—as the sons of another Mary, a follower of Christ (Mt 27:56). Thus both the biblical evidence and the constant teaching of the church argue strongly for the virginity of Mary and the special intervention of God in the conception of Jesus.

It is important to note what Jesus himself said about his true kinsmen:

> "Anyone who does the will of my Father in heaven is my brother and sister and mother" (Mt 12:50).

How Did Jesus' Public Ministry Begin? *[CCC 522-523; 535-550; 565-567]*

After the incident when Jesus was found in the Temple, he next appears on the scene in the "fifteenth year of Tiberius Caesar's reign" (from AD 27-28) when he was in his 30s. Jesus was baptized by John the Baptist, his immediate precursor, sent to prepare the way. By submitting to John's baptism, Jesus accepted and previewed his ongoing mission of God's Suffering Servant. At his baptism the Spirit descended upon Jesus in the form of a dove and a heavenly voice proclaimed, "This is my beloved Son," thus showing Jesus as the Messiah and God's only Son. Jesus then began his ministry.

In the gospel account of Jesus' temptations in the desert (Lk 4:1-13), Jesus is revealed as the New Adam. He remained faithful to God when he rebuffed Satan. He emerged from the desert and preached the advent of God's reign, a reign open to everyone, especially the poor, the lonely, and sinners. To underscore his message about the kingdom, Jesus performed many **miracles**—mighty works, wonders, and signs—that revealed the presence of God's kingdom in his person, thus proving that he was indeed the Messiah, Son of God.

The story and meaning of Jesus' public ministry of preaching and wonder-working—a ministry that led to his death—occupies center stage in the gospel accounts of Jesus' life.

What Special Qualities of the Human Jesus Do the Gospels Reveal? *[CCC 514-515]*

In Jesus, God embraced human nature in all its fragility. The New Testament paints a portrait of Jesus reaching out to those most in need. He did this on their terms and experienced all the same difficulties that they did. He was tired. He cried. He felt pain when he was slapped and scourged. He also shared the joy of being human. He shared meals with friends.

Jesus' whole life revealed the Father; everything he said and did was pleasing to God. Likewise, when we choose to live like the human Jesus, we become Christ-like. This is discipleship-in-action. **Disciple** is "one who learns." Disciples of Christ learn from the Master, imitating him in word and deed.

Jesus' actions and teachings during his short public life disclose an incredible generosity. St. Peter summarized Jesus' personality and works:

> "Because God was with him, Jesus went about doing good and curing all who had fallen into the power of the devil" (Acts 10:38).

Jesus was a healer. Jesus never explained to his disciples the meaning of suffering, but he did heal any suffering he encountered. He received everyone who came to him with love and compassion. He cured not only friends—like Peter's mother-in-law—but also lepers, the blind, the deaf, epileptics, the crippled, the possessed, and many others with various afflictions. He also brought the dead back to life (see, for example, Lk 7:11-17). Jesus' healings were considered miraculous by the people, and they were. Jesus demonstrated God's love in concrete actions on behalf of his people and also showed that God's love has the power to overcome evil.

Jesus was compassionate. Jesus' marvelous deeds show us a compassionate Savior. He associated with the real "losers" of his day, outcasts who for one reason or another were despised by the establishment. The poor, the sinners, the abandoned, widows, and children—all flocked to receive his love and understanding. Crowds smothered him with attention; when he discovered that 5,000 of those who had come to hear him had no food, he fed them. But more importantly, he gave them what they really needed: the healing touch of God's forgiveness and the good news that they were loved.

Jesus was honest with his emotions. For example, when the money-changers violated the sanctity of the Temple, Jesus expressed his anger. He was also impatient at the apostles' slowness to understand him (Mt 16:5-12). When he witnessed the sadness at the death of his friend Lazarus, he was moved deeply and cried (Jn 11:1-44).

Jesus was courageous. He stood up to the false teachers of his day, calling them blind guides and hypocrites and pointing out their error. He rescued the woman who was about to be stoned to death because she was caught in adultery. He boldly preached the Father's will, knowing it would lead to his death. And he did not back down, even though he feared death just as any normal person would:

> "Abba, Father!" he said, "For you everything is possible. Take this cup away from me. But let it be as you, not I, would have it" (Mk 14:36).

Jesus was humble. He was poor and owned no possessions. He came from Nazareth, a nondescript place that was ridiculed even by his disciples (see Jn 1:46). At the Last Supper, he gave his followers a true sign of humble service: He washed their feet, a task that even a slave was not required to do.

Jesus was self-giving. His love, his concern for all people, his miracles, his message of God's forgiveness, his preaching about God's kingdom—all of this got him in trouble with the leaders of his nation. They plotted his death. Jesus knew of the plot but freely allowed himself to be arrested. This arrest led to a trial before the Jewish leaders and before Pontius Pilate, the Roman governor in charge of the Jewish nation. And this trial led to his incredible suffering and an excruciatingly painful death on a cross. He freely gave his life for all people everywhere.

> "No one can have greater love than to lay down his life for his friends (Jn 15:13)."

There was nothing more that he could give.

What Do the Name and Titles of Jesus Reveal About Him? [CCC 430-455]

The name Jesus comes from the Hebrew word *Yehoshua* (Joshua) which means "God saves" or "God is salvation." Thus God's own name is present in the person of the Son. The angel Gabriel revealed this name to Mary (Lk 1:31), thus signifying Jesus' identity and mission. From his conception, God had destined that Jesus would save the world from sin and death.

When the early Christians reflected on Jesus' life and the meaning of his death and resurrection, the Holy Spirit led them to deeper insights into *who* Jesus is. The titles they used when they spoke of Jesus teach us valuable truths about his identity.

Christ. This is one of the most important titles given to Jesus. **Christ** is the Greek word for the Hebrew title *Messiah*. The Messiah was the "anointed one of Yahweh" through whom all God's promises made to the Chosen People were fulfilled. Jesus was anointed with the Spirit of God to accomplish our salvation through a life of suffering service. He accomplished his task through his threefold office of prophet, priest, and king. As the Great Prophet, Jesus spoke for his Father and shared the full message of salvation. As the High Priest, Jesus offered his life for all of us on the altar of the cross. (Today he continues to fulfill the role of High Priest at each celebration of the eucharist.) As True King, Jesus is the rightful ruler of the universe, one who rules gently and compassionately. He uses the power of love and service to attract followers to his way.

Suffering Servant. Jesus was not the kind of Messiah his contemporaries expected; that is, an earthly leader who would throw off the yoke of their foreign oppressors. Jesus, rather, was the Suffering Servant of Isaiah who took on the burdens of his people and redeemed them.

> "The Son of Man came not be served but to serve, and to give his life as a ransom for many" (Mt 20:28).

Son of God. Through his work and words, Jesus revealed himself to be the unique Son of God.

> "The Father and I are one" (Jn 10:30).

Lord. The term Lord has various meanings. A ruler or someone with great power is often called "lord." The term can also be used as a polite and respectful form of address, much like "sir."

However, when used to describe Jesus the title *Lord* means much more than any of these definitions. Rather, Lord refers to its Greek translation, *Kyrios,* which in turn renders the Hebrew *Adonai.* Adonai was the word spoken aloud by Jews whenever the most sacred name Yahweh would appear in the Hebrew scriptures. Thus, to call Jesus Lord (*Kyrios*) is to state that *he is God.* Christians claim that Jesus has the same sovereignty as God and that his death and resurrection have won eternal life for humanity, a gift only God can grant. Christians believe that Jesus is the only one *true* Lord, the only one deserving our total allegiance.

Word of God. John's gospel underscores the divinity of Jesus:

> In the beginning was the Word:
> the Word was with God
> and the Word was God (Jn 1:1).

Human words reveal our thoughts. They express in a symbolic way what is hidden. In a similar way, the Word of God (Jesus) perfectly reveals God the Father. To see the human Jesus is to see God, for Jesus is God-made-man.

Son of Man. Jesus used this title of himself more than any other. Borrowed from Daniel 7:13, it means two things. First, it refers to Jesus as a human being, one like us who will suffer for and serve all people. Second, it describes his role as the judge and the savior through whom God will fully establish his kingdom at the end of time.

How Was the Faith of the Apostles Preserved? *[CCC 688]*

The first few centuries of the church's history were marked by a growth in numbers and in an understanding of Jesus and the meaning of the paschal mystery. The **Fathers of the Church**, leading church thinkers and writers, preserved the apostolic faith in Jesus as they attempted to explain his message to the people of their day.

What Is a Heresy? *[CCC 465-467]*

During the first five centuries or so of Christianity, a number of false teachings about who Jesus was arose in the church. These false beliefs, called heresies, did not reflect the Jesus that the apostles experienced or believed in.

The heresies about Jesus clustered into two main categories— one denying Jesus' true humanity, the other his true divinity. The earliest group of heresies—Gnostic Docetism—denied that Jesus was really a human being. Its followers believed that he only took the *appearance* of a man and only *appeared* to suffer and die for us. On the other hand, Arianism denied the divinity of Jesus. It held that Jesus was the greatest of God's creatures, but he was not God himself.

Other heresies included Nestorianism (the false belief that there were *two* persons in Christ and that Mary was not really the Mother of God) and Monophysitism (the false belief that Jesus' human nature was absorbed into his divine nature, thus, in effect, denying Jesus' true humanity).

How Was Heresy Dealt With? *[CCC 90, 884, 891]*

These heresies confused and misled people. The official church had to counteract these false notions. Thus, under the guidance of the Holy Spirit, the bishops called a series of ecumenical (world-wide) councils to carefully define the nature of Jesus Christ. These councils were Nicaea (325), Constantinople I (381), Ephesus (431), Chalcedon (451), Constantinople II (553), and Constantinople III (680-681). The teachings of these councils state the classic dogmas of Catholics and other Christians about Jesus Christ. A **dogma** is a central doctrine (teaching) of the church which is issued with the highest authority and solemnity by the church leaders.

What Did These Early Councils Teach? *[CCC 464-483]*

Following is a summary of the teaching about Jesus that came from the ecumenical councils mentioned above.

- *Jesus is the only Son of God.* Although Christ had a natural human mother, Mary, he had no natural *human* father. Rather, Jesus' father is the First Person of the Trinity, God the Father. All humans are the adopted children of God; only Jesus is the natural son. Jesus shares in the very nature of God.

- *Jesus Christ is true God.* He was born of the Father and is of one substance with the Father. There was never a time when he was not God.

- *Jesus Christ is true God, "God from God, Light from Light."* The Son, like the Father, has a divine nature. The Son proceeding from the Father is of one substance with the Father. Jesus Christ is true God just as light is identical to the light from which it comes.

- *Jesus is "begotten, not made, one in Being with the Father."* The always-existing Son "proceeds" from the Father—he always proceeded and always will proceed. The Father did not "generate" the Son the way human fathers generate their sons. Christian faith holds that the Son is not *made* by the Father because the Son is not a created being. Rather, the Father "begets" the Son who is one in being with the Father.

The Council of Nicaea distinguished between *begotten* and *created*. The Father begets his Son and creates the world. The Son always existed in relationship to the Father from whom he proceeds. If Jesus is truly the only Son of God, then he must always have been so. As John's gospel so eloquently states:

In the beginning was the Word [the Son]:
the Word was with God
and the Word was God (Jn 1:1).

- *All things were made through the Son.* Since the Son is one in being with the Father, he also shares in the creation of the world. John's gospel puts it this way:

    Through him all things came into being,
    not one thing came into being except
    through him.
    What has come into being in him was life,
    life that was the light of men (Jn 1:3-4).

- *There is only one person in Christ, the divine person,* the Word of God, the second Person of the Blessed Trinity. Thus, everything in Christ's human nature is to be attributed to his divine person, for example, his miracles and even his suffering and death.

- *Mary, by conceiving God's Son, is truly the Mother of God.*

- *There are two distinct natures in the one person of Christ.* Jesus has a divine nature and a human nature. He is perfect in divinity and perfect in humanity. Jesus Christ is true God and true man.

- As a true human being, body and soul, *Jesus embodies the divine ways of God in a human way.*

- As true God and man, *Jesus has a human intellect and a human will.* Both are perfectly attuned and subject to his divine intellect and will, which he has in common with the Father and the Holy Spirit.

- The union of the human and divine natures in the one person of Jesus is so perfect that it is said *in Jesus God truly shared humanity*, truly suffered, truly underwent death, and truly rose victorious over death.

- *Jesus, God-made-man, is our Savior.* By uniting ourselves to his death and resurrection through faith, we will share in the eternal life he has promised.

Concluding Reflections

"But you, who do you say I am?" Jesus put this question to his apostles on the road to Caesarea Philippi. Peter confessed, "You are the Christ, the Son of the living God" (Mt 16:16). Jesus asks this same question of each of us today? "Who am I? Do *you* believe in me?"

The New Testament strengthens our faith in Jesus. It tells us that Jesus was a real, historical person. The gospels, faith summaries testifying to the good news of Jesus, proclaim that Jesus is the Savior of the world. They paint a picture of a remarkable person: a generous healer; a compassionate, forgiving and down-to-earth friend of everyone he met; a courageous individual who lived the love he preached; a humble servant who sacrificed his very life for all people; the "man for others" who witnessed to God's active love for his children.

The New Testament also reveals what early Christians believed about Jesus. Jesus is the Christ, the Messiah promised to the Chosen People. He is the Suffering Servant, the Son of God, the Lord (God), the Word of God, the Son of Man.

In the early centuries of Christianity, doctrines about Jesus developed in response to certain heresies concerning Jesus. Ecumenical councils met to teach in a definitive way that Jesus is truly God and man; that Jesus is one divine person who has both a divine nature and a human nature; that Jesus has two wills; and that Jesus is our Savior.

Many people throughout history have said yes to Jesus; others have rejected him and his message; still others have not heard his good news. What about you? *What do you think of Jesus Christ?*

Is Jesus Christ the Lord of your life? Many of us today think of Lord as a title of power, of one who "lords it over others." But once again, Jesus reveals a unique kind of lordship. "Here I am among you as one who serves" (Lk 22:27). At the Last Supper Jesus says, "You call me Master and Lord, and rightly; so I am" (Jn 13:13), but he shows what true greatness is by washing the feet of his disciples. And he commands us to do likewise.

Prayer Reflection

Praying with scripture. "If you remain in me and my words remain in you, you may ask for whatever you please and you will get it" (Jn 15:7).

Christians believe that the Bible is God's living word. For this word to speak to us, though, we must read and reflect on it. We must pay attention to what the Lord is saying to us through the particular scripture reading. **Meditation** uses the mind and heart to help us hear the word of the Lord. It engages the faculties of thinking and imagination (our minds), the love we have for God (our hearts), and also the resolutions we make to live better Christian lives (our "hands and feet").

Here is a suggested procedure to pray the scriptures:

1. *Select* a passage. (For example, try Mt 4:1-11, Jesus' temptation in the desert.)
2. *Calm yourself.*
3. *Pray to the Holy Spirit* to help you hear what the Lord is saying to you.

4. *Read* the scripture passage *slowly and meditatively.*
5. *Observe.* Step into the story. Choose one character and consider the story from his or her point of view.
6. *Reflect.* What does the story mean? What strikes you as the main point?
7. *Listen.* Ask: "What, Lord, are you saying to *me* in this reading?"
8. *Resolution.* Resolve to do something about the insights you have gained.
9. *Thanksgiving.* Thank the Lord for your time of prayer and insights you have received.

For Discussion

1. What do you admire most about Jesus? How would you like to be like him?
2. Christians believe that Jesus is God-made-man. If God became one of us, what does this tell you about God? about yourself?
3. Which title of Jesus best answers for you the question, "Who do you say I am?" Explain your choice.
4. What is your favorite gospel story about Jesus? What does it reveal about him? What might this choice be saying about your own image of Jesus?

Further Reading

Read Mark's gospel. (It is the shortest of the gospels and can be read in one sitting. It gives a basic picture of Jesus.)

Chapter Four

Jesus: Teacher and Savior

In fact, however, Christ has been raised from the dead, as the first-fruits of all who have fallen asleep. As it was by one man that death came, so through one man has come the resurrection of the dead.
— 1 Corinthians 15:20-21

For our sake he was crucified under Pontius Pilate:
he suffered, died, and was buried.
On the third day he rose again in fulfillment of the Scriptures;
he ascended into heaven and is seated at the right hand of the
Father.
He will come again in glory to judge the living and the dead,
and his kingdom will have no end.
— from the Nicene Creed

Jesus changes people. Simon bar Jonah encounters Jesus and his life changes forever. He becomes Peter, which means "rock." He will eventually die for his Lord.

Jesus finds a Samaritan woman at a well. He reads her soul and sees her faults, but he accepts her and loves her, even though her people are enemies of the Jews. The Lord asks her to believe in him. She does and spreads the good news of the advent of the Savior to the village and countryside.

Jesus meets a man born blind, a beggar. Jesus makes a mud pack, applies it to the wretched man's eyes and instructs him to wash in a pool. The man does and for the first time in his life he can see. The Pharisees are upset because Jesus cured on the Sabbath. Is he or is he not God's man? The beggar knows. "Lord, I believe" (Jn 9:37).

The historical Jesus met and touched people. His touch always demanded some kind of response. The Lord continues to touch us today—through his church, in his holy word, in the sacraments, through other people. He continues to teach us. He awaits our response.

The artist Holman Hunt painted a thought-provoking picture entitled "The Light of the World." In it we see a patient, gentle Jesus standing before a closed, ivy-covered door. He is wearing a priestly breastplate and holds in one hand a lamp. He is standing at the door and is knocking.

But no one answers. Yet, Jesus still knocks. His eyes shine with compassionate love; his face beams welcome.

As you study the painting you soon notice there is no knob or latch on the outside of the door. It can only be opened from within.

This chapter will look to the teaching of Jesus and what he wants from those who believe in him. It will also touch on one of the greatest truths his life reveals: To follow Jesus means to partake in the paschal mystery. If we unite ourselves to our Lord, we will share in his everlasting life.

As you read this chapter, ask yourself whether you will open the door of your heart to this wonderful Teacher and Savior.

Why Is Jesus Called a Teacher? *[CCC 427]*

The Jesus of history was both a healer and a teacher. He gathered around him twelve apostles and carefully instructed them so that they could carry on his work and preach his message. In addition, he traveled throughout the Holy Land preaching to the people in the fields, on the hillsides, by the seashores, in the marketplaces, and in the synagogues.

What Characterized Jesus' Teaching Style? *[CCC 546]*

Jesus' teaching style was imaginative and provoked much interest. His whole life, every action and word he spoke, was his teaching. People took notice when he healed lepers or associated with sinners or dined with tax collectors. They listened when he boldly scolded the hypocrites. But they were especially delighted with his parables. Jesus' parables were short stories with a religious message and a surprising ending. They were drawn from ordinary life: fishing, farming, weddings, banquets, housekeeping, children at play. They were memorable and caused people to ponder his message.

Why Is Jesus' Teaching Important? *[CCC 561]*

Christians believe that what Jesus taught—by his life, his preaching, his miracles, his loving acceptance of people, his prayer, his death for our salvation—conveys the most important message God ever delivered to us. One of Jesus' titles, Word of God, stresses that Jesus communicates the good news of salvation, the message that saves us and wins for us eternal life. The Word of God is the message of God.

The gospels proclaim the meaning of the life, suffering, death, resurrection, and glorification of Jesus. But they also record the words of the Word of God. These words are life giving. They show us the way to true happiness; they unlock the meaning of life. When we read the gospels with faith or hear them proclaimed at Mass, we are listening to the Lord himself who said he was the Good Shepherd, the gate. "Anyone who enters through me will be safe" (Jn 10:9).

What Did Jesus Teach? *[CCC 541-545; 551-553; 562; 567]*

Here is a short summary of some of the major points of Jesus' teaching, his good news. Read and prayerfully reflect on the scripture passage given for each point.

- *The reign of God is here.* The term **reign (or kingdom) of God** refers to God's active participation in life, both in heaven and on earth. God's presence can be detected in the actions of justice, peace, and love. Jesus himself ushers in God's reign. His healing of people's physical, emotional, and spiritual hurts were signs of the kingdom. Jesus taught that although the reign of God starts small and will meet resistance, it will inevitably grow and powerfully transform all humanity. (Read Mark 4:1-20; 26-32.)

- *God is a loving Father.* Jesus' address of God as **Abba** ("dear Father") highlights God's love for everyone as a parent tenderly loves a child. God's love is so great that Abba sent his only Son to live among us and gain eternal life for us. We can approach God with confidence, knowing in faith that Abba will provide for us and answer our most pressing needs. (Read Luke 11:1-13.)

- *God is merciful.* The parable of the lost son shows the depths of God's mercy. In the parable, the father accepts the wayward son back into his household even though the son squandered his inheritance in a sinful, wasteful life. Because God is so forgiving, Jesus taught that we should be joyful, happy people who imitate the Father by forgiving those who have hurt us and showing mercy to all. (Read Luke 15:11-32.)

- *God's love is for everyone.* God's reign embraces not only the Chosen People but all people as well. Jesus told a parable in which all people were invited to the heavenly banquet. Entrance into God's kingdom is a free gift from a merciful God; we cannot earn it. We show our appreciation for this gift when we unite our love of God and neighbor.

  "You must love the Lord with all your heart, with all your soul, and with all your mind. This is the greatest and the first commandment. The second resembles it: *You must love your neighbor as yourself"* (Mt 22:37-39).

  And who is our neighbor? Everyone, even our enemy. (Read Luke 10:29-37 and Matthew 22:1-14.)

- *Repent, believe the good news, and imitate Jesus' life of service.* If we want God's reign to touch our hearts, then we must turn from our sins and put on the mind of Jesus Christ. We should be humble and admit that we need God's help to live good lives. We must believe that Jesus is God's Son, the way to happiness, and we must become his disciples. We must be light to the world, allowing the Lord to shine through us by serving others. What we do to others, especially the "least of these," we do to the Lord. (Read Luke 18:9-14 and Matthew 25:31-46.)

- *The Lord is present in his church.* Jesus promised that he will be with us until the end of time. One way he does this is through his church, which he established through the apostles. He entrusted special authority to Peter and his successors (the popes). The bishops and their helpers (priests) can forgive sin in Jesus' name, teach in matters of doctrine, and guide in matters of church discipline. The Lord is also active in the communal life of the church, participating in the lives of all its believers. The church, the body of Christ and temple of the Holy Spirit, is the seed and beginning of God's kingdom. (Read John 21:15-19.)

- *The Lord is present through the Holy Spirit.* Until Jesus comes again in glory, he has sent the Holy Spirit—a comforter—to unite his people in love with one another and with the Father and the Son. The Holy Spirit—the third person of the Trinity dwells within us—guides, strengthens, and sanctifies us as we try to follow in the Lord's footsteps and joyfully await the day of his arrival. (Read John 14:16-18, 25-26; 16:7-15)

- *To accept Jesus is to accept the cross.* To follow Jesus means to do God's will. This means living morally and serving others. Moral living and service will lead first to renouncing sin and the world's false enticements to happiness and then, inevitably, to suffering. Doing God's will requires self-denial and sacrifice, walking in the very footsteps of the Lord. "Whoever wishes to come after me must deny himself, take up his cross, and follow me" (Mt 16:24 *NAB*). But Jesus promises that he will make the burden "light and easy" and that we will share in the peace and joy of the resurrection. A life of service means dying to selfishness, but it leads to an eternal life of happiness. (Read Luke 12:13-21; 13:22-30; 16:19-31.)

The gospels also quote Jesus on the following subjects:

Discipleship "If anyone wants to be a follower of mine, let him renounce himself and take up his cross every day and follow me" (Lk 9:23).

Enemies "Love your enemies and pray for those who persecute you" (Mt 5:44).

Faith "If you had faith like a mustard seed you could say to this mulberry tree, 'Be uprooted and planted in the sea,' and it would obey you" (Lk 17:6).

Forgiveness Then Peter went up to him and said, "Lord, how often must I forgive my brother if he wrongs me? As often as seven times?" Jesus answered, "Not seven, I tell you, but seventy-seven times" (Mt 18:21-22).

How to Live: "So always treat others as you would like them to treat you" (Mt 7:12).

Humility "Many who are first will be last, and the last, first" (Mk 10:31).

Judgment "Do not judge, and you will not be judged" (Mt 7:1).

Love "My command to you is to love one another" (Jn 15:17).

Possessions "Watch, and be on your guard against avarice of any kind, for life does not consist in possessions, even when someone has more than he needs" (Lk 12:15).

Prayer "Ask, and it will be given to you; search, and you will find; knock, and the door will be opened to you" (Mt 7:7).

Sincerity "Be careful not to parade your uprightness in public to attract attention; otherwise you will lose all reward from your Father in heaven" (Mt 6:1).

True Happiness "More blessed still are those who hear the word of God and keep it!" (Lk 11:28).

Worry "Set your hearts on his [the Father's] kingdom first, and on God's saving justice, and all these other things will be given you as well. So do not worry about tomorrow: tomorrow will take care of itself. Each day has enough trouble of its own" (Mt 6:33-34).

Why Did Jesus Become Man? *[CCC 456-463]*

The dogma of the Incarnation holds that God took on human flesh, assuming a human nature for *us* and for *our* salvation. The Word of God, the second person of the Trinity, entered human history for our benefit, to show us God's love, and to serve as a model of holiness. The Father sent the Son out of pure love for us and thus kept the divine covenant promises made to Abraham, Moses, and David. God became one of us so we can participate in the divine life, so we might become God's children. In the words of Vatican II:

> For Jesus Christ was sent into the world as a real Mediator between God and men. Since he is God, all divine fullness dwells bodily in Him. . . . He is the new Adam, made head of a renewed humanity, and full of grace and truth (Jn 1:14). Therefore the Son of God walked the ways of a true Incarnation that He might make men sharers in the divine nature. He became poor for our sakes, though He had been rich, in order that His poverty might enrich us (2 Cor 8:9). The Son of Man came not that He might be served, but that He might be a servant, and give His life as a ransom for the many—that is, for all . . . (Decree on the Missionary Activity of the Church, 3).

What Is Salvation? *[CCC 457]*

Jesus' name is highly symbolic in that it means "God saves." This is most appropriate since Christians acknowledge Jesus Christ as our Savior. Jesus came to rescue us from those evil forces within and outside us that keep us from being the kind of people God wants us to be. Jesus came to reconcile humans to God, to heal our brokenness, to renew all of creation.

When we speak of **salvation** we mean the good and happiness that God intends for us, the healing of our hurts, the attainment of God's peace. Salvation is the mending of broken relationships that keep us alienated from God and other people. It is the showering of God's blessings and attention, God's grace, adoption into the divine family, the sharing of his life with us. Salvation means the forgiveness of our sins and redemption from the power of evil and death.

Jesus is the Savior. It is his love, his service, his sacrifice, his presence, his death and resurrection that have won eternal life for us. No one else and nothing else can accomplish what Jesus has accomplished: the forgiveness of sin and the gift of eternal life. Jesus is the good news the apostles preached after his resurrection. "For of all the names in the world given to men, this is the only one by which we can be saved" (Acts 4:12).

Why Did Jesus Suffer and Die for Us? *[CCC 599-623]*

The way a person dies punctuates his or her life. Jesus' death is an exclamation point of profound love for us and unwavering obedience to the Father who sent him to win our salvation. He came to give us abundant life, the very life of God, and he accomplished this by *freely* surrendering his life for us.

> "I am the good shepherd
> the good shepherd lays down his life for his sheep. . . .
> No one takes [my life] from me;
> I lay it down of my own free will,
> and as I have power to lay it down,
> so I have power to take it up again" (Jn 10:11, 18).

In Old Testament times, Jews offered their prized lambs at the Temple as sin offerings. Jesus' death eliminated that need once and for all. Jesus' death was a perfect sacrifice undertaken by the Lamb of God for our benefit. An early New Testament explanation is that Jesus' death was a "ransom," a "redemption" that defeated the powers of evil. Jesus Christ substituted for each of us, taking on our guilt, dying a death we deserve, in order to buy our freedom with his very person and eternal love. St. Paul knew the depths of this love when he wrote:

> You could hardly find anyone ready to die even for someone upright . . . So it is proof of God's own love for us, that Christ died for us while we were still sinners (Rom 5:7-8).

Jesus Christ died for all human beings. He took *our* sins to the cross and, as the New Adam, represented us to the Father. In his suffering and death, Jesus' humanity became the free and perfect instrument of divine love, a self-surrendering gift of love on our behalf. It opened eternal life to us, a supreme gift that we sinners do not deserve. Anyone who reflects on Jesus' death must be drawn to Jesus as the perfect human. He is the exemplar of love, the gracious Lord who gave all that we might live.

Who Killed Jesus? *[CCC 571-598]*

Jesus came to fulfill the Law, but by preaching it definitively with divine authority, he antagonized certain lawyers of the day. He also profoundly respected the Jerusalem Temple, but his prophecy that it would be destroyed as a sign of the last days was distorted by witnesses at his trial before the Jewish high priest. Moreover, by associating with sinners and extending God's love to them through forgiveness and speaking as God himself, Jesus severely alienated certain Jewish leaders. These actions plus Jesus' expelling of demons, his healing on the Sabbath, and his teaching on the ritual laws of purity, led some of his contemporaries to accuse him of false prophecy and blasphemy (making himself God). Under Jewish law, these religious crimes were punishable by death through stoning. However, under Roman law of occupation, only Romans could exercise the death penalty. Thus, some Jewish authorities—acting out of ignorance and a hardened unbelief—turned Jesus over to the Roman procurator, Pilate, for execution as a political criminal, a threat to Caesar.

Historically, Pontius Pilate, the Roman procurator of Judea, Samaria, and Idumea from AD 26-36, sentenced Jesus to death, probably in April of AD 30. He knew Jesus to be innocent, and hence violated his conscience in doing the politically expedient thing.

The real crime has been to assign the blame of Jesus' death on the Jews as a people. The gospel record clearly shows that Jesus' trial was very complex. He had a number of supporters among the adversarial religious sect, the Pharisees (for example, Nicodemus), and at least one ally among the Sanhedrin Jewish court (Joseph of Arimathea). Furthermore, all of Jesus' apostles, disciples, and early converts were Jews. Jesus forgave his executioners on the cross, acknowledging that they did not know what they were doing.

The real culprits for Jesus' death are all of us—sinners. In fact, we who have the gift of faith and know who the savior is, crucify Christ in our hearts whenever we relapse into our sins and give way to our vices. Vatican II teaches:

> What happened in His passion cannot be blamed upon all the Jews then living, without distinction, nor upon the Jews of today. . . . Jews should not be presented as repudiated or cursed by God, as if such views followed from the holy Scriptures (Declaration on the Relationship of the Church to Non-Christian Religions, 4).

Jesus freely accepted his crucifixion. In the ancient world, crucifixion was the most severe, painful, and humiliating form of capital punishment. It was devised to torment a criminal to the point of insanity and prolong the agony of death for hours and even days. Romans reserved this punishment for slaves; thus, Jews saw it as especially loathsome and degrading. Jesus accepted this form of punishment, with its inconceivable pain and humiliation, to prove beyond doubt his immense love for us.

Did Jesus Truly Suffer? *[CCC 572, 612]*

The Creed pointedly states that Jesus really suffered. Jesus endured the *physical* pains of scourging, the crowning with thorns, and the crucifixion. He also suffered the *psychological* pains of rejection by the people and abandonment by his friends. Jesus consented to feel the suffering of crucifixion. In the garden of Gethsemane he anticipated the torture he would endure. Like any normal human would, Jesus recoiled from the torture that lay before him. He prayed, "Father, if you are willing, take this cup away from me." But Jesus revealed his true character when he added, "Nevertheless, let your will be done, not mine" (Lk 22:42). Jesus was obedient. And Jesus was faithful to his preaching and his life of self-sacrificing love for all.

By saying that Jesus suffered, the Creed is underscoring that Jesus was *truly human* and that he loves us beyond what we can imagine.

Did Jesus Really Die? *[CCC 624-637]*

Because of original sin, death touches all humans. Jesus allowed death to touch him to pay for our redemption and also to prove that through his resurrection he conquered sin and death. Jesus died a real death. He allowed the greatest consequence of sin—death—to touch him, too. Thus, Jesus experienced the condition of death, the separation of his soul from his body, between the time of his death on the cross and his resurrection.

All four gospels agree that Joseph of Arimathea, a member of the Sanhedrin, buried Jesus and that others witnessed his burial, including Nicodemus, the Blessed Mother, and Mary Magdalene. Jesus' burial and Matthew's account that Pilate posted guards at the tomb all help show that Jesus was truly dead. However, because Jesus' human soul and body were still linked to the person of the Son, Jesus' mortal corpse was preserved from corruption.

The Apostles' Creed tells us that the dead Christ went to the abode of the dead (*Sheol* in Hebrew, *Hades* in Greek) and there proclaimed the gospel to the just who were awaiting the redeemer.

> And this was why the gospel was brought to the dead as well, so that, though in their bodies they had undergone the judgment that faces all humanity, in their spirit they might enjoy the life of God (1 Pet 4:6).

The good news of the gospel of Jesus Christ is that Jesus rose from the dead. He, the author of life, destroyed the evil one (Satan) who has the power of death, and freed those who are enslaved by the fear of death.

What Is the Meaning of the Resurrection of Jesus?
[CCC 638-653; 656-657]

The **resurrection** of Jesus from the dead is the bedrock fact of our faith. It is the heart of the good news about Jesus.

The resurrection was a real event, with historically verifiable manifestations. It took the apostles and disciples by surprise. Hiding and frightened in Jerusalem after the crucifixion, the apostles did not immediately believe the women when they reported an empty tomb. The empty tomb, however, was an essential sign of Jesus' resurrection—a first step in acknowledging God's work in bringing the Son back to life.

The apostles and disciples did believe, however, when the risen Lord himself appeared to them—in the upper room, to Peter, to Mary Magdalene (the first to see Christ), to disciples on the road to Emmaus, to the apostles in Galilee, to Saul who had been persecuting Christians, to more than 500 disciples at one time (1 Cor 15:5-8). Along with the Spirit's gifts of faith and fortitude, these appearances transformed frightened, confused, and disappointed followers of Jesus of Nazareth into bold, courageous witnesses who willingly lived and died proclaiming, "Jesus Christ is Lord!"

Jesus' resurrection to a glorious body, not limited by space or time and filled with the power of the Holy Spirit, proves that he has conquered sin and death. Christ's resurrection confirms Jesus' works and teachings. It fulfills the Old Testament promises and Jesus' preaching. It proves Jesus' divinity. Additionally, while Jesus' death frees us from sin, his resurrection gives us new life, justifies us in God's grace, and adopts us into the divine family.

Finally, the gospel promises that if we join ourselves to the risen Lord and live according to his message of love, we will also share in our own final resurrection at the end of time. Jesus' resurrection is the promise of our eternal life with God.

What Is the Paschal Mystery? *[CCC 654-655; 658]*

Collectively, the passion, death, resurrection, and glorification (ascension) of Jesus Christ is known as the **Paschal Mystery** (or Easter Mystery). Through these events, Jesus "passes over" from our own world into the Father's glory. These salvation events have redeemed us from slavery to sin and the evil one. They illustrate perfectly the meaning of love. Love is self-giving unto death. The Father blesses those who love with superabundant life.

We celebrate this great mystery of faith in the sacraments, especially in the eucharist when we thank the Father in the Holy Spirit for the Son whose sacrifice has won us salvation. We live the Paschal

Mystery when we allow the risen Lord to live in us and help us worship God in truth and love. We live the Paschal Mystery when we serve our neighbors.

What Is the Meaning of the Ascension of Jesus? *[CCC 659-667]*

The ascension of Jesus refers to the time when Jesus stopped appearing to the disciples in visible form and his glorified body took its rightful place in heaven as equal to the Father. Jesus, too, has prepared a place for us with him in heaven and continuously intercedes for us and prays for us.

In his glorified state, Jesus, who is true God and true man, is not limited to time and space. He lives and reigns forever. He comes to us in many ways. By power of the Holy Spirit, the Lord comes into our hearts at baptism and forms us into his own image. In a special way, he comes to us in the eucharist under the forms of bread and wine. He speaks to us through his holy word, the scriptures. He leads and guides us through the teaching of his holy church and the leaders he has appointed to speak his truth. And he meets us in a special way through our neighbors, especially the "least of these." These include those whom society looks down on (the poor, the powerless, the discriminated against, the lonely, the suffering). Though Jesus reigns as the king of the universe from his heavenly throne (by "the Father's right hand"), he is actively and spiritually present in our life and in the life of the world around us.

When Will Jesus Come Again? *[CCC 668-682]*

Our profession of faith proclaims that Jesus will come in all his glory at the end of time. This second coming of Christ, known as the **Parousia**, will mark the end of the world as we know it. On this day, all creatures in the universe will acknowledge the Lordship of Jesus Christ. Scripture tells us that God's full reign will be established then, bringing about the definitive order of justice, love, and peace to all people. As to its exact day and hour, however, no one knows it. Jesus himself said this knowledge was hidden (Mk 13:32) and that we should live each day as though it were our last. We should always be ready to meet our Lord.

The twenty-fifth chapter of Matthew's gospel gives the criterion for the Lord's judgment of all people and nations: *agape* love, selfless love for others. He will ask questions like this: Did we give food to the hungry and drink to the thirsty? Did we extend hospitality to strangers? clothe the naked? visit the sick and imprisoned? In brief, did we respond to Jesus through others, especially the "least" of our brothers and sisters?

Concluding Reflections

Jesus is a teacher *par excellence*. He verbally delivered a life-saving message; more importantly, he lived what he preached. We have been privileged to hear Jesus' message and to reflect on what he did for us. What difference does Jesus make in your life? For those who believe, Jesus' message is a life-changing one. It is truly "good news."

Jesus revealed that God is a loving Abba, "daddy," one whose love knows no limits, one whom we can approach in utter confidence. God's love for us has no strings attached to it; God loves us for who we are. This is great news—we are worth so much that God's only Son gave up his life for us.

Jesus has saved us. He announces God's forgiveness and heals us of all the hurts which evil and sin can cause. He has conquered sin and death. If we join ourselves to him in faith, accept his forgiveness, and turn from sin, we need fear nothing. Jesus' life witnesses to the greatest news possible: Good triumphs over evil; life wins out over death!

Jesus teaches us how to live. As God's Son who entered fully into our human life, he shows us the path to follow: a life of loving service to others. "Love God above all things and our neighbor as ourselves." God is love and will help us to love. Do this and we will live happy, meaningful lives.

Jesus is our friend. We can meet the risen Lord in prayer, in the depths of our heart. We can encounter him in scripture and in the sacraments. We can receive him in the eucharist. We can find him in one another, in the Christian community of which he is the head. We can meet him in a special way in all the needy, hurting people who come into our lives.

Jesus invites us to change so that we may find true life. Conversion is a lifelong challenge. One question remains: Are we willing to cooperate with the Holy Spirit who is at work in us?

Prayer Reflection

A major challenge on our journey through life is constantly to be aware of Jesus' presence. A true test of our sincerity in turning to our Lord is our ability to see him in others and our willingness to respond to him through them. In life we meet many people who are Jesus-in-disguise.

Meditate on the following quotation. Then, in the presence of the Lord, examine yourself on the questions which follow.

"In truth I tell you, in so far as you did this to one of the least of these brothers of mine, you did it to me" (Mt 25:40).

Who are the "least of these," the brothers and sisters you encounter on a daily basis? Picture them in your mind. See the image of our Lord shining through their faces.

What are their most pressing needs? Ask the Lord to give you insight on how these brothers and sisters need you, your touch, your smile, your acceptance, your support.

Will you respond to these needs? Ask the Lord to empower you with the strength of the Holy Spirit to manifest his love to the least of these.

Conclude your prayer session by making a resolution to do something with the insights the Lord sent you.

For Discussion

1. Jesus is the Savior of the world. What does it mean for you to say "Jesus saves me"?
2. Jesus calls us to conversion. What needs changing in your life right *now* so that you can better respond to the Lord Jesus?
3. Jesus came to "comfort the afflicted and afflict the comfortable." How does Jesus comfort you? How does he challenge you?
4. The Lord says we can call God *Abba*. What does this mean to you? In what way is God's love also like the love of a mother?
5. How can you live the paschal mystery in your daily life?

Further Reading

Read the following parables of Jesus:

The Laborers in the Vineyard (Mt 20:1-16)
The Rich Man and Lazarus (Lk 16:19-31)
The Good Samaritan (Lk 10:29-37)
The Good Shepherd (Jn 10:1-21)
The Prodigal Son (Lk 15:11-32)

Chapter Five

The Holy Spirit:
The Power of Love

Nobody is able to say, "Jesus is Lord," except by the Holy Spirit.
—1 Corinthians 12:3

. . . by the power of the Holy Spirit he was born of the Virgin
Mary and became man.
We believe in the Holy Spirit, the Lord, the giver of life, who
proceeds from the Father and the Son.
With the Father and the Son he is worshipped and glorified.
He has spoken through the Prophets.
— from the Nicene Creed

Life is full of mystery. The natural world is full of silent, invisible power. The imperceptible power of erosion which was at work for eons carved out the magnificent Grand Canyon. The potency hidden in the acorn causes the inevitable growth of the oak tree. The unseen explosions of nuclear energy in our sun millions of miles away give life to our planet. Hidden, silent, powerful realities lurking in the background account for the wonderful and awesome things we see about us.

God is also actively working in the world, but in a way that is veiled from direct human observation. Christians believe in the active presence of the Holy Spirit whose life-giving friendship works for us until the end of time. The Father and the Son have sent the Spirit—the power of God's love—to draw us to God. The Spirit transforms our lives from within. The Spirit's gifts enable us to accomplish God's saving work for others and the world in which we live. The Spirit is the mystery of God's love alive in the world.

A fair question to ask, however, is "How do I know the Holy Spirit is alive in me?" It is similar to asking whether or not there is music on a CD given to you by a friend. You can't know for sure that there is music digitally imbedded on the disk just by looking at it.

You can believe the label on the disk that lists the tunes and you must play the CD on a player and hear it for yourself. In a similar way, you can know that the Spirit lives in you by believing the Father who speaks through his Son, a Son who promised to send us an Advocate, a Comforter, a Spirit of truth to dwell within us. And you can allow the Spirit to sing through you by allowing your life to be a song of love that makes a difference in this world.

This chapter will discuss the Holy Spirit, the Third Person of the Blessed Trinity, and the Spirit's role in our lives.

What Does "Spirit" Mean? *[CCC 691]*

A common philosophical definition describes *spirit* as "the life force of living beings." We occasionally use this same concept when we talk about groups like student bodies or athletic teams. Without spirit, there is no enthusiasm, no life.

Spirit can also mean the real sense or significance of something. The expression "the spirit of the law" reflects this meaning; so does the expression "the spirit of '76."

In a religious sense, we often refer to God as Spirit. The New Testament has many references to the Spirit in connection with Jesus and his followers. Jesus is conceived by the Holy Spirit; God's Spirit descended on him at his baptism; and the Spirit leads him into the desert. Jesus was filled with the Spirit as he preached and performed miracles. Jesus himself promised to send his followers the Spirit of truth who will glorify him.

Our bedrock Christian belief is that the Holy Spirit is the third person of the Blessed Trinity, of the same "substance" (nature) as the Father and the Son. The Holy Spirit is the breath (Spirit) of the Father with whom Jesus is totally filled. The Spirit is active in the Word and is the gift given by the Father and Son to all of Jesus' followers.

How Was the Holy Spirit Present in the Early Church? *[CCC 731-732]*

One of the most important passages concerning the outpouring of the Holy Spirit comes from the Acts of the Apostles, a work written by the evangelist Luke. Acts records the exciting early days of the church, a story which began in an upper room in Jerusalem and spread to the very ends of the Roman empire. It reports in faith-filled language the exciting, dynamic presence of the Holy Spirit who led the early church to proclaim the gospel of Jesus Christ.

In the upper room, the place of the Last Supper, the apostles were gathered there, praying with some of the women, including the Blessed Mother. Perhaps they were still frightened and confused about the events leading to our Lord's death and resurrection.

Suddenly there came from heaven a sound as of a violent wind which filled the entire house in which they were sitting; and there appeared to them tongues as of fire; these separated, and came to rest on the head of each of them. They were all filled with the Holy Spirit and began to speak different languages as the Spirit gave them power to express themselves (Acts 2:2-4).

The apostles went out and spoke to the crowds in tongues so that people from all the different places in the Roman empire each heard their own language. At first the crowds were skeptical; in fact, they thought the apostles were drunk. Peter explained that what was happening was clearly promised by the prophet Joel:

"In the last days—the Lord declares—
I shall pour out my Spirit on all humanity.
Your sons and daughters shall prophesy,
your young people shall see visions,
your old people shall dream dreams. . . .
And all who call on the name of the Lord will be saved" (Acts 2:17, 21).

What Is the Significance of Pentecost? *[CCC 731-732]*

Pentecost proves that Jesus kept his word. The Holy Spirit whom he promised to send had indeed come.

"On that day, the Holy Trinity is fully revealed" (CCC 732).

The rich symbolism of the Pentecost event evokes the power and promises of God. For example, *fire* recalls the holy presence of God at the time of covenant at Mt. Sinai when Yahweh appeared to Moses in a fiery bush. *Tongues* evoke the story of tower of Babel when the pride of the people led to division and confusion. In contrast, the work of the Spirit poured out on the people brings unity, understanding, and insight.

The *wind* ("ruah" in Hebrew) evokes the presence of the Spirit of God hovering over the dark, chaotic waters at the time of creation (Gn 1:2). In the first creation account (see Gn 1:1–2:4a), the Spirit is linked with God's word which brings light, order, and life into existence. In the second creation account (see Gn 2:4b-25), God breathes life into Adam after making him from clay (Gn 2:7). This "breath of life" is God's gift to us, God's spirit in us that enables us to live and to communicate with and to love God.

The Pentecost images inform us that with the coming of the Holy Spirit, God completes all the covenants made with humanity. The Holy Spirit, the Spirit of the risen Jesus and his Father, is a

Spirit of love. The Spirit is a Spirit of unity who creates the disciples into a community, the community we call church. Jesus calls the Holy Spirit a *Paraclete*, a legal term meaning advocate, counselor, lawyer, defender.

This Spirit inaugurates a new age, the age of the church, uniting Jesus' followers into a family of love.

What Was the Holy Spirit's Role in Jesus' Public Ministry? *[CCC 689-693; 717-730; 743; 745-746]*

With the gift of the Holy Spirit, the early Christians could see more clearly how the Holy Spirit figured in Jesus' entire ministry from beginning to end. For example, the Holy Spirit's power enabled Mary to conceive and bring Jesus, God's Son, into our midst (Lk 1:35). The Holy Spirit was present at Jesus' baptism (Lk 3:21-22). Filled with the Holy Spirit, Jesus was led into the desert for prayer and fasting (Lk 4:1). Jesus returned to Nazareth to begin his preaching in the Spirit's power (Lk 4:14). Jesus testified that the Spirit was upon him, anointing him to preach good news to the afflicted, proclaim liberty to the captives, give sight to the blind, and let the oppressed go free (Lk 4:16-21).

When we reflect on the above passages we can see that whenever the Father sends the Son, he also sends the Holy Spirit. The Son and Holy Spirit have a joint, but distinct mission. It is Christ Jesus who is visible, the image of God; however, it is the Holy Spirit who reveals him to us.

In his public ministry, Jesus gradually revealed the mystery of the Holy Spirit, for example, when he conversed with Nicodemus (Jn 3:5-8) and the Samaritan woman (Jn 4:10, 14, 23-24), and when he taught the crowds about the eucharist (Jn 6:27, 51, 62-63). Finally, before the hour of his glory Jesus promised to send the Holy Spirit who would comfort and teach the disciples. John's gospel gives the Holy Spirit center stage. At the Last Supper, the Lord promised:

"I shall ask the Father, and he will give you another Paraclete to
be with you for ever" (Jn 14:16).

A paraclete is someone who will give aid, help, comfort. Another word for paraclete is advocate. Jesus himself fits these terms well, but he promised to send *another* paraclete—

"the Spirit of truth
whom the world can never accept
since it neither sees nor knows him;
but you know him,
because he is with you, he is in you" (Jn 14:17)

Jesus told his friends that he must go the way of suffering, death, and resurrection:

> "Still, I am telling you the truth:
> it is for your own good that I am going,
> because unless I go,
> the Paraclete will not come to you;
> but if I go,
> I will send him to you. . . .
> When the Spirit of truth comes
> he will lead you to the complete truth" (Jn 16:7, 13).

The Spirit remained with Jesus throughout his ministry and even to his death. When a soldier stabbed him with a spear, blood and water gushed out of Jesus' wound, symbolizing the life and waters of the Holy Spirit flowing out to the world (Jn 19:34). Through the Spirit, God raised Jesus from the dead with the risen Lord taking on a spiritual, glorified body. As resurrected Lord, Jesus is, through the power and presence of the Holy Spirit, the invisible head of his body, the church. And, drawing on the image of St. Augustine, the Holy Spirit is the soul of the church.

How Is the Spirit Represented in the Old Testament? *[CCC 702-716]*

The concept of the Holy Spirit developed gradually in the Old Testament. Most typically the biblical authors use the Hebrew word *ruah* (wind or breath) to speak of God's mysterious, powerful, and life-giving presence in creation and at work among the Chosen People. In later writings, the Hebrew scriptures develop the notion of Yahweh's spirit in personal terms—guiding and instructing.

Also, the Old Testament authors saw the Spirit more as a force, a divine power, and a presence. They lacked a clear idea of the Spirit as a separate person of the Blessed Trinity. This can only be recognized when Jesus reveals the Spirit as a distinct person of the Blessed Trinity.

However, with the eyes of Christian faith, we can look back over the Hebrew scriptures and gain wonderful insights into the Spirit's activity. For example, we can see the Spirit of God working at creation (Gn 1:2) and giving the breath of life to Adam and Eve (Gn 2:7). It is God's Spirit that helped God's people keep his Law (Ez 36:26-28).

God's Spirit also keeps the world in existence, working in a special way through humans. For example, God inspired and gave strength to judges like Samson (Jgs 13–16) and to kings like Saul and David (1 Sm 16:13-14) who were to rule in Yahweh's name. In addition, God's spirit "anointed" Israel's prophets like Elijah (2 Kgs 2:9) and Elisha (2 Kgs 2:15) who spoke on God's behalf by instructing people to remain faithful to the covenant.

Salvation history tells how the Chosen People suffered setbacks because of their sinfulness. Consequently, they came under the rule of various foreign powers like the Assyrians, Babylonians, Persians, and Greeks. The prophets, in turn, promised the coming of a Messiah. On this person God's Spirit would rest in a special way.

> Here is my servant whom I uphold,
> my chosen one in whom my soul delights.
> I have sent my spirit upon him,
> he will bring fair judgment to the nations.
> He does not cry out or raise his voice,
> his voice is not heard in the street;
> he does not break the crushed reed
> or snuff the faltering wick.
> Faithfully he presents fair judgment;
> he will not grow faint, he will not be crushed
> until he has established fair judgment on earth (Is 42:1-4).

What Are Some Images of the Holy Spirit? *[CCC 694-701]*

The Bible has many rich images of the Holy Spirit that help us understand the Spirit's action in salvation history. Previously mentioned was the Hebrew term *ruah* which denotes breath, air, wind, soul. The Old Testament uses *ruah* 379 times to image God's activities. God's Spirit is present in wind at creation. Psalm 18:11 describes how wind connotes power and mystery. Also, breath (see Ez 37) is the principle of life; its absence means death. We need God to live; God's breath (Spirit) gives us life. Here are some other scriptural images of the Holy Spirit.

- *Fire.* God appeared to Moses in a burning bush and led the Israelites through the desert by pillars of fire. Fire purifies to make one holy. It punishes the wicked, as in Sodom. In brief, fire represents the transforming energy of the Holy Spirit.

Jesus referred to himself as the light of the world. He gave the Holy Spirit to his disciples to empower them to enlighten the world. The Spirit is the inner light who enables us to know Jesus and to burn with love for him and others.

- *Tongues of fire.* The tongue empowers us to speak. Filled with the Spirit, Jesus spoke his Father's truth. He had the power to forgive sin, to cure, to control nature, and to bring the dead back to life.

The Holy Spirit enables us to reverse the prideful confusion of Babel (see Gn 11:1-9). The Spirit empowers us to proclaim Christ, to speak the truth, and to create community in the Lord's name.

- *Anointing.* "Christ" means "anointed one." Though there were several "anointed ones" in the Old Testament, Jesus is God's Anointed in a unique way: the humanity the Son assumed was entirely anointed by the Holy Spirit. The Holy Spirit established him as "Christ" (*CCC* 695).

- *Water.* The rich symbol of water signifies both death and life. For example, God punished humanity in the time of Noah by sending the Flood. But God also created the world out of the watery chaos. God sent springs of water to the Chosen People in the desert.

Jesus clearly associated water and the Spirit when he said to Nicodemus:

> "No one can enter the kingdom of God without being born through water and the Spirit" (Jn 3:5).

This is a clear reference to the sacrament of baptism which brings about death to an old life of sin and rebirth to eternal life. The waters of baptism initiate us into Christ's body, the church, and bestow on us the gift of the Holy Spirit.

- *Hand.* Jesus healed through touch. In his name, so did his apostles. Through the imposition or laying on of hands, the Holy Spirit was given. This is a sign used in several sacraments to signify the giving of the Holy Spirit.

- *Dove.* In the Hebrew scriptures, a dove released by Noah returned with an olive tree branch to show that the flood waters were receding. This symbol of life is also frequently mentioned as a purification offering for the poor (for example, Lv 5:7).

The gospels describe the Spirit's descent on Jesus at the time of his baptism as being "like a dove." The descending dove suggests God's hovering Spirit over the waters at creation. It is also a symbol of gentleness, virtue, and peace—all gifts of union with the Holy Spirit.

Three other symbols of the Holy Spirit mentioned in the *Catechism of the Catholic Church* are the *seal* (which signifies the indelible effect of anointing with the Spirit), the *finger of God* (which writes the divine law on our hearts) and the *cloud and light* (which reveal the saving God, yet veil the divine glory).

Is the Holy Spirit God? [CCC 243-248]

The Nicene Creed professes that the "Holy Spirit is Lord and Giver of Life." While the Council of Nicaea (325) clearly taught the divinity of Jesus to counteract the Arian heresy, the Council of Constantinople (381) strongly affirmed the divinity of the Third Person of the Blessed Trinity—the Holy Spirit. The Holy Spirit is *not* some *creature* like angels who serve as God's messengers. *Nor* is the Holy Spirit some impersonal force. Rather, the Holy Spirit is *Lord*, God, whose important role is to give us a share in God's own divine life. The Holy Spirit does this by conforming us to Christ, by making us Christ-like. Drawn to the Son, we thus have access to the Father: "To the Father through the Son in the Holy Spirit."

How Does the Holy Spirit Give Us Life? [CCC 733-736; 742]

The Spirit is the Giver of Life. As a life-giver, the Spirit teaches, directs, and strengthens church leaders (especially the pope and bishops) as well as individual Christians. The Holy Spirit is the internal teacher, the one who makes it possible for us to recognize the truth about Jesus:

> Nobody is able to say, "Jesus is Lord" except in the Holy Spirit (1 Cor 12:3).

The Holy Spirit also leads individual Christians to judge how best to live the Christian life and directs the pope and bishops to lead the Christian community with wisdom and compassion. Finally, the Holy Spirit both inspires us to live Christ-like lives and gives us the spiritual gifts to do so.

The Holy Spirit is truly God's grace to us. Grace is a traditional term meaning good will or benevolence—a gift given. Grace is a good word to apply to the Holy Spirit because we can see how gracious God is to us by sending the Holy Spirit to live within us, thus enabling us to be temples of the all-holy God. At baptism, the Spirit comes to us as God's gift. The grace of the Holy Spirit *justifies* us, that is, cleanses us of our sins and communicates to us God's righteousness through faith in Jesus. The Spirit initiates the lifelong conversion and healing process that leads us to eternal life, and elevates us to share in God's own life.

The most incredible effect of the Spirit is, in fact, adoption into God's own family. By virtue of God's unmerited friendship and love, the Spirit changes our identities from that of slaves and mere creatures to that of sons and daughters of a gracious, loving Father. The Spirit enables us to call God, "Abba."

> You received the spirit of adoption, enabling us to cry out, "Abba, Father!" The Spirit himself joins with our spirit to bear witness that we are children of God. And if we are children, then we are heirs, heirs of God and joint-heirs with Christ, provided that we share his suffering, so as to share his glory (Rom 8:15-17).

The Holy Spirit and the Lord Jesus continue their divine mission in the church. The church is called the body of Christ and temple of the Holy Spirit. The Holy Spirit builds, gives life to, and sanctifies the church. Through the church, the Spirit draws us to Christ, reveals the Lord to us, and makes present the Paschal Mystery of Christ, especially in the sacrament of the eucharist, a sign of the Holy Trinity's intimate friendship with us.

What Is the Holy Spirit's Role in the Forgiveness of Sins? [CCC 976, 1485]

A second story of the giving of the Holy Spirit appears in John's gospel. On Easter Sunday the risen Lord appeared to the apostles who were afraid and confused in the upper room. Twice he offered them his greetings of peace, and then he sent them on a great mission: "As the Father sent me, so I am sending you" (Jn 20:21). After saying this he breathed on them and said:

> "Receive the Holy Spirit.
> For those whose sins you forgive,
> they are forgiven;
> for those whose sins you retain,
> they are retained" (Jn 20:22-23).

Just as God breathed life into our first parents at the beginning of creation, so Jesus creates his disciples anew. He gives them a new life, a life of the Spirit, a life as children of God. The Holy Spirit helps Christians on the great mission of continuing Jesus' work of forgiveness and reconciliation.

How Does the Holy Spirit Help Us to Live Like Christ? [CCC 737-741; 747; 1830-1832; 1845]

The Holy Spirit showers us with many gifts that help us live a Christian life. Their purpose is to build up Christ's body and to keep us from prideful self-glory. These gifts include:

- *Gifts that make us holy.* These are the traditional seven **gifts of the Holy Spirit**, that is, permanent dispositions that incline us to respond to the Holy Spirit's promptings. *Wisdom* enables us to look on reality from God's point of view. *Understanding* helps us to reflect on the deeper meaning of our faith. *Knowledge* notes how God is working in one's life and in the world. *Counsel (right judgment)* helps us form our conscience in light of church teaching. *Fortitude* is the strength to follow one's own convictions. *Piety (reverence)* moves us to respect the Lord through praise and worship and enables us to respect the dignity and worth of others. *Fear of the Lord (wonder and awe)* shows concern about the reality of sin in one's life.

- *Gifts that help us serve the church.* St. Paul lists other gifts which build up the body of Christ (see 1 Cor 12:4-11). These include wisdom, knowledge, faith, healing, miracle-working, prophecy, discernment, speaking in tongues, and interpreting tongues. These charisms (or special gifts) point to God working in the community. They are for the benefit of the community.

- *Gifts that manifest spiritual fruit.* St. Paul lists some **fruits of the Holy Spirit**, perfections that result from the Holy Spirit living in us. These are the first fruits of eternal glory (see Gal 5:22-23). Church tradition lists them as: charity, joy, peace, patience, kindness, goodness, generosity, gentleness, faithfulness, modesty, self-control, and chastity.

These lists are not mutually exclusive. All signs of a faithful Christian life result from spiritual union with Christ, the true vine (Jn 15:1). The Spirit of love is God's gift to us through Jesus. Love is the central gift—bestowed on us freely and independently of our talents or personal merits. God does not love us because we are good. In contrast, we are good because God loves us. If we allow the Spirit to reign in our hearts, then love and all its many rich facets will shine forth in our lives. St. Paul described beautifully the fruits of love alive in us:

> Love is always patient and kind; love is never jealous; love is not boastful or conceited, it is never rude and never seeks its own advantage, it does not take offense or store up grievances. Love does not rejoice at wrongdoing, but finds its joy in the truth. It is always ready to make allowances, to trust, to hope and to endure whatever comes (1 Cor 13:4-7).

How Does the Holy Spirit Work in Human History?
[CCC 687; 744]

The Holy Spirit has been at work throughout human history. In a special way, the Spirit "spoke" to all ages in the history of the Chosen People. And the Spirit speaks today to the spiritual descendants of the Jews, the Christian community. The letter to Hebrews affirms:

> At many moments in the past and by many means, God spoke to our ancestors through the prophets; but in our time, the final days, he has spoken to us in the person of his Son (Heb 1:1-2).

Prophets like Moses, Isaiah, Jeremiah, and Ezekiel spoke for God. They tried to call the kings and people back to fidelity to God's covenant. But too often the leaders put their faith in power, money, and armies. The people worshipped false gods, ignored the Law, and scorned the weak and the poor.

The Spirit spoke to the hard-hearted Israelites by promising a new and everlasting covenant (Jer 31:31-34, Ez 36:26-27). Responding to the graces of the Holy Spirit, Mary said "yes" to God at the annunciation. Thus, by the power of the Spirit working in her, the Father gave the world the Son, Emmanuel, "God-with-us." Jesus, of course, was the prophet *par excellence*.

Jesus speaks perfectly for God because he has the fullness of the Holy Spirit. He, the Word of God, could say:

> "Do you not believe
> that I am in the Father and the Father in me?
> What I say to you I do not speak of my own accord:
> it is the Father, living in me, who is doing his works"
> (Jn 14:10).

How Does the Holy Spirit Speak to Us in Scriptures?
[CCC 105-108; 135-137; 141]

The Holy Spirit continues to instruct us through the sacred scriptures. The Holy Spirit inspired the biblical authors. Though limited by their own cultures and literary abilities, they used their unique talents to write what God wanted written for our benefit. Thus, the Bible contains God's prophetic word, histories, maxims, and other writings that help make up the sacred deposit of faith.

Today, the Spirit helps us understand the scriptural word and helps it come alive in our hearts. When we read, meditate on, and live the scriptures, then we are responding to the Holy Spirit who continues to enlighten us. In addition, the Spirit guides the pope and the bishops, the successors to Peter and the apostles, when they teach us the meaning of the sacred scriptures and their application to daily life.

What Are Other Ways the Holy Spirit Speaks to Us Today?
[CCC 688]

The Holy Spirit speaks God's word in many ways. The beauty of creation, the special people who come to us, the triumphs and tragedies of our personal lives—all these can be God's word to us. The Holy Spirit also teaches each age through the "signs of the times." These build God's reign, advance justice, and extend the Lord's healing, comforting touch to the oppressed and suffering.

Faith enables us to recognize these signs in the advances of science, in cries for equality and justice, in international cooperation, and in many other ways. The Holy Spirit is especially active through the church, the temple of the Holy Spirit. As noted above, we can experience the Spirit today in the inspired scriptures, in Tradition, in the church leaders whom the Spirit assists, and in the words and symbols of the sacraments which make us holy. The Holy Spirit also intercedes for us through prayer, guides the missionary activity of the church, and reveals his holiness through the witness of the lives of the saints who cooperate so well with God's plan of salvation.

Concluding Reflections

In the Bible, the Lord reveals the Holy Spirit to us in a number of images. The Spirit, the power of love is, life-giving breath, a wind that creates and guides. The Spirit is the fire that enables us to love, burning in our hearts to create community with others and the Lord; the life-giving water that brings growth; and tongues of fire that embolden us to proclaim the prophetic word with courage.

Common human experiences with these elemental images can reinforce our understanding and appreciation of the role of the Holy Spirit in our lives. For example, just as a cool breeze refreshes us on a sweltering day, so does the Spirit comfort us when we are troubled. Just as the sailor needs the breeze to fill the sails, so do we need the gentle guidance of the Spirit on our journey to the Father.

The warmth of a fireplace in the dead of winter conjures up nostalgic images of home and hearth and love. It is the Holy Spirit who thaws our cold hearts, teaching us how to love. The secret attraction of a roaring bonfire at a family picnic celebrates family unity. The Holy Spirit burns in the hearts of Christians, drawing them into community around the Lord's table.

A word of comfort to a troubled colleague or a hurting family member demonstrates the healing power of human speech rightly used. The Holy Spirit, who appeared as tongues of fire, inspires us even today to seek out and speak on behalf of the "least of these" in our midst, for example, speaking in defense of the unborn.

All of us have relished a sip of cold, refreshing water for our dry throats. The Holy Spirit is living water. The Spirit quenches our thirst for meaning in life by attracting us to Jesus Christ. A gentle rainfall on a dusty day brings growth to crops; the Holy Spirit gives growth to our faith, especially when we feel spiritually dry.

These powerful images of the Holy Spirit remind us that God's presence sustaining our very lives is a dynamic power of love.

Prayer Reflection

Pray the following with deep faith and conviction:

Come, Holy Spirit, fill the hearts of your faithful
and kindle in them the fire of your love.
Send forth your Spirit, O Lord, and renew the face of the earth.
O God,
on the first Pentecost
you instructed the hearts of those who believed in you
by the light of the Holy Spirit;
under the inspiration of the same Spirit,
give us a taste for what is right and true
and a continuing sense of his joy-bringing presence and power,
through Jesus Christ our Lord. Amen.

For Discussion

1. What is the most meaningful image of the Spirit for you? Explain.
2. The Holy Spirit enables us to be members of God's family. This means that all others are our brothers and sisters. What is the practical meaning of this truth in your daily relations with other people?
3. The Holy Spirit is a spirit of truth, a truth that leads to freedom. How can you personally witness to the truth? Give personal examples of how the truth set you free.
4. The Holy Spirit enables God's children to love. Loving others often increases our faith. Give examples of times in your life that your love of others increased your faith in a loving God.

Further Reading

Old Testament: Exodus 19–20
Isaiah 11:1-3; 61:1-2
Ezekiel 36:26-28; 37:1-14
Joel 3:1-3
New Testament: 1 Corinthians 12:4–13:13

Chapter Six

The Blessed Trinity: Unity in Community

Glory be to the Father,
and to the Son,
and to the Holy Spirit,
as it was in the beginning,
is now,
and ever shall be,
world without end. Amen.

Some people are so proud of their intelligence that a pundit once observed that they are like condemned criminals who are proud of the vastness of their prison cells.

The famous poet Milton taught that the end of all learning is to know God, and out of that knowledge to love and imitate him.

True knowledge of God does not begin with intellectual prowess but with humility. It is the one sure path to God. When asked what is the first thing in religion, St. Augustine replied, "The first, second, and third thing therein—no, all—is humility."

Christians learn this lesson well when they contemplate the fathomless mystery of the Blessed Trinity. Trying to explain this mystery is like trying to explain a kiss. The dictionary defines a kiss as "a caress with the lips; a gentle touch or contact."

But this hardly captures the essence of a mother tenderly placing her lips on her newborn. Nor is this adequate to capture a young man saying "goodnight" to his newfound love.

In the same way, anything we say about the Blessed Trinity is inadequate to the reality. We will never be able to fully comprehend, explain, or even define the nature of God. The best we can do is to trust God's Word, Jesus our Lord and Savior, who through the Holy Spirit revealed to us that our loving God is a trinity of persons—the

Father, the Son, and the Holy Spirit. This is the central mystery of Christian faith and life. All other teachings of the church are derived from it. God's true nature is a deep mystery, beyond mere human knowledge (*CCC* 261). Yet, the Lord Jesus in the Spirit has privileged us with the profound truth that "The Father is God, the Son is God, and the Holy Spirit is God, and yet there are not three gods but one God" (Athanasian Creed).

This chapter will highlight some major teachings of the last few chapters. It will then look to Jesus to see that he reveals the *one* true God as a Blessed Trinity. Finally, it will present what the church teaches about this mystery: unity in community.

Who Is God? *[CCC 210-221]*

When Moses asked for the divine name, God responded, **Yahweh**, a name so sacred that pious Jews avoided even saying it. Yahweh means "I am who am." This means simply, God is being who God is. Yahweh is truth and love, a "God of tenderness and compassion, slow to anger, rich in faithful love and constancy" (Ex 34:6).

Everything Jesus did and everything he taught reveals to us the truth and love of God. It is through Jesus, united in the Holy Spirit, that we learn of God's true nature. The questions that follow highlight some of his teachings concerning the Trinity, one God in a community of three persons.

Who Is God the Father? *[CCC 238-242]*

Though not named as such, the God of the Hebrews is actually God the "Father" because God created the world, fathered a covenant with the Chosen People and gave them the Law, and served as their king.

The New Testament reveals that the God of the Hebrew scriptures is the Father of the Lord Jesus Christ. God is not only the Father Creator; God is eternally Father to his only Son. Jesus is God's unique Son, a Son who shares in the nature of the Father.

Jesus reveals his unity with the Father in his prayer when he addresses God as *Abba*, a simple term of endearment. Furthermore, when speaking about his special and *unique* relationship with the Father, Jesus says, "My heavenly Father" (Mt 15:13) and "Your Father in heaven" (Mt 5:45).

Jesus, God's only Son, however, came to preach "good news." This good news is indeed great news because Jesus tells the apostles that they—and we his disciples—can address God as *Abba*, too. The Blessed Trinity has adopted us into the divine family, a community of love.

What is our Father like? Jesus teaches that the Father loves us in a way that is beyond our comprehension. He is like the father in the parable of the prodigal son who welcomes back his wayward child with open arms—no questions asked. He is like a good shepherd who goes out of his way to seek a lost sheep. The Father loves immeasurably and unconditionally. We can't earn this love; it is a gift showered on good and evil people alike.

Jesus' whole life centered on doing his Father's will. He wants us to obey the Father's will, too. He wants us to pursue his kingdom, giving up everything else if necessary, like the man who sold everything he had to buy the pearl of great price. He wants us to imitate his Father—our Father by adoption—by forgiving those who hurt us, by refraining from judging others, by seeking perfection in everything. He tells us not to fret because our loving Father will take care of all our needs; after all, he provides for the birds of the field, and we are more important than they.

Jesus tells us to pray to the Father, that he will answer us. He urges us not to give up. God knows our needs and will give us what is good for us.

St. Paul reminds us that the Father creates all things and wills the salvation of everyone through his Son. He sent his only Son to redeem us and call us to faith and glory. God is the Father of all people, but he is the special Father of Jesus Christ. The Father, who raised Jesus, will also raise us on the last day.

> Thank God, then, for giving us the victory [over death] through Jesus Christ our Lord (1 Cor 15:57).

Is It Also Proper to Refer to God as "Our Mother"? *[CCC 239]*

Without a doubt, Jesus frequently used the idea of Father in his teaching about God. But at times, for example when he compared God's love to that of a woman who rejoiced over finding a lost coin, Jesus used feminine images for God. The medieval mystic Julian of Norwich and others point out that the idea of God as Mother also adds to our understanding of God's love for us. Willing to sacrifice her own life, a mother gives her child life by entering the valley of the shadow of death. A good mother tenderly protects, unblinkingly forgives, and unconditionally accepts her child. Every child who experiences true motherly love knows that it is the most natural, available, compassionate, and self-giving kind of love known to us. God's love is exactly like that. A Jewish proverb says it best: "God could not be everywhere, and therefore he made mothers."

The church teaches that the image of motherhood is indeed an apt way to describe God's eternal and parental love for us and God's tender and intimate relationship to us. But we should remember that God is pure spirit, neither male nor female. The best of human parents have their limitations. God embodies all the positive traits we traditionally associate with both fathers and mothers—creativity, sustenance, nurture, guidance, availability, tenderness, compassion, love. But God possesses these traits without limit. God's love is unimaginably greater than the love of any human father or mother.

How Is Jesus the Son of God? *[CCC 240-242]*

Christians believe that Jesus is "the human face of God." When Philip asked Jesus to show him and the other apostles the Father, Jesus replied:

> "Anyone who has seen me has seen the Father, so how can you say, 'Show us the Father'? Do you not believe that I am in the Father and the Father is in me?" (Jn 14:9-10).

It was only after the resurrection of Jesus and the outpouring of the Holy Spirit on Pentecost that the apostles and other disciples began to really understand who Jesus was. Yet Jesus had done many startling things while he was with them: He cured lepers, made deaf people hear, gave sight to the blind, enabled the lame to walk, drove out demons. He demonstrated his power over nature when he calmed the storm and multiplied the loaves and fishes. He claimed unity with the Father and backed up his claim by forgiving sin, something only God could do. He raised the dead to life. He claimed to be the resurrection and the life, the living water that leads to eternal life, the light of the world.

As we have seen, Jesus called God Father and is related to him in a unique way. He taught that only the Son knows the Father, that all the Father has is his, that the Father has given him all power, that his words are the words of the Father who sent him. If we know Jesus, we know the Father. And if we love Jesus, both Jesus and the Father will take up their dwelling within us.

The early Christians, who had seen Jesus risen from the dead and who were filled with the power of the Holy Spirit, proclaimed with no hesitation: Jesus is Lord! Jesus is the Son of God! Jesus is God!

Everything about Jesus reveals the Father. His presence, his words, his healing touches, his forgiving glances and especially his death and resurrection show us what is really real. They reveal God because Jesus is the Word of God. Christians believe:

> For this is how God loved the world:
> he gave his only Son,
> so that everyone who believes in him may not perish
> but may have eternal life (Jn 3:16).

Jesus is Emmanuel, "God-is-with-us." Jesus is God-made-man who comes to deliver us from sin and death and bestow on us a share in the eternal life he shares with the Father from all time. And he gives the greatest of all promises: "And look, I am with you always; yes, to the end of time" (Mt 28:20).

How Does the Holy Spirit Reveal the True Mystery of the Trinity? *[CCC 243-244]*

The last chapter featured many references to the Holy Spirit in the teaching of Jesus and the early Christians. For example, the Spirit empowered the early Christians on Pentecost Sunday and was with the Lord throughout his ministry. Moreover, Jesus promised to send the Paraclete to his followers. He promised that the Spirit of truth and love would take up his dwelling in God's people.

One very important gospel passage testifies to the Spirit's presence at the Lord's baptism:

> Now it happened that when all the people had been baptized and while Jesus after his own baptism was at prayer, heaven opened and the Holy Spirit descended on him in a physical form, like a dove. And a voice came from heaven, "You are my Son; today have I fathered you" (Lk 3:21-22).

These verses are important for two reasons: First, they explicitly mention all three persons of the Trinity: Father, Son, and Holy Spirit. Catholics use this, and other passages, to help root their belief in the key doctrine of the Trinity, three divine persons in one God. Second, this passage shows how Jesus was filled with the Spirit as he launched out on his public ministry. The Spirit was with Jesus in the desert and during his entire teaching and healing ministry. For example, Jesus cast out demons by the power of the Holy Spirit.

Before his sacrifice on the cross, Jesus promised the Holy Spirit who would come to console his disciples. The Lord had to leave them because he was going the way of suffering, death, and resurrection. But he did not *really* leave them, nor does he leave us. After his resurrection and ascension, his glorified body is no longer visible to us as it was to the disciples who knew him on earth. But Jesus very much remains with his followers. The

Holy Spirit, who *always* existed with the Father and Son, is the very presence of the risen, glorified Lord.

The Holy Spirit attracts us to the Son so that we are able to recognize him as the Messiah, our Savior. The Spirit also enables us to proclaim that God is our Father and is the source of all good gifts given us by our gracious, loving Triune God.

In sum, the sending of the Holy Spirit after Jesus' ascension revealed to Christians the full mystery of the Blessed Trinity.

What Is the Blessed Trinity? *[CCC 232-234]*

> In the name of the Father
> and of the Son
> and of the Holy Spirit. Amen.

Note that Christians are baptized in the *name* of the Father and of the Son and of the Holy Spirit and not in their *names*. There is only *one* God: the almighty Father, his only Son, and the Holy Spirit—the Most Blessed Trinity. Thus, in this short prayer formula, Christians profess their belief in the greatest of all mysteries—the mystery of the Blessed Trinity.

The doctrine of the Trinity is central to Christian faith. It, like other articles in the Creed, is a dogma, a core church teaching; no Christian doctrine is more central than that of the Blessed Trinity.

The closing words of Matthew's gospel strongly attest to the Blessed Trinity. Before ascending to heaven, Jesus said: "Go, therefore, make disciples of all nations; baptize them in the name of the Father and of the Son and of the Holy Spirit" (Mt 28:19).

Belief in the Trinity finds its roots in the first Christians' experience of Jesus. Guided by the Holy Spirit they discovered in his life, death, and resurrection the mystery of one God who exists in a relationship of three persons: Father, Son, and Holy Spirit. St. Paul shared this early belief when he ended a letter to the Corinthians with the following blessing:

> The grace of the Lord Jesus Christ, the love of God and the fellowship of the Holy Spirit be with you all (2 Cor 13:13).

How Can We Begin to Understand the Mystery of the Holy Trinity? *[CCC 236-237]*

Trying to see God as God is impossible for humans. It is like looking directly into the sun. No one can do so without going blind.

And remember, the sun is only a creation of God who is the Light of the World, the Light beyond Light.

We can never fully comprehend God's inmost being as Holy Trinity, a strict mystery hidden in God. It took the Incarnation of God's Son and the gift of the Holy Spirit for humans even to have access to God as God really is.

When reflecting on the Trinity, the Fathers of the Church distinguish between two aspects of God: economy and theology. "Economy" refers to the many works through which God is revealed and communicates the divine life. "Theology" (derived from the Greek *theos,* meaning God) refers to God's inner life as Trinity. Both branches of study help us deepen our understanding of the Blessed Trinity.

God's works reveal who he is in himself; the mystery of his inmost being enlightens our understanding of all his works (CCC 236).

How Do God's Works Reveal the Trinity? *[CCC 257-258]*

God is more intimate to us than we are to ourselves. God chose to approach us through Jesus and take up his dwelling in us through the Holy Spirit. This is the mystery of love itself: We have been given a glimpse of God's own life.

Jesus reveals the mystery of God. When we develop a relationship with the Lord Jesus, we become aware that the one God who is at work in Jesus is also present in his followers. The Holy Spirit brings life to each Christian and to the body of Christ, the church. The coming of the Holy Spirit on Pentecost Sunday, after Jesus' glorification, reveals the full mystery of the Holy Trinity.

When the church reflects on God as we experience God in Jesus, it is reflecting on the divine economy, the **salvific Trinity**, God-for-us. The one God is experienced as three distinct persons who are all involved in the common work of salvation, but each divine person performs the common work in line with his unique personal property. Thus, we say that God the Father creates everything and continues to give life and being to everything in creation. God the Son lived among us, taught us of the Father's love, and won for us eternal salvation. God the Holy Spirit is the love of God who dwells in us and in the church. The Spirit is the source of unity, courage, truth, and love for all humanity.

How Are Three Persons in One God? [CCC 251-254; 258-259]

The salvific Trinity, God-for-us as Creator, Redeemer, and Sanctifier, is one way of looking at the mystery of God. Another way is to look at God as God is in himself, the **immanent Trinity**.

Though the Trinity is one being, having a divine substance or nature, God is three distinct persons: Father, Son, and Holy Spirit. But we must not think of person in the same sense as humans are persons. *Person* in the Trinity refers to distinctions between the members. Thus, there are not three separate centers of consciousness in God. *There is only one simple divine being.* There are not three separate intelligences or wills in the one God. When one person of the Trinity acts, the other two persons also act. Each person is *distinct* but does not act separately from the others. God is one, a community-in-unity. The divine persons are inseparable in both what they do and in what they are.

God loves us with the same love and knows us with the same knowledge. God acts as one, though we *appropriate* certain actions to each of the persons. For example, we appropriate creation to the Father, redemption to the Son, and sanctification to the Holy Spirit. These are the **missions** of each of the three divine persons. But even here all three persons act as one and are fully present in all the missions. For example, in creation, each person performs the common work according to unique personal properties. Thus, the church taught at the Second Council of Constantinople (as quoted in the *Catechism of the Catholic Church*), there is

> "one God and Father from whom all things are, and one Lord Jesus Christ, through whom all things are, and one Holy Spirit in whom all things are." It is above all the divine missions of the Son's Incarnation and the gift of the Holy Spirit that show forth the properties of the divine persons (cf. CCC 258).

What Are the Relationships Within the Trinity? [CCC 254-256]

We confess one God with three divine persons who are really distinct from one another. In a mysterious way, we can say "God is one but not solitary" (*Fides Damasi* quoted in *CCC* 254). The divine persons are distinct in their relations of origin.

Traditional Catholic teaching explains the relationships among the three persons on the Trinity this way:

The Father. The First Person of the Trinity is absolutely without origin. From all eternity he "begets" the Son, the Second Person of the Trinity. The Son proceeds from the Father. There was never a time when the Son did not proceed from the Father.

The Son. We can think of the Father's begetting the Son as God knowing himself perfectly. The Father expresses himself perfectly to himself, and this is the Son, the Word of God. Thus the Son is the Father's perfect, divine expression of himself. They are one, yet distinct.

The Holy Spirit. The relationship of the Father and Son is a perfect relationship. The Father and Son love each other with an eternal, perfect, divine love. The love *proceeds* from the Father and the Son and is the Third Person of the Trinity, the Holy Spirit. The Holy Spirit proceeds from both the Father and the Son as the perfect expression of their divine love for each other. Thus, the Holy Spirit is the Spirit of love between the Father and the Son; the Spirit binds them into a community of unity.

In a classic expression of faith, the Athanasian Creed expresses the relationships of the three persons of the Trinity this way:

> The Father is not made by anyone, nor created, nor begotten. The Son is from the Father alone, not made, not created, but begotten. The Holy Spirit is from the Father and the Son, not made, not created, not begotten, but proceeding. . . . The entire three Persons are co-eternal with one another and co-equal, so that . . . both Trinity in Unity and Unity in Trinity are to be adored.

What Are Some Images of the Blessed Trinity? *[CCC 1702, 2205]*

We should never confuse an image with the reality. This is especially true when speaking of God who is a mystery beyond our human ability to comprehend. But God's divine revelation has given us a glimpse into the divine life—a life we are invited to share. God is a community of persons.

You might be familiar with St. Patrick's famous attempt to communicate the Trinitarian mystery through the image of a shamrock—one leaf consisting of three petals. A modern analogy uses the image of a woman. Though one person, she has simultaneous, though different, relationships to others. For example, this one person is a mother, a wife, and a friend. Finally, consider the images used by St. John of Damascus:

> Think of the Father as a spring of life begetting the Son like a river and the Holy Ghost like a sea, for the spring and the river and the sea are all one nature. Think of the Father as a root, of the Son as a branch, and of the Spirit as a fruit, for the substance in these three is one. The Father is a sun with the Son as ray and the Holy

> Spirit as heat. The holy Trinity transcends by far every similitude and figure. . . . [T]he concept of the Creator is arrived at by analogy from his creatures.

Concluding Remarks

Our minds can never fully grasp the mystery of God. We can never explain three divine persons in the one divine nature. We simply believe it as a truth that Jesus in the Holy Spirit revealed to us.

We believe that our one God is a Father who loves us and will never forget us. We believe that God is our Savior Jesus Christ who loved us so much that he gave up his life so that we can have eternal life. We believe that God is a Spirit of love who dwells within us.

This privileged knowledge of our God can fill us with a sense of peace and confidence about our future. Friends may abandon us; family members may disappoint us; setbacks will inevitably come our way. But God will never let us down. God lives in us. We need but spend some time in prayer to be aware of God's presence and allow God's love to penetrate us.

Our God is a God who knows and loves. God is a community of persons. To be godlike means to know, love, and serve God by joining others in community. Our eternal destiny is to pray *to* the Father, *through* the Son, *in* the Holy Spirit of love. The Holy Spirit unites us to the Father and to Jesus and to every other person. The Holy Spirit helps us look at others and ourselves with love and appreciation. Our knowledge of God is a great gift we have been given, and it can help us live our lives in a hopeful way.

Jesus came to reveal the nature of reality. He came to tell us about God and about ourselves, God's children. In revealing the nature of God as unity-in-community, community-in-unity, Jesus told us a profound truth about human life as well. As we journey on our pilgrimage to the Father, with Jesus our brother, in the Holy Spirit, we should remember that a goal of Christian life is to join with our fellow pilgrims in approaching our Father. A Christian should not simply approach God alone.

Prayer Reflection

This chapter began with a Christian doxology, a prayer of praise to the Blessed Trinity. It now concludes with the "Greater Doxology," a hymn in praise of Jesus Christ who is in union with the Father and Holy Spirit. This hymn is recited or sung at most Sunday liturgies.

Glory to God in the highest,
and peace to his people on earth.
Lord God, heavenly King,
Almighty God and Father,
we worship you, we give you thanks,
we praise you for your glory.
Lord Jesus Christ, only Son of the Father,
Lord God, Lamb of God,
you take away the sin of the world:
have mercy on us;
you are seated at the right hand of the Father:
receive our prayer.
For you alone are the Holy One,
you alone are the Lord,
you alone are the Most High,
Jesus Christ,
with the Holy Spirit,
in the glory of God the Father. Amen.

For Discussion

1. One of the most popular and important of all Christian prayers is the simple yet profound sign of the cross. What do you do *in the name of* the Father, the Son, and the Holy Spirit?
2. What does the doctrine of the Blessed Trinity reveal to you about God? about reality? about your own life?
3. In your own prayer life, how do you relate to each person of the Trinity?

God the Father is our creator. God the Son is our redeemer. God the Holy Spirit is our sanctifier. When do you thank the Father for the gift of life? In what areas of your life to you need a savior? In what ways do you allow the Spirit to help you become holy?

Further Reading

Sirach 11:12-28 (trust in God alone)
Galatians 4–5 (sons of God and Christian liberty)

Chapter Seven

People of God:
The Christian Community

"All authority in heaven and on earth has been given to me. Go, therefore, make disciples of all nations; baptize them in the name of the Father and of the Son and of the Holy Spirit, and teach them to observe all the commands I gave you."
— Matthew 28:18-20

He cannot have God for his father who refuses to have the church for his mother.
— St. Augustine of Hippo

A plumber, whose older brother happened to be a renowned and well-published philosopher, was talking with his supervisor. "You must be proud to have such a famous brother," remarked the boss. But not wanting to offend the plumber's pride, he continued, "But we must remember that talent is not often distributed evenly, even in the same family."

"You're right," replied the less-famous brother. "Why, my brother can't even stop a leaky toilet. He's lucky he can hire somebody like me to take care of such important things as that."

What a refreshing attitude displayed by the younger brother. He appreciated his own gifts and felt no envy toward his accomplished brother.

It should be that way in the church as well since the church is a family of believers in Jesus Christ, a true community gifted by the Holy Spirit and formed in the Lord's name.

A typical parish on a Sunday morning illustrates well the variety-in-unity that comprises the Christian community. Present are all types of people: young and old; male and female; financially well-to-do, others less so; various national and ethnic groups; those who participate wholeheartedly, others who appear bored. The parish is a microcosm of the church: many unique individuals with unique talents. Though different, they have a vital common interest. By virtue of their baptism into the Christian family, they come together as one to acknowledge, celebrate, and live the Lordship of Jesus Christ.

This chapter will examine the church, a community formed and sustained by the Spirit of Jesus. The Lord loves us both individually and communally. He brings us together in the Spirit and unites us into his people—a true family—to carry on his work here on earth. We are united with our Christian sisters and brothers who have preceded us in death and with those who will follow us. It is both a privilege and honor to belong to this special community we call church.

What Is the Church? *[CCC 751-752; 777]*

Many concepts come to mind when you mention the word *church* to people. Some think of a building, others think of priests and nuns. Some people imagine strict rules or dogmas. Others with more theological sophistication notions might have in mind "God's people" or "body of Christ." In some ways, the church embodies all of these ideas.

The word **church** itself translates the scriptural word *ekklesia* which literally means "those called out," a convocation, or assembly. The Old Testament applied the term to the Chosen People. When Christians first used the term, they were proclaiming that they were the new chosen people of God. God calls Christians to proclaim openly to all people that Jesus Christ is the Lord, to assemble as a believing community who lead a sacramental life, and to commit themselves to fellowship and service for the sake of God's kingdom.

The word *church* today means three realities: the assembly of believers at the liturgy, the local parish community, and the universal community of believers.

What Are Some Images of the Church? *[CCC 753-766; 778]*

Above all else, the church is a mystery of God's loving grace, both the means and goal of God's plan. Instituted by Christ to communicate divine life to us, the church was born out of Christ's great gift of self-sacrificing love, a love we celebrate in the eucharist. Because it is unlike any other human community, no one definition or description can exhaust all its rich meaning. Thus, the bishops at the Second Vatican Council described the church by using biblical images: mystery, the people of God, the body of Christ, the temple of the Holy Spirit, the sacrament of Jesus Christ.

Although these are the key images of the church which we will discuss below, the Bible holds to many other images of the church: pilgrim, God's building and farm, Christ's bride, the flock of Christ, Christ's vineyard, God's family, and our mother. Each of these adds to our understanding and appreciation of the mystery of the church. For example, the pilgrim image stresses that the church is a community on its way to a final destination. The building and farm images connote that the Lord has constructed his community and that he still cultivates it like a farmer tending his crops. The bride imagery speaks of the great love Jesus has for his church and the intimate union with him which is a major benefit of being a member of the Christian community. The flock image reminds the community that it has a sacrificing shepherd whose voice must be listened to if it is to escape being lost and even destroyed. The vineyard image underscores that it is the Lord who gives life and fruitfulness to the branches.

What Does It Mean to Call the Church a "Mystery?" *[CCC 770-773; 779]*

St. Augustine defined a **mystery** as a visible sign of some invisible grace. Pope Paul VI had something similar in mind when he described the church as "a reality imbued with the hidden presence of God." Therefore, to call the church a mystery is to say that the invisible, almighty God is working through this faith community, this visible institution that exists to continue the saving work of Jesus Christ. This "nuptial union" of the earthly and heavenly has one purpose: the holiness of Christ's members.

The mystery of the church is intimately related to the mystery of God working through Jesus Christ. In Ephesians 1–3, St. Paul describes how God the Father unfolds the divine plan of salvation and reconciliation of everyone through the Son, Jesus Christ. Paul calls God's plan the mystery hidden for ages, a mystery that is now being unfolded in the church, the mystery of Christ.

> So then you are no longer strangers and sojourners, but you are fellow citizens with the holy ones and members of the household of God, built upon the foundation of the apostles and prophets, with Christ Jesus himself as the capstone. Through him the whole structure is held together and grows into a temple sacred in the Lord; in him you also are being built together into a dwelling place of God in the Spirit (Eph 2:19-22, NAB).

The human/divine dimensions of the church are manifest in a hierarchically structured society that is—simultaneously—Christ's mystical body, in a visible society that is a spiritual communion, and in an earthly church endowed with heavenly riches.

How Is the Church a Sacrament? *[CCC 774-776, 780]*

The Latin word *sacramentum* translates the Greek word *mysterion*. **Sacrament** is a special kind of sign or symbol. A symbol, by definition, is something concrete that points to another reality. A stop sign, for example, uses shape, color, and a word (all symbols) to point to the *idea* of stopping. A wedding ring points to the reality of perpetual love. A country's flag brings to mind the values of that particular nation. However, these symbols do not cause what they point to. A stop sign does not *cause* a driver to stop; a wedding ring does not guarantee marital happiness; a nation's flag does not automatically bring about patriotism or devotion to the values of the country.

A sacrament is also a symbol, an *efficacious symbol*. An efficacious symbol brings about what it points to; an efficacious symbol embodies the very reality that it represents. Hence, a sacrament is a very special symbol. It is a concrete reality that, in some way, *is what it represents*. Thus it is accurate to say that Jesus is the sacrament of God's love. Jesus not only points to God; he is God. He not only symbolizes God's love; he is God's love. He is what he represents. He is the first and most important sacrament of all. "Anyone who has seen me has seen the Father" (Jn 14:9).

The church is like a multi-faceted stone. We get a different view each time we consider it from a new perspective. The Second Vatican Council shed more light on the nature of the church with its insight about the church as sacrament:

> By her intimate relationship with Christ, the Church is a kind of sacrament or sign of intimate union with God, and of the unity of all mankind. She is also an instrument for the achievement of such unity (Dogmatic Constitution on the Church, 1).

Simply put, the church is a concrete sign of Christ's presence to all people. It is an outward, visible sign of God's loving gift of himself in human history. Like every other sign and symbol, the church must point to something. This is especially true of an efficacious symbol that embodies what it represents. Thus, the church must lead us to what it signifies, that is, to Christ who is united to people through the church. The church helps put us in touch with the Lord whom it represents. It is an instrument in the hand of the Lord whose love visibly reaches out to all humans through the Christian community united to him. (And one way the church does this is through the seven sacraments, the special signs and instruments through which Christ's grace comes to those in the church.)

How Does the Church Lead Us to Christ? *[CCC 767-768; 849-854]*

To be "the universal sacrament of salvation," the church must be true to its essential *missionary* nature. A "missionary" is one who is sent. The church has its origin in the mission of the Son and the Holy Spirit who came to allow all humans to share in the divine life. By the power of the Holy Spirit, the Lord commissions the Christian community to share his love so that all people can be saved and come to know the truth.

The church is an effective sacrament of Christ—his visible presence in the world—when it presents the message of God's love in Jesus Christ, builds up the Christian community, serves all people (especially those in need), and worships the Triune God.

Message. Down through the centuries the church has announced the good news that the God of love invites all people to the fullness of life. Some people have never heard this good news; others have only heard it in a partial or confused way. A major mission of the church is to proclaim the good news of God's love in Jesus Christ. Jesus himself commanded his disciples to do this when he told them:

"As the Father sent me,
    so am I sending you" (Jn 20:21).

The heart of the good news is found in the **kerygma**, the central message of the gospel proclaimed by the apostles. We find a masterful summary of the kerygma in Peter's first sermon on Pentecost Sunday (Acts 2:14-41). Peter reviewed the high points of Jesus' life, death, and resurrection. He proclaimed that Jesus was Lord, the key to the mystery of life. He invited people to turn from their sinful lives, to accept Jesus Christ in faith, and to be baptized with water in the Holy Spirit. The church must continue to preach this message to all people everywhere. By doing so the church helps lead people to the Lord Jesus.

Community. The church builds up the community of believers when it lives the gospel it proclaims. If Christians do not live the gospel message, the church cannot be a believable symbol of Christ. To be an effective and credible sign of the gospel, others must see in the church a community united by faith, hope, and love.

"It is by this love you have for one another, that everyone will recognize you as my disciples" (Jn 13:35).

If nonbelievers see loving, caring people, they naturally take notice and ask themselves what this group stands for. The technical term for this reality of Christian community is *koinonia*, or fellowship.

Service. The third task of the church is *diakonia*, which means service. The image of servant best describes this task. Jesus showed us the way when he, the King of kings, took off his cloak and washed the feet of the apostles at the Last Supper. Foot washing was a menial task that even servants did not have to do. Nevertheless, Jesus washed the feet of his disciples to show that to be great in the kingdom of God, a person must become a servant to others.

A Christian should be one who serves. A follower of Jesus must minister to the needs of others. The church must witness to God's love by translating its words of love into concrete acts of service for all, especially the poor, the lonely, the imprisoned, the sick and suffering. Actions speak louder than words. The church which announces that our loving God cares for people in their misery must be willing to take that message and make it real by the deeds it does for others. It must walk the road Jesus walked, a way of poverty, obedience, service, and self-sacrificing love.

Worship. In worship we recognize and acknowledge that God, the source of our being and every gift, is worthy of our adoration, praise, and thanksgiving. The liturgy, from the Greek *leitourgia* ("work of the public"), is the official public prayers and rituals of the church. It is "the summit toward which the activity of the church is directed; at the same time it is the fountain from which all her power flows" (*Constitution on the Sacred Liturgy*, 10). Through the liturgy, especially the eucharist which both celebrates and creates Christian community, the work of our salvation is exercised. The liturgy inspires Christians to unite in love to the Lord and each other. Doing so, they become Christ for others, "to become in deed what they proclaim in creed."

How Is the Church the People of God? *[CCC 781-786; 802-804]*

The image of the church as the people of God has its roots in the Old Testament covenant between God and Israel. In this covenant God wished to sanctify and save not only individuals, but individuals formed into a loving community. The Hebrew scriptures tell a story of God teaching, preserving, and cherishing his people. This was in preparation for the new people of God formed through the blood of Jesus Christ. The new covenant calls all people to unity in the Holy Spirit.

The Greek word for people is *laos*, from which we get the word *laity*. This image emphasizes the dignity of each individual Christian, a child of God, who has been called into a fellowship of life, love, and truth through faith and baptism. The Lord Jesus invites the members to continue his work of redemption in the world, to be light of the world and salt of the earth. To be vital and active members of the church means we must help bring others to the Lord Jesus both by example and direct effort. We must love as the Lord loves.

The people of God are those who are baptized and acknowledge that Jesus Christ is Lord and Savior. Thus, we share in the Lord's priestly, prophetic, and royal office. Our mission is to live our lives so the Lord's light shines forth in the world through us. When we love, God's love can be seen. When we act like Christ, we are like salt. Just as the presence of salt in food enhances its flavor and brings out the best taste, so the presence of God's people should bring to the world the exciting news that Jesus is the Savior and that God's kingdom has been established in our midst.

Are the Church and the Kingdom of God the Same? *[CCC 763-764; 769; 782]*

God's kingdom or reign, God's saving activity in human history which draws all people to the Triune God, is different from the church. The church includes only baptized members. Thus, the kingdom of God is broader than the church. The kingdom of God extends to all people who are saved, from the time of Adam to the end of the world. But there is an intimate connection between the church and the kingdom of God. That connection is, simply, that the church is Christ's reign already present in mystery (*Dogmatic Constitution on the Church*, 3). It is the seed and initial budding forth of the kingdom.

The church is Christ's little flock. As its Good Shepherd, he teaches its members to work for the kingdom in an explicit, conscious way. The church grows slowly, straining toward the fulfillment of the kingdom. As God's people, we hope for a day of glory when we will be united to our king. Because the church ministers to the world on behalf of the Lord, the church helps advance the fulfillment of the kingdom in all persons of good will. The full flowering of the kingdom will take place at the end of human history. It is the privileged task of Christians to help promote God's saving activity for all people everywhere and in all times.

What Does It Mean to Call the Church the "Body of Christ"? [CCC 787-796; 805-808]

This important image of the church can be traced to Jesus. Jesus often identified himself with his followers. For example, he proclaimed:

"In truth I tell you, in so far as you did this to one of the least of these brothers of mine, you did it to me" (Mt 25:40).

And he said to his disciples:

"Anyone who listens to you listens to me; anyone who rejects you rejects me" (Lk 10:16).

At the Last Supper Jesus spoke of the unity between himself and those who accept him in faith and love:

"I am the vine,
you are the branches.
Whoever remains in me, with me in him,
bears fruit in plenty;
for cut off from me you can do nothing" (Jn 15:5).

Just as the vine and branches are one living reality, so it is with Christ and his church. By giving the Holy Spirit, Jesus achieves an intense unity with his disciples. This unity is mystically realized especially through the marvelous gift of the eucharist through which Christ lives in us and we live in him.

St. Paul considered the body of Christ imagery central. He was powerfully influenced by the risen Lord's question put to him when he was on his way to persecute the Christians in Damascus:

"Saul, Saul, why are you persecuting me? . . . I am Jesus, whom you are persecuting" (Acts 9:4-5).

By persecuting Christians, Saul (Paul) had been persecuting the Lord himself. This revelation prompted Paul to write to the Corinthians:

Now Christ's body is yourselves, each of you with a part to play in the whole (1 Cor 12:27).

The risen, glorified Lord is present in the world today through Christians. We are his hands, his loving touch, his understanding glance, his sympathetic word of comfort to the lonely and suffering, his instrument used to preach the good news of salvation and forgiveness.

Christ is the head of the body. We are its members. We become incorporated into the body through baptism. The Holy Spirit unites the members into *one* body:

> We were baptized into one body in a single Spirit, Jews as well as Greeks, slaves as well as free men, and we were all given the same Spirit to drink (1 Cor 12:13).

The Holy Spirit, then, is the soul of the church, a Spirit of unity who overcomes all natural divisions of race, color, nationality, and sex.

The church as the body of Christ also underscores the dignity of each individual member. Just as each member of a person's body has a specific and important function to play, so, too, in the church each member has a specific and important role to play. Some are apostles, some prophets, others teachers, and still others miracle workers, healers, assistants, or administrators. We all have specific gifts, but the greatest gift of all is the capacity to love with the love of our God.

As the head of the Body, Jesus unites us with his Passover and dispenses the gifts we need for growth.

Although the church is one mystical person with Christ, there is a clear distinction between Christ and his disciples. This distinction is often expressed in the image of bridegroom and bride. As the loving Bridegroom, Jesus sacrificed himself for his bride (the church), purifying her by his blood and making her the fruitful mother of God's children.

How Is the Church the "Temple of the Holy Spirit"? *[CCC 747; 797-801; 809-810]*

Just as the human spirit penetrates every fiber of our bodies so we may have life, so the Holy Spirit is present in the body of Christ: in the head who is the risen Lord, and in the body made up of his members. The Holy Spirit is the "soul" of Christ's mystical body, building up, animating, and sanctifying its members by uniting them to Christ. Because the Spirit lives in the church, we can call it the temple of the Holy Spirit. The church as a temple is, in fact, "the sacrament of the Holy Trinity's communion" with us (CCC 747). It is "a people brought into unity from the unity of the Father, the Son, and the Holy Spirit" (cf. CCC 810).

The Holy Spirit works through the church to accomplish the works of salvation. The Spirit's means are many: scripture, the sacraments, graces, the virtues that help us accomplish good, and charisms given to individual Christians, to be used for the common good under the direction of church leaders.

Is the Church Perfect? [CCC 853]

The Spirit gives each of us gifts to accomplish the Lord's work in our own special way. When we use them generously and loving-ly, we help build up the body of Christ and work to spread Christ's reign on earth. However, sometimes we fail to love. Because the church includes a human as well as a divine dimension, individual Christians can sin by not being Christ for others. The story of the Christian people through history reveals that we are both holy and sinful. This is the paradox of Christian life: Jesus Christ comes to us through people like ourselves, people who are weak and sinful and not loving. We are a pilgrim people, a people on our way to total union with God. Our deeds performed in human weakness to do not always match the lofty message of love that we proclaim. Be-cause Christians are sinners and imperfect, we need constant conversion, accomplished with penance. We are not finished prod-ucts. In humility, we must acknowledge our sinfulness and allow ourselves to be touched and renewed by the power of the gracious God we are privileged to preach to the world.

Can Non-Christians Be Saved? [CCC 846-848]

Traditionally Catholics have taught that the church is neces-sary for salvation. This belief is based on the teaching of both scripture and tradition. We believe that Jesus is present in his body, the church, and that he is the one Mediator and the unique way to salvation.

> For of all the names in the world given to men, this is the only one by which we can be saved (Acts 4:12).

Since the time of the Lord's ascension into heaven and his glori-fication with the Father, he is met on earth in an *explicit* way only through his body, the church. As people seek salvation, they will be drawn to Christ and membership in his body. The church is a *sign*, a *sacrament* of God's love. Its task is to witness to the mystery of God's love and salvation in human history through Jesus Christ. Its mandate is to show others the way to Jesus.

Furthermore, Jesus himself taught the need for faith and bap-tism (Jn 3:5). Consequently, the church teaches that anyone who knew "that the Catholic Church was made necessary by God through Jesus Christ, [and] would refuse to enter her or to remain in her could not be saved" (*Dogmatic Constitution on the Church*, 14).

What about all those many people who have never heard of Jesus Christ? What about those who have been given a distorted picture of him by followers who didn't always live what they preached? Can they be saved? The church answers yes.

> Those can also attain to everlasting salvation who through no fault of their own do not know the gospel of Christ or His Church, yet sincerely seek God and, moved by grace, strive by their deeds to do His will as it is known to them through the dictates of conscience. Nor does divine Providence deny the help necessary for salvation to those who, without blame on their part, have not yet arrived at an explicit knowledge of God, but who strive to live a good life, thanks to his grace. Whatever goodness or truth is found among them is looked upon by the Church as a preparation for the gospel. She regards such qualities as given by Him who enlightens all men so that they may finally have life (Dogmatic Constitution on the Church, 16).

Thus God's kingdom includes those who are mysteriously drawn to it through the workings of the Holy Spirit in their lives. Their task is to seek the kingdom of God as they know it. Their vocation is to live as lovingly as they possibly can.

> God is love
> and whoever remains in love remains in God
> and God in him (1 Jn 4:16).

However, if a person truly knows and accepts the gospel which has been given to him or her as a gift, then he or she should recognize the necessity of the church for salvation. For those who have been privileged to receive the gift of faith, it would be seriously wrong to turn away from the body of Christ, the church.

> "Anyone who listens to you listens to me; anyone who rejects you rejects me, and those who reject me reject the one who sent me" (Lk 10:16).

Concluding Reflections

Song lyrics are sometimes so inane that we chuckle at them. At other times, though, they seem to reveal profound truths. For example, the song "People" was right on target when it said that "people who need people are the luckiest people in the world." The church recognizes this reality. Christians need the love of Jesus, the support and strength of the Holy Spirit, and the encouragement of fellow-believers on their pilgrimage to the Father.

Christians need the church, the temple of the Holy Spirit, which is primarily a mystery of God's profound love for us in Jesus Christ. We can never totally fathom this love; we can accept it in faith and with God's grace try to put it into practice. The Christian community is a special people—God's people—set aside to witness in word and deed to God's activity in the world.

The church is also the body of Christ. Jesus established the church and is its head. Each baptized Christian is a member of Christ's body, gifted in a special way to carry on the work of the Lord.

In addition, the church is a sacrament of Christ—his visible presence in the world. All Christians are called to be signs of God's love by heralding the good news of God's love in Jesus Christ, by building up Christian community, by serving all people, especially "the least of these," and by worshipping God in a spirit of truth and love.

Christians need the support of their fellow-believers to continue to be faithful symbols of Jesus Christ. The world also needs the Christian community because the church is entrusted to proclaim and live the good news of eternal salvation for all people.

Prayer Reflection

The body of Christ is St. Paul's favorite image of the church. In the following passage Paul writes of the different gifts the Holy Spirit gives to Christians.

Read the passage slowly and meditatively. In the presence of the Lord, reflect on the two questions that follow.

> There are many different gifts, but it is always the same Spirit; there are many different ways of serving, but it is always the same Lord. There are many different forms of activity, but in everybody it is the same God who is at work in them all. The particular manifestation of the Spirit granted to each one is to be used for the general good. To one is given from the Spirit the gift of utterance expressing wisdom; to another the gift of utterance expressing knowledge, in accordance with the same Spirit; to another, faith, from the same Spirit; and to another, the gifts of healing, through this one Spirit; to another, the working of miracles; to another, prophecy; to another, the power of distinguishing spirits; to one, the gift of different tongues and to another, the interpretation of tongues. But at work in all these is one and the same Spirit, distributing them at will to each individual (1 Cor 12:4-11).

Ask the Lord to help you identify your greatest gift. How are you using it to help others?

Think of a fellow Christian with whom you might currently be having a problem. With the eyes of faith, what good can you see in this person?

For Discussion

1. *It is impossible to be a Christian and not be a member of the Christian church.* Do you agree with this statement or not? Explain.
2. If you were to create a new image for the church, what would it be? How does it reveal something about Christ who lives in this community?
3. What factors do you see present in today's church which might be keeping it from being a more effective *sacrament* of Christ? What must Christians do to help remedy this situation?
4. What do each of the images of the church say about the church as a *community*?
5. The family is the "domestic church." What can you do to strengthen the community of your family?
6. What more can you do to help build up God's people in your local parish?

Further Reading

Exodus 2:23-25; 3–12; 15–20; 24 (creation of God's people, Israel)

Ephesians 1–3

Chapter Eight

The Church:
One, Holy, Catholic,
and Apostolic

We believe in the one, holy, catholic, and apostolic church.
— from the Nicene Creed

For the whole church which is throughout the whole world possesses the same faith.
— St. Irenaeus

A father asked his son to break a bundle of sticks, tied together with twine. A little while later he found a frustrated boy still at the task. The child had lifted the bundle up and smashed it on his knee, but the result was only a bruised knee. He had also propped the bundle up against the garage wall and stomped on it hard with his foot, but to no effect except a sore ankle.

The father took the bundle from his son and untied it. The sticks scattered in a mess at his feet. Then he easily began to pick up each stick and break them—one at a time.

This is a wonderful image for the church. When united, we are strong. When divided, we easily fail or can be broken.

For most Catholics, the local parish is where we experience church. If it is a center of guidance and light, of inspiration and strength, then the reality of church as a vital, active community will touch us and strengthen us as we journey through life.

However, Christians do not just take from the church. We must give to it as well. It is true that Christ allows the Christian community to participate in his priestly, prophetic, and kingly ministries. But it is required that not only ordained leaders or professed religious who are asked to perform these tasks. Each and every Christian must join with our church leaders to build up Christ's body by heralding the gospel, growing in holiness, and serving others.

This chapter will look first at the organization of the church, and then at the prophetic, priestly, and regal ministries of the church which both individuals and the hierarchy must undertake on the Lord's behalf. Further, it will also discuss the four traditional "marks" of the church—one, holy, catholic, and apostolic. These marks highlight essential features of the church and its mission. Rooted in Christ, they help reveal the church as a credible witness of her mission to further God's reign on earth (CCC 811-812).

Who Is a Member of the Church? *[CCC 871-873; 897-900; 914-934; 944-945]*

Catholics are baptized, accept the Lordship of Jesus, and commit themselves to continue Christ's work in the world. Baptism endows each member of the church with equal dignity and a special share in Christ's priestly (sanctifying), prophetic (teaching), and kingly (governing) ministries. The different ministries build up Christ's body and extend Christ's work of salvation to all people.

Some members of the church belong to the **hierarchy** (order of ministries) which Christ established for the apostles and their successors. Christ has assigned the office of sanctifying, teaching, and governing to the hierarchy.

The church also consists of the laity, defined as all the faithful except those in holy orders or those who belong to a church-approved religious state. The special vocation of lay people is to engage in the social, political, and economic affairs of the world and to direct them according to God's will.

Finally, in the church are some from both the hierarchy and laity who consecrate themselves to the vows of poverty, chastity, and obedience and live a stable life specially dedicated to God. Those in the consecrated life strive toward a more intimate dedication of their lives to God, a form of self-perfection rooted in their baptismal call. Consecrated life includes hermits, consecrated virgins, secular institutes, and various apostolic societies. It also includes those in religious life, members of religious orders like the Society of Jesus, the Franciscans, or the Ursulines. Religious life is distinguished by its liturgical character; public profession of the gospel counsels of poverty, chastity, and obedience; fraternal life in common; and a unique witness to the Lord's union with his church.

How Is the Church a Prophet? *[CCC 904-906; 942]*

A prophet speaks the word of God. Each church member shares in the prophetic (teaching) mission of Jesus. For example, qualified lay people can share in a special church ministry like catechesis ("instruction of the faith"). Moreover, all Christian parents have the privilege and responsibility to share their faith with their children. Because all of us are baptized into God's family, Jesus asks everyone to witness to his truth. We must do this in word and in action.

> "In the same way your light must shine in people's sight, so that, seeing your good works, they may give praise to your Father in heaven" (Mt 5:16).

Over the centuries the church has been blessed with Christian heroes who have boldly witnessed to the gospel. They have shared their Christian faith with non-Catholics and non-Christians and have called the church to be true to its mission. One example is St. Francis of Assisi who united himself with the poor to show that the kingdom of God belongs to those who depend on God for everything. Another example is St. Catherine of Siena who counseled the pope and reminded him that petty quarrels among the hierarchy hurt the unity of the church. In the twentieth century, Mother Teresa of Calcutta opened the world's eyes to her example of humility. Christian heroes like these inspire all of God's people to bring the Lord and his message to every circumstance of daily life.

What Is the Role of the Church Hierarchy? *[CCC 874-882; 936-939]*

Jesus entrusted to his church the task of authentically and truthfully teaching and witnessing the good news. The teaching of the church, its ongoing life and its worship as they have been handed on from the time of the apostles to our own day—all these make up the Tradition of the church. Everything that contributes to holiness and helps increase the faith of God's people is part of the church's tradition.

The Holy Spirit has led the church through the centuries. The Spirit helps the church authentically recognize and hand on what is essential to the Christian life. Jesus himself promised to be with his church in a special way when he established the church, choosing Peter to be chief shepherd. Thus, the Lord is the true source of all ministry in the church. He founded the church, gave it authority, mission, orientation, and goal.

The church is organized along hierarchical lines to ensure the carrying on of his ministry. Hierarchy refers to the ordered grade of ordained leaders in the Catholic church. Catholics believe that Jesus chooses to teach, to rule, and to sanctify his church through this sacred leadership of the pope and bishops and their assistants, the priests and deacons. These men lead through service. It is Christ who empowers these ministers to proclaim the gospel in the Lord's name; no one minister can act on his own authority. Two major benefits of hierarchical leadership are the preservation of authentic tradition and insurance that the true gospel will be spread as Christ mandated.

Today, the hierarchy continues the ministry of Peter and the apostles. Catholics believe that the successor of Peter, the pope, has a special role in the church. As the bishop of Rome—the place where Peter ministered and was martyred—the pope has primacy over the whole church. We base this belief on Christ's own teaching:

> "Simon son of Jonah, you are a blessed man! Because it was no human agency that revealed this to you but my Father in heaven. So I now say to you: You are Peter and on this rock I will build my community. And the gates of the underworld can never overpower it. I will give you the keys of the kingdom of Heaven; whatever you bind on earth will be bound in heaven; whatever you loose on earth will be loosed in heaven" (Mt 16:17-19).

The pope and the bishops form a single entity called the college of bishops. The bishops in communion with one another and with the pope have the task of teaching truthfully the word of God. They do this when they come together in an ecumenical (worldwide) council. The pope's special role is to be a sign of unity when the bishops speak as one. He is the head. He speaks with the bishops as the voice of Jesus Christ alive in the church.

How Does the Church Teach? [CCC 892; 935]

Normally the pope and bishops teach through the ordinary magisterium of the church. **Magisterium** refers to the office of teaching in the church which the Lord gave to the apostles and their successors. This teaching can be found in encyclicals, pastoral letters, sermons, and the like. It is aimed at the correct proclamation of the gospel, the building up of Christian love and service, and the proper administration of the sacraments and other spiritual and temporal benefits administered by the church. Catholics recognize the right of the pope, bishops, pastors, and priests to teach for the Lord Jesus. Our general attitude to the teachings of our leaders is prayerful listening and obedience, that is, religious assent.

What Is Infallibility? *[CCC 888-890]*

Based on our Lord's promise that the church could not go astray because of his continuous presence, Catholics believe that on essential matters of faith and morals, the church is infallible. **Infallibility** refers to the belief that a certain doctrine (teaching) is free from error.

The bishops as a group, in union with the pope, teach infallibly when teaching or protecting Christ's revelation concerning belief or morality. The same Holy Spirit who directs the pope and the whole body of the faithful also directs the college of bishops.

Although the individual bishops do not enjoy the prerogative of infallibility, they can nevertheless proclaim Christ's doctrine infallibly. This is so, even when they are dispersed around the world, provided that while maintaining the bond of unity among themselves and with Peter's successor, and while teaching authentically on a matter of faith or morals, they concur in a single viewpoint as the one which must be held conclusively (*Dogmatic Constitution on the Church*, 25).

This kind of teaching is best exemplified when the bishops meet together and teach with the pope in an ecumenical council.

What Is Papal Infallibility? *[CCC 891]*

The pope speaks infallibly when he teaches *ex cathedra*, that is, "from the chair of Peter." These conditions exist when:

- he teaches as pastor of all the faithful
- he intends to use his full authority in an unchangeable decision
- the subject is a doctrine pertaining to faith or morals.

Infallible teaching is rare. One example of an infallible papal statement is the declaration of Mary's assumption into heaven (in 1950 by Pope Pius XII). Catholics owe assent, the obedience of faith, to infallible statements since they are backed by our Lord's own promise to remain with his church through the Holy Spirit. Refusal to give assent of faith to such a teaching is heresy.

Finally, please note that papal infallibility refers solely to the pope's power or gift as successor of Peter to teach correctly Christ's revelation, especially when that revelation is being attacked or denied, thus leading to confusion among God's people. The pope's personal opinions and beliefs, like any person's, can be wrong, for example, in politics, science, or sports. In addition, because the pope is human, he can sin and make mistakes, even in the way he governs the church. Like all gifts of the Holy Spirit, the gift of infallibility builds up the body of Christ. It helps give us access to the truth of Christ.

How Does the Church Share in the Priesthood of Christ?
[CCC 893; 901-903; 941]

A primary purpose of the church is to foster the sanctification of people. Jesus came to make us holy, that is, to make us one with his Father in friendship, to give us a life of love and holiness. He wished to form a priestly people so that everyone could come into contact with the saving deeds of his passion, death, resurrection, and glorification—deeds which redeem and make holy the entire universe. A priest is a mediator between God and people. The Christian vocation is to help bring others to Christ.

All Christians share in the common priesthood of Jesus:

> But you are a chosen race, a kingdom of priests, a holy nation, a people to be a personal possession to sing the praises of God who called you out of darkness into his wonderful light (1 Pt 2:9).

Many activities in the church lead to holiness. For example, the teaching and ruling office of the church has as its purpose the leading of people to the source of truth and holiness: Jesus Christ. But teaching and ruling do not exhaust all the sanctifying powers given by the Lord. Jesus instructed his disciples to baptize, to celebrate the eucharist, to pray, to help others, to forgive sins.

Some are called to act as official teachers in the church, to preside at the eucharistic sacrifice, and to forgive sin in our Lord's name. Jesus calls apart bishops, priests, and deacons to serve their Christian brothers and sisters through example, prayer, and their special ministry of the word and sacrament. This special priesthood within the Christian community is not meant for the sake of the individual's personal glory but for the good and sanctification of all.

Though Christ calls some to holy orders, everyone in the church—clergy and laity alike—has the baptismal call to holiness. The measure of our personal greatness in God's eyes is not the special gifts we have been given, but rather the intensity of love we have for God and others. Lay people share in Christ's priestly ministry by dedicating to Christ their work, prayer, family life, recreation, and hardships. A married couple has a unique opportunity to unite their common life to the Lord as a special ministry and source of holiness for their children. In addition, the church invites the laity to serve in various liturgical ministries, for example, by being a lector or a eucharistic minister.

What Is the Purpose of the Church's Governing Structure? [CCC 894-896; 908-913; 943]

When we think of a king, we think of a ruler, an authority figure. Jesus reminds us that all authority resides in him, "All authority in heaven and on earth has been given to me" (Mt 28:18). However, the Lord has chosen to share his teaching authority with shepherds in the church—the pope and bishops and their helpers, priests and deacons. He also shares his ruling authority. All institutions need a governing structure for tasks to be done.

The office of ruling in the church has but one purpose: the growth of faith and holiness. Church law, sometimes called canon law, includes those precepts and rules that regulate the life of the community of the church. Canon law, along with the legitimate commands of the pope and bishops, exists for the sake of God's people and deserves our respectful obedience.

The church's governing must be done with humility, love, compassion, and understanding. The church's standards must be those of Christ, never the standards of worldly rulers:

> Jesus called them to him and said, "You know that among the gentiles the rulers lord it over them, and great men make their authority felt. Among you this is not to happen. No; anyone who wants to become great among you must be your servant, and anyone who wants to be first among you must be your slave, just as the Son of man came not to be served but to serve, and to give his life as a ransom for many" (Mt 20:25-28).

Lay people participate in Jesus' kingly ministry by striving through self-denial to overcome sin in themselves and in the world, and to work for justice so God's kingdom may come on earth. Qualified lay people can also serve on parish finance committees, councils, and other church organizations.

What Are the Marks of the Church? [CCC 811-812]

Traditionally the church has been known by four signs or marks that help identify its true nature: one, holy, catholic (universal), and apostolic. These marks of the church help to strengthen the faith of Catholics and can attract the attention of nonbelievers.

But the signs are paradoxical in nature, both realizations and challenges. They refer to the divine element—Christ and the Holy Spirit—working in the church. And yet the church is made up of human members who sometimes betray the very marks which should point to the Lord. For example, the church is holy, and yet it is the home of sinners. The church is one, and yet there is a wounded unity among various Christian denominations. The church is open to all people, and yet individual Christians show prejudice to nonbelievers.

The church is apostolic, yet some Christian denominations ignore the leadership of its apostolic successors. These marks need some more explanation.

How Is the Church One? *[CCC 812-818; 820; 866]*

The church is one because its roots are in the unity of a Triune God. It is also one because Christ founded it and the Holy Spirit animates it. The Lord continues to pray for this church:

> "May they all be one,
> just as, Father, you are in me and I am in you,
> so that they may also be in us,
> so that the world may believe it was you who sent me" (Jn 17:21).

Love (charity) is the "spiritual glue" that harmoniously binds all in the church. Other bonds of communion include the following visible bonds which the church shares:

- profession of one faith traceable to the apostles (expressed, for example, in the Nicene Creed);

- common celebration of divine worship, especially the sacraments;

- and the succession of the bishops from the apostles through holy orders.

Unity does not mean uniformity. The Lord has given the church a diversity of gifts and a variety of people who receive them. Given the many differences in God's people, there is room for a variety of local and cultural expressions of the faith. A good example is the celebration of the Mass in the vernacular language. This practice recognizes healthy differences between people and respects their desire to understand the Mass in their own language.

Church history has revealed a wounded unity in God's people caused by **heresy** (the denial of essential truths), **apostasy** (abandonment of faith), and **schism** (a rift in unity). Fault lies on both sides—Catholic and Protestant—of these ruptures to unity, so blaming those living today for these divisions is wrong. **Ecumenism** is the movement that works to restore the unity of Christ's church (see Chapter 9). However, Catholics believe that the true church of Jesus Christ subsists in the Catholic church because in it can be found the *fullness* of the means of sanctification and apostolic succession traceable to St. Peter.

When conflicts arise because of differences in the church, Catholics look to the pope. He is both the symbol and servant of unity.

How Is the Church Holy? *[CCC 823-829; 867]*

Jesus Christ, the founder of the church, is the model of all holiness in the church. He and the Father send the Holy Spirit to dwell in the church, filling it up and uniting it. God is the ultimate source of holiness in the church. In a sense, only God is holy, but because the Holy Spirit lives in the church we can call the church holy. The church is a special presence of the risen Jesus Christ.

We sometimes speak of a person being holy because he or she lives wholly for God. But people cannot make themselves holy. Only God can sanctify a person, and a major way God chooses to do this is through the church. Thus, we may also say the church is holy because in it can be found the means to holiness, the means to the wholeness of personal development. In all centuries, saints have been our models of holiness and our intercessors before God. Mary, our Mother, is the preeminent model: "in her, the Church is already the 'all-holy'" (CCC 829).

God wants us to develop as fully as possible as individuals and as a community. As sinners, we must strive for holiness through penance and renewal. The church assists this effort because it uniquely possesses the means necessary to achieve full personhood: in scriptures, in the apostolic tradition, in the writings of great saints and theologians, in the teaching office of the church, in the liturgy, and in the various kinds of prayer practiced by Catholics.

The true test of a Christian's holiness is a life of service to others. Jesus teaches that "it is not anyone who says to me, 'Lord, Lord,' who will enter the kingdom of heaven, but the person who does the will of my Father in heaven" (Mt 7:21). The Father's way to holiness translates into deeds of active service: "So always treat others as you would like them to treat you" (Mt 7:12).

How Is the Church Catholic? *[CCC 830-835; 868]*

The word **catholic** means "general" or "universal." St. Ignatius of Antioch, a martyr who wrote in the first part of the second century, was the first to apply this adjective to the church.

The church is catholic because Christ is present in the body as its head, giving it the fullness of the means of salvation: a complete and correct confession of faith, an ordained ministry traceable to the apostles, and a full sacramental life, especially the gift of the eucharist.

Second, the church is catholic because it follows the Lord's command to teach all nations. It reaches out to all people at all places in all times. Poor and rich, learned and unlearned, all people everywhere are invited to be members of the Lord's body.

Third, the church is catholic in the sense that it continues to teach all that Christ taught. The same essential faith and worship are held by a wide variety of people, separated geographically across our wide globe, culturally across the races, and historically across almost 2,000 years.

Our Lord's presence guarantees that the church will always be catholic. Yet the church must live up to its mission to preach the gospel to everyone. It must work to restore Christian unity and respectfully carry on a conversation with those who have not yet heard or who are not yet open to the good news.

Finally, the church in each particular area, that is, each diocese united to its bishop, is also catholic because of its union with the church of Rome. The church's catholicity manifests itself in a variety of cultures, liturgical rites, disciplines, and spiritual traditions.

How Is the Church Apostolic? *[CCC 857-865; 869]*

The present leadership of the Catholic church can trace itself back to the first leaders of the church, the apostles. Christ founded his church on the apostles who in turn appointed successors. The hierarchy of the church is in direct succession to the apostles.

The church is also apostolic in the sense that it professes the same doctrine and Christian way of life taught by the apostles. It has preserved the good news of Jesus and his salvation and has not changed anything essential in his preaching or that of his closest disciples. The church, in other words, is founded on and continues the faith of the apostles. It does so by teaching, sanctifying, and guiding the faithful through the pope and bishops, and the priests and deacons who help them.

Apostle means "one who is sent." All Christians share in the apostolate of sharing Christ's good news with others. The success of our mission depends on our union with Jesus and the life we draw from him, especially in the eucharist, and in the wise use of the gifts and talents the Holy Spirit has given us to continue the Lord's work.

Concluding Reflections

The church is a Christian community organized hierarchically to carry on the Lord's work. The hierarchy plus all the individual members of the church share prophetic, priestly, and kingly roles. The church as prophet must represent the Lord's truth. The church as priest must serve as a mediator between God and people. The church as king must exercise the Lord's authority, an authority of loving service to all.

The church can be recognized by four marks: one, holy, catholic, and apostolic. These marks reveal the church's deepest identity because God's kingdom, which has come in Jesus Christ, already exists in the church, growing until it fully comes at the end of time.

The hierarchy—the official leaders of the church—has the responsibility to see that the church is true to its nature and mission.

It is a privilege to know the good news of God's love for us and to be a member of his body which has the task of teaching and demonstrating that love to others. This privilege also brings a challenge for us to be a prophetic, priestly, and kingly people. United with other Catholics, nourished by the eucharist, and strengthened by the gifts of the Holy Spirit, we have the task of spreading the Lord's word by the way we live. Jesus calls us to be his helping hands, his forgiving voice, his understanding eyes, his loving gesture. Through us the gospel message can come alive in the world.

Prayer Reflection

The biblical word of God contains many wise words for harmonious Christian living. Reflect on the following passage:

> Finally: you should all agree among yourselves and be sympathetic; love the brothers, have compassion and be self-effacing. Never repay one wrong with another, or one abusive word with another; instead, repay with a blessing. That is what you are called to do, so that you inherit a blessing. For Who among you delights in life, longs for time to enjoy prosperity? Guard your tongue from evil, your lips from any breath of deceit. Turn away from evil and do good, seek peace and pursue it. For the eyes of the Lord are on the upright, his ear turned to their cry. But the Lord's face is set against those who do evil (1 Pt 3:8-12).

For Discussion

1. What are some benefits of clear lines of authority and definite leadership in the church? Apply your observations to your local parish.
2. The church as prophet should speak the truth; the church as priest should draw people to God; the church as king should use its authority to serve the needs of people. In today's world, on which issues should the church take a prophetic stand? Which spiritual needs should the church address? Which people should the church serve in a special way?

3. How can you be a sign of holiness to others; that is, how can you best exercise your own priestly ministry?
4. How can you personally help to enhance a unity in the community to which you belong?

Further Reading

Jeremiah 1–2 (the call of a prophet and his initial preaching)
Hebrews 3–5 (Christ as the model of priestly ministry)

Chapter Nine

Ecumenism: The Church and Other Religions

My dear friends,
let us love each other,
since love is from God
and everyone who loves is a child of God and knows God.
Whoever fails to love does not know God,
because God is love.

— 1 John 4:7-8

Posted on a bulletin board in the back of a popular chapel in the heart of a city is a sign that reads:

Be silent.
Be thoughtful.
Be reverent, for this is the Lord's house.
Before the service, speak to God.
During the service, let God speak to you.
After the service, speak to one another.[1]

Pilgrimage is an important image for the spiritual life. Pilgrims are on a journey to a specific destination, but along the way they will encounter many interesting people whose stories make the journey much more fascinating. It is worth listening to these fellow travelers tell their stories, and it is equally vital to share what we as Christians have learned at the feet of the Lord. Whether we realize it or not, we travel through space and time on the "spaceship" earth. We are naturally bound with others and their stories.

This journey theme is important for understanding and living our Catholic faith. Jesus also reminds us that we do not travel alone. Our Christian brothers and sisters help us make it to our destination; we also have the obligation to sustain them on their journey. Numerically there are many Roman Catholics, fellow-travelers who share the same faith, for Catholicism is the largest Christian denomination in the world and the largest branch of any of the world religions. Many Catholics consider it a privilege and an honor to be members of this religious body, one we believe the Holy Spirit guides on its journey.

We must be aware, however, that most of the world's population is not Catholic. Millions of people belong to other religions. Yet they are our brothers and sisters too. We share the same gift of God's creation, and our mutual journey has a common destination—union with God. To think that one is superior because he or she belongs to one religious group rather than another is to fall victim to the sin of pride. Worse yet, negative judgments about our fellow travelers can often lead to prejudice. And this is a bad sin that results in the religious bigotry which has permitted so many horrible evils over the centuries.

The attitude of the church today towards other religions is one of respect and reverence. Just as the bee gathers honey from thorny rose bushes, so too Catholics and other Christians can and should gain much nourishment from respecting and learning about other religious traditions. This chapter briefly treats the topic of ecumenism whose aim is mutual understanding among religions.

What Are the Major World Religions? *[CCC 839-842]*

We typically divide the major world religions into those of the West and those of the East. The religions of the West include Judaism and its two spiritual descendants: Christianity and Islam. Judaism defines itself as a people of the Covenant: Yahweh formed and sustained the Jewish people in return for their love and worship. Yahweh is their God, and Israel is God's people. Christianity professes that Jesus of Nazareth, a first-century Jew, is the Messiah who fulfills all the promises made to Israel. The Moslems share with Judaism and Christianity a strong faith in one God. Though Islam acknowledges Jesus as a prophet and honors Mary his mother, it maintains that Mohammed is Allah's greatest prophet.

The religions of the East include Hinduism and Buddhism which were born on the Indian subcontinent, Taoism in China, and the Shinto religions in Japan.

To these major religions we could add the many minor religions, sometimes called primitive religions. These include the religions of the American Indians and various aboriginal people, for example, of Australia and Africa.

What Are the Major Christian Denominations? *[CCC 834-838]*

Numerically, Christianity is the largest major world religion. It has three major denominations or divisions: Catholic, Orthodox, and Protestant.

Catholicism, the largest Christian denomination, includes those Christians who acknowledge the primacy of the pope. Most Catholics are of the Roman or Latin rite, the predominant rite of the Western church. Of the five major Eastern rites, the Byzantine rite is the largest; it includes a number of Catholic groups of diverse ethnic origin. The term *rites* refers to the forms and rules regarding liturgical worship and the various ways of expressing the rich theological, spiritual, and disciplinary heritages of the churches of the East and West. These different rites developed over the course of history as the church adapted itself to the various cultures it encountered through time.

The *Eastern Orthodox* (or Orthodox) are Eastern rite churches (notably the Greek and Russian Orthodox churches) that are in schism from Rome, that is, not in union with the pope. Of all Christian groups, the Orthodox are closest to Roman Catholicism in faith, theology, and church structures.

The Reformation of the 16th century resulted in the formation of the mainstream *Protestant* churches. These denominations share many beliefs in common with Catholics, notably the articles of faith in the Nicene Creed, but they differ on other points of belief and practice.

How Did Division Among Christians Come About? *[CCC 817-818]*

We would have to relate a long and complex history to show how the church of Christ splintered into the various Christian denominations. These ruptures to the unity Christ intended for his church resulted from heresy, apostasy, and schism. The history would include at least two major parts.

A major chapter of the story tells of the schism (split) between the Western and Eastern churches. Both political and church differences arose due in some measure to the rivalry between the two capitals of the Roman empire—Rome and Constantinople. Various cultural, sociological, and theological differences finally led to the great schism of 1054. These differences focus on the role of papal authority. This schism has divided the Roman Catholic and the Eastern Orthodox churches ever since.

The second chapter in this history would tell of the *Protestant Reformation* and its aftermath. Because of corruption and some laxity in the 16th-century church, the Catholic church was in need of reform itself at that time and had, in fact, begun the process. However, at the same time some reformers like Martin Luther and John Calvin protested in such a way that their firmly-held beliefs resulted in their separating from the Roman Catholic church. Sadly, they had followers who went with them.

Before long a number of Protestant churches came into existence, varying considerably in their beliefs and practices. The most prominent today are the Lutheran, Presbyterian, Methodist, Baptist, and United Church of Christ. The present-day Anglican church, known as the Episcopal Church in America, was begun by King Henry VIII as a result of a conflict with the pope who refused to annul Henry's marriage. It has much of the institutional form of the Roman Catholic church, but maintains independence from the pope.

Other significant Protestant faiths include the Pentecostal and Holiness groups. Still other groups are described as sects. These sects are typically small, have become separated from a larger church, and are difficult to classify according to traditional definitions of a Christian church. For example, they do not believe in the divinity of Jesus Christ as the *unique* Son of God. These groups include the Mormons (the Church of Jesus Christ of the Latter Day Saints) and the Jehovah's Witnesses.

What Is Ecumenism? *[CCC 820-822]*

Ours is an age of ecumenism. *Ecumenism* comes from a Greek word that means "universal." The ecumenical movement generally means two things: First, it refers to the attempt among all world religions to understand one another better and to overcome needless opposition. Second, when applied to Christians, the ecumenical movement refers to the efforts of Christian denominations to work for greater unity among themselves and to understand better and improve relations with the other major world religions. In the words of Pope John Paul II, "Ecumenism is directed precisely to making the partial communion existing between Christians grow toward full communion in both truth and charity" (*That All May Be One*, 14).

The Christian Ecumenical movement began among Protestants in Edinburgh, Scotland, in 1910. Meetings were held periodically, culminating in 1948 with the founding of the World Council of Churches. The Catholic church did not officially participate in non-Catholic ecumenical efforts until the Second Vatican Council (1962-1965). The *Decree on Ecumenism* made efforts for

Christian unity to become a top priority for the church and praised efforts on behalf of ecumenism. Today, the church holds that ecumenism is "an organic part of her life and work, and consequently must pervade all that she is and does" (*That All May Be One*, 20).

What Is the Relationship of Other Christian Churches to the Catholic Church? [CCC 819; 870]

Work on behalf of ecumenism does not mean that the church denies its unique role in God's plan of salvation. For example, the church teaches that the fullness of the truth and grace of Jesus Christ subsists (can be found) in the Roman Catholic church:

> For it is through Christ's Catholic Church alone, which is the all-embracing means of salvation, that the fullness of the means of salvation can be obtained. It was to the apostolic college alone, of which Peter is the head, that we believe our Lord entrusted all the blessings of the New Covenant, in order to establish on earth the one Body of Christ into which all those should be fully incorporated who already belong in any way to God's people (Decree on Ecumenism, 3).

Nevertheless, the church also teaches that the Holy Spirit works in all people of good will to build up God's kingdom. Other churches share in the building up of the kingdom to the degree that they are related to the one true church of Jesus Christ, centered primarily in the Roman Catholic church. Many elements of holiness and truth can be found in other faiths, for example, the Bible; grace; the theological virtues of faith, hope, and love; gifts of the Holy Spirit; and visible elements as well. The Holy Spirit uses these ecclesial communities and churches to bring salvation to people.

> [Their] power derives from the fullness of grace and truth that Christ has entrusted to the Catholic Church. All these blessings come from Christ and lead to him, and are in themselves calls to "Catholic unity" (CCC 819).

What Is the Goal of Ecumenism? [CCC 820-821]

The goal of Christian ecumenism is a common commitment among Christians to live out the gospel and to be open to the unifying action of the Holy Spirit. Much already unites Christian churches, for example, agreement that the true nature of the church of Christ is to be "salt of the earth" and "light of the world."

How Can We Work for Christian Unity? [CCC 820-822]

Every Catholic can work for Christian unity, can be part of the ecumenical movement. Vatican II defined this movement as "those

THIS IS OUR FAITH

activities and enterprises which . . . are started and organized for the fostering of unity among Christians" (*Decree on Ecumenism*, 4).

A primary duty of Catholics in the work for unity is to make sure that the Catholic church itself is living the gospel message by renewing itself according to the gospel vision of Jesus Christ. Christ has given the church the gift of unity, "but the Church must always pray and work to maintain, reinforce, and perfect the unity that Christ wills for her" (*CCC* 820). Work for Christian unity belongs to both the clergy and all the faithful. In the words of Vatican II, "Let all Christ's faithful remember that the more purely they strive to live according to the gospel, the more they are fostering and even practicing Christian unity" (*Decree on Ecumenism*, 7).

Thus, all Catholics must try to live holy lives to draw others to Jesus and his church. Infidelity to Christ leads to divisions. Furthermore, Catholics can acknowledge the spiritual gifts which our Lord has endowed on our Christian brothers and sisters and remember that their faith, hope, and love can inspire us. In addition, we can do the following:

Pray. The most important thing any of us can do to foster Christian unity is to pray. We can pray *for* Christian unity, asking the Spirit to guide our efforts, and we can pray *with* our Christian brothers and sisters. Common prayer for unity is, in the words of Vatican II, the "soul" of ecumenism (*Decree on Ecumenism*, 8).

Study. We have a duty to know our own faith well and to share its truths with others. This is a lifelong quest—to know better the depths of our own faith and to appreciate the meaning of church doctrines so that we can help others to understand them as well. Knowledge of other religions can also be very helpful for mutual understanding.

Communicate. Since Vatican II, Catholic theological experts and those of many different religions have engaged in dialogues to better mutual understanding and to arrive at common professions of faith. These efforts should continue. As individuals we can share our own Catholic beliefs and engage in open exchanges with members of other faiths as occasions arise. The Council encourages us to eliminate prejudicial language from our conversation. We can share points of view in Christian harmony, charitably and with understanding.

Cooperate. The church calls on us to work with our Christian brothers and sisters of other communions on projects of social action and service. Putting the gospel into action in joint efforts of Christian charity can go a long way in bringing Christians together.

Who Belongs to the Catholic Church? *[CCC 836-837]*

God calls all people to the catholic unity of God's people. In different ways, the Catholic faithful, other Christians, and all people—called by God's grace to salvation—belong to or are ordered to this unity.

> [Catholics] are those who, possessing Christ's Spirit, accept her entire system and all the means of salvation given to her, and through union with her visible structure are joined to Christ, who rules her through the Supreme Pontiff and the bishops. This joining is effected by the bonds of professed faith, of the sacraments, of ecclesiastical government, and of communion (Dogmatic Constitution on the Church, 14).

However, belonging to the Catholic faith does not guarantee salvation. A person must live a loving, Christ-like life to be a church member in heart and spirit, and not just in body.

What Is the Relationship Between the Eastern Orthodox Churches and the Roman Catholic Church? *[CCC 838]*

The Catholic church respects the Eastern Orthodox churches. Though there are some differences in belief, the Eastern Orthodox churches keep all the basic beliefs and traditions of the Roman Catholic church up to the separation of 1054. They celebrate all of the sacraments and have a valid hierarchy and priesthood. The basic difference is over the role of the pope whom they claim does not have jurisdiction over the whole church. Major efforts toward reunion have been made in the years since the Second Vatican Council.

What Is the Relationship Between the Catholic Church and Most Protestant Churches? *[CCC 817-819]*

The church acknowledges, respects, and praises what we have in common with most Protestant churches: faith in God the Father, his Son Jesus Christ, and the Holy Spirit; the Bible as the living word of God; a life of prayer and grace; faith, hope, and charity and other gifts of the Holy Spirit; baptism; commemoration of the Lord's Supper; work for the kingdom and a looking forward to the day of its glory; concern to live moral lives according to God's revelation.

The church teaches that all Catholics should honor Protestants who are saved by faith and baptism. They "are accepted as brothers by the children of the Catholic Church" (*Decree on Ecumenism*, 3).

What Is the Church's Attitude Toward Judaism? *[CCC 839-840]*

All Christians owe the Jewish faith special reverence and respect. The Christian religion finds its spiritual roots in Judaism. The Jewish people were the first to hear the word of God: "it was they who were adopted as children, the glory was theirs and the covenants; to them were given the Law and the worship of God and the promises. To them belong the fathers and out of them . . . came Christ who is above all" (Rom 9:4-5). Jews have not ceased to be God's Chosen People.

> The Jews still remain most dear to God because of their fathers, for he does not repent of the gifts He makes nor of the calls He issues [cf. Rom. 11:28-29] (Declaration on the Relationship of the Church to Non- Christian Religions, 4).

The Jewish faith is already a response to God's revelation in the original covenant. The Jewish people witness to the Father of Jesus and revere the books of the Hebrew scriptures (what we call the Old Testament). Furthermore, they live by the same moral code, the Ten Commandments.

The church in our day speaks out strongly against anti-Semitism, prejudice directed against Jews. The church reminds us that any persecution against the Jews, and any form of discrimination because of race, color, condition of life, or religion is contrary to the will of Christ and a direct violation of his call to love.

Through the ages many Christians wrongly blamed the Jews as a people for the death of Christ. What happened in Jesus' passion "cannot be blamed upon all the Jews then living, without distinction, nor upon the Jews of today" (*Declaration on the Relationship of the Church to Non-Christian Religions*, 4).

What Is the Church's Attitude Toward Moslems? *[CCC 841]*

The church also esteems the Moslems who worship the one and merciful God. Moslems do not acknowledge the divinity of Jesus Christ, but they do revere him as a great prophet, and they honor his mother Mary. With Christians they await judgment day and resurrection, prize the moral life, and worship God through prayer, almsgiving, and fasting.

The Council recognized that the history of Christians and Moslems has seen conflicts and hostilities, but the church now calls for cooperation. All are urged to forget the past and to strive sincerely for mutual understanding. The Council urges Moslems and Christians to work in common for social justice, moral values, and the causes of peace and freedom.

How Does the Church View Other Religions and People With No Religion? *[CCC 842-843]*

The church recognizes that in God's own mysterious way, God extends salvation to all people everywhere. All people are God's children who share a common destiny: a loving God. Thus, the church

> rejects nothing which is true and holy in these religions. She looks with sincere respect upon those ways of conduct and life, those rules and teachings which, though differing in many particulars from what she holds and sets forth, nevertheless often reflect a ray of that Truth which enlightens all men (Declaration on the Relationship of the Church to Non-Christian Religions, 2).

Even those with no professed faith deserve respect as persons. God extends grace to them and if they strive to live good and loving lives, they are responding to God's gift of salvation. Whatever is good or true found among these people is seen as a preparation for the gospel.

> Those also can attain to everlasting salvation who through no fault of their own do not know the gospel of Christ or His Church, yet sincerely seek God and, moved by grace, strive by their deeds to do His will as it is known to them through the dictates of conscience (Dogmatic Constitution on the Church, 16).

What Special Role Does the Church Have Toward People of Other Faiths? *[CCC 844-845; 855-856]*

Division among God's children has often resulted from Satan's ploy to tempt humans to trust in their own efforts or to choose to serve a creature rather than the Creator. The Lord established the church as a special community to reunite all God's children, to be a seaworthy ship guided by Christ and the Holy Spirit to navigate the rough seas of this world.

Thus, the church is essentially missionary. It has the message of Christ's salvation to deliver in word and deed to a world thirsty for ultimate meaning. It must respectfully listen to and learn from people of other faiths, but it must also proclaim the good news of Jesus to those who do not know it. In so doing, the church evokes the truth and goodness God plants in the hearts of all and helps lead them to their eternal happiness in Christ Jesus.

Concluding Reflections

A tragedy of Christian history is division among the followers of Jesus. Today there is a wounded unity in the body of Christ. Undoubtedly this happened because Christians preached their own message instead of heeding the gospel call of the Lord to repentance and service.

More than ever before the members of the human community need to grow closer to one another, if simply for the survival of the species. Human community is fostered by unity. Christians believe that the Lord Jesus through the power of the Holy Spirit—the Spirit of love—can bring about what human efforts cannot. Like a magnet that draws particles of iron to itself, the power of love can attract Christians to Christ and thus unite them one to another. United, Christians stand as a beacon to a world searching for light; divided, Christians fall and scatter the fire of hope.

For love to work its mysterious wonders, Christians must strive to live according to the gospel of Jesus. Mutual respect, a genuine desire to learn from others, shared prayer, and humble works of service for those suffering—all these are essential for Christian unity. The religious antagonism of the past has no place in a world struggling against the forces of evil for its mere survival. All people of good will must join hands to help work for God's kingdom. By centering on Jesus and letting go of superior attitudes toward others, Christians place themselves in a much better position to be the light of the world they are called to be.

Prayer Reflection

The parable of the Good Samaritan (Lk 10:29-37) has as its central character a man who is traveling. He is waylaid by an anonymous thug, but more importantly, he is ignored by the established religious figures who were his compatriots. Only the stranger—an enemy—stopped to help him. There are many lessons in this parable, including two that drive home the message of this chapter. First, religious prejudice is ugly and wrong according to the teaching of Jesus. Second, one way to transcend religious differences is through service of one another.

Let us turn to St. Ignatius of Loyola for a simple yet profound prayer for generous service of others.

> Lord, teach me to be generous,
> Teach me to serve you as you deserve,
> To give and not to count the cost,
> To fight and not to heed the wounds,
> To toil and not to seek for rest,
> To labor and not to ask for reward,
> Save that of knowing that I do your will.

For Discussion

1. Think of a person of another faith who seems to really live his or her beliefs. How might Catholics learn from this person?
2. How should today's church reach out to people of other faiths?
3. What can you do in a practical way to work for Christian unity? How do you witness to your faith on a daily basis?

Further Reading

Jonah (God proclaims his message to everyone)
John 17 (Jesus' priestly prayer for unity)

Chapter Ten

The Communion of Saints and the Blessed Mother

I believe in the communion of saints.
— from the Apostles' Creed

Mary said, "You see before you the Lord's servant, let it happen to me as you have said."
— Luke 1:38

An oft-repeated story tells of a teacher who said she was going to write the word *church* on the blackboard. She then printed "CH . . CH." The youngsters began to giggle and informed the teacher that she left out two letters at the middle of the word—"U-R." The clever teacher responded to the children, "You're right. *You are* at the center and heart of the church."

This story reminds us that the Lord wants each member of his church to help him accomplish his work of salvation. The church, the body of Christ, is a family, a communion formed in Jesus Christ. The Lord sends the Holy Spirit, the Spirit of love, to endow each member of the family with the necessary gifts to continue his work for the kingdom. Jesus sanctifies the members of this communion through the grace of his friendship and the presence of the Holy Spirit.

Jesus calls all Christians to live lives of holiness, that is, to imitate his heavenly Father, to live morally, to worship God, and to serve others. Jesus calls us to the vocation of sainthood and the epistles commonly call Christians "the saints." The claim being made was *not* that Christians were already perfect. Rather, the early church writings called Christians saints because the Lord calls us to holiness—the word *saint* means "holy one." Through our baptismal initiation into Jesus' own life of holiness, Christians have been given a privileged vocation: to become saints in imitation of our Lord.

This chapter discusses the Catholic doctrine of the communion of saints, the union of all God's people. It also treats the special role Mary plays in the church as the perfect model of Christian holiness.

What Is the Meaning of the Communion of Saints? *[CCC 946-953; 960-961]*

Jesus, the head of the church, communicates his abundant gifts and graces to the members of the church. Because all Christians form one body in Christ, the goodness and gifts of each member are communicated and shared with one another.

Among the gifts the members share are faith, sacramental graces, benefits from each other's special gifts (charisms), their love for each other, charitable giving, and social concern.

The term **communion of saints** means, therefore, communion among the holy persons in the church ("the saints," which includes us all) and communion in the holy things, especially the eucharist.

Who Belongs to the Communion of Saints? *[CCC 954-955; 962]*

The communion of saints includes all those who are now living on earth (the pilgrim church), those who are being purified in **purgatory** (the church suffering), and those who are blessed in **heaven** (the church in glory).

The term *communion of saints* also underscores that the people of God, the church, is a *eucharistic* community. The church is a community of people, a real communion, gathered around the eucharistic table of the risen Lord. This community is called, gathered from around the world, and unified by the Holy Spirit. The risen Lord comes to us in his word proclaimed at the eucharist and in the consecrated bread and wine. Through the power of the Holy Spirit, the church is united into a communion of love and holiness as it partakes of the gift of the risen Lord, the source of all holiness.

Where Does Belief in the Communion of Saints Originate? *[CCC 958-959; 1475]*

The doctrine of the communion of saints flows from our belief that we Christians are closely united as one family in the Spirit of Jesus Christ. The bond of love makes us one. In a certain sense, all of God's people are dependent on one another. Those of us who are still living depend on the prayers and good works of our Christian brothers and sisters who are united to us in the friendship of the Lord. "The heartfelt prayer of someone upright works very powerfully" (Jas 5:16). We also believe in the value of prayer for our departed brothers and sisters who are being purified in purgatory. Finally, we believe that those Christian heroes whom we call saints in heaven are vitally interested in those of us who are still living or in purgatory. The saints pray for us in our weakness. And for our good, they offer the merits they earned on earth through Jesus, our one Mediator and Savior.

Who Is a Saint? *[CCC 828; 957]*

Jesus calls each of his disciples to be a saint, that is, to be holy. A saint is a good person. Saints are people who always choose the better of two courses open to them. Saints are Christian models of holiness. To believe in Christian heroes and to learn from their lives can inspire us to do heroic deeds of service ourselves on our own journey to holiness.

Under the guidance of the Holy Spirit the Catholic church will sometimes declare that a person who lived a good life and died a death joined to Jesus is a saint. The process leading to adding a person's name to the list of saints (a process known as **canonization**) involves a careful study of that person's life and a sign from God (usually miracles performed in that person's name) that this person is truly a saint. Saints are those who practiced heroic virtue and faithfully lived a grace-filled life. Therefore, the Christian hero is worthy of our imitation and can serve as our intercessors. When the church honors a saint, the church is praising God who shares his life of holiness with us, his creatures.

Every person in heaven is truly a saint, whether canonized or not. Some of these saints may be our own deceased friends and relatives. The church honors all these good people on All Saints' Day. In some countries, including the United States, All Saints' Day is celebrated as a holy day, a day of truly celebrating the countless number of people who have lived good, holy lives and are now sharing in God's life and happiness in heaven.

Why Do We Pray to the Saints? *[CCC 955-957]*

Devotion to the saints is a traditional means to holiness. We venerate, that is, honor these men and women. We do *not* pray to the saints as though they were God. Rather, we petition them to intercede for us with our heavenly Father. They are living a deep, personal, and loving relationship with God; they have proven their friendship by the extraordinary goodness of their lives while on earth.

We pray to the saints to befriend us, too, especially those to whom we feel particularly close. We ask these personal heroes to take our petitions to the Father on our behalf. We also ask them to inspire us by the example of their lives. They were flesh-and-blood people who rose to the challenge of the Christian life. They can be a great source of inspiration and can provide us with an example of single-hearted commitment to God's kingdom. Erasmus made a telling observation when he said: "No devotion to the saints is more acceptable and proper than if you strive to express their virtue" (*Enchiridion*).

What Is Mary's Role in the Church? *[CCC 511; 964-965; 967-968; 973]*

Mary, foremost among the saints, has a special place in the story of salvation history. Her role in the church flows and is inseparable from her union with her son. Her "yes" at the annunciation consented to the Lord's Incarnation, thus collaborating with her Son's work from the beginning.

The New Testament reports that she was singled out and graced by God for the special and unique privilege of being the mother of the Savior. Not fully understanding how she—an unmarried woman—was to conceive a child, she became the perfect symbol of faith when she said yes to the invitation to bear God's Son. With her husband, Joseph, Mary raised Jesus in a loving, prayer-filled home, teaching and caring for him.

When Jesus launched his public ministry, Mary faithfully witnessed and supported him. With courage and sorrow in her heart, she stood at the foot of the cross in Jesus' dying moments. Finally, the Bible tells us that Mary was with the apostles praying in the upper room after Jesus' resurrection, expectantly awaiting the descent of the Holy Spirit. The church teaches that Mary is the greatest Christian saint. She is the perfect model of Christian faith and love because she obeyed the Father's will, cooperated with her son's redemptive work, and responded to the graces of the Holy Spirit.

What Are Some of Mary's Titles? *[CCC 969]*

The church honors Mary with many titles such as Our Lady, Mother of God, Our Lady of the Immaculate Conception, Blessed Mother, Mother of the Church, Ever Virgin, Queen of Heaven and Earth. These titles reflect what the church believes and teaches about her.

As our loving Mother, Mary continues to intercede for us before her Son, our Lord Jesus. This is why the church also prays to her under the titles *Advocate, Helper, Benefactress,* and *Mediatrix.*

What Is the "Immaculate Conception"? *[CCC 490-493; 508; 722]*

The church teaches that Mary was conceived without original sin, the **Immaculate Conception**. This means that from the first moment of her existence Mary was full of grace, that is, free of any alienation from God caused by original sin. Because of Mary's special role in God's saving plan, she was graced with this divine favor in anticipation of her son's death and resurrection. In addition, Mary was so attuned to God that she was free of all personal sin. She lived a blameless life. The proclamation of the angel—"Rejoice, you who enjoy God's favor! The Lord is with you" (Lk 1:28)—proclaims that Mary is the most blessed of all humans, for she plays a central part in God's plan of salvation. She, the Mother of God, is all-holy.

What Does the Church Teach About Mary's Virginity? *[CCC 484-489; 494; 496-499; 502-503; 510; 723]*

The Apostles' Creed states that Jesus was conceived by the Holy Spirit and born of the Virgin Mary. Mary conceived Jesus without a human father, and the church has traditionally taught that she was a virgin "before, in, and after" the birth of the Lord. This virginal conception of Jesus is God's work, beyond "all human understanding and possibility" (CCC 497). We can understand its true meaning only with the gift of faith.

The theological significance of Mary's virginity is intimately related to the divinity of Jesus. What the Catholic faith believes about Mary is rooted in its beliefs about Jesus. From all eternity God chose Mary to be Jesus' mother. She was a true daughter of Israel, one in a line of holy women who helped prepare for her mission of cooperating with God's plan for our salvation. Her free cooperation—"Let it be done to me according to your word"—helped God's plan bear fruit.

By maintaining its belief in Mary's virginity the Catholic church teaches that God alone took the initiative in the Incarnation. God alone is the Father of our Lord and Savior Jesus Christ.

How Is Mary Mother of God and Mother of the Church?
[CCC 495; 501; 509; 724-726; 963]

In reflecting on the identity of Jesus, the early church, under the inspiration of the Holy Spirit, taught that Jesus is *one* divine person who has both a human nature and a divine nature. Further, the early church taught that Jesus was divine from the very first moment of his conception. Thus, at the Council of Ephesus (AD 431) the church solemnly taught that Mary is "Mother of God" (*Theo-tokos* = *"bearer of God"*).

By being the mother of Jesus, Mary is truly the mother of God. It is most appropriate for Christians to address Mary with the lofty title: Mother of God.

But Mary is also our mother, the Mother of the Church. As he hung dying on the cross, Jesus gave his mother to all people everywhere to serve as their spiritual mother. "This is your mother," he said (Jn 19:27). Mary is the new Eve who fully cooperated with the Holy Spirit to bring Christ into the world and the world to Christ. By giving Mary to us as our mother, the Lord wishes the church to learn what God does for those he loves. The church also has a maternal role. As such the church can learn much from Mary, the perfect model of faith, obedience, fidelity, compassion, and prayerfulness. Mary is the model of Christian holiness and an image of God's love for his people.

What Is the Assumption? *[CCC 966; 974]*

In 1950 Pope Pius XII officially proclaimed the doctrine of the **Assumption**: "The Immaculate Mother of God, the ever Virgin Mary, having completed the course of her earthly life, was assumed body and soul into heavenly glory." This doctrine, which has its roots in ancient Catholic belief, shows the connection between Mary's unique role as God's mother preserved from original sin and the reality of our final resurrection in Christ. In her assumption, Mary was preserved from the decay of death. Mary, the mother of the Savior, is the first to share in the Lord's resurrection. She is the living model for all people whose future destiny is union with the risen Lord. Her assumption to heaven is an anticipation of our own resurrection.

Why Do Catholics Have Special Veneration for Mary? *[CCC 970-972; 975]*

Catholics venerate Mary because she is the Mother of God and our mother. "All generations will call me blessed" (Lk 1:48). By praying to and honoring Mary in a special way, we are led to love her and to imitate her many virtues, especially her total commitment to God's will and her single-hearted faith in God's work. "You see before you the Lord's servant . . . let it happen to me as you have said" (Lk 1:38). As his mother she is uniquely close to him; she is the perfect model of those who center their lives on Jesus.

Mary's role as our mother is not meant to hide Jesus' role as our one mediator. Rather, her maternal function shows forth the Lord's love and shares his graces. Mary is a special grace to humanity; she uniquely attracts us to her son. Note how classical Marian art—the *Pietà* or any of the famous icons of Mary and Jesus—depicts Mary drawing our attention to her son. The focus of the painting or the statue is Jesus, not Mary. *Mary's role in salvation is to give her son to humanity. She leads us to him, shows us how to live in response to him, and intercedes on our behalf.*

Sometimes Catholics are accused of worshipping Mary as though she were a god. True devotion to Mary *honors* Mary; we *worship* God alone. When we pray in Mary's honor, we are really thanking and praising God for blessing one of our sisters. The doctrine of the communion of saints teaches us that those who are close to God will intercede on our behalf. The New Testament reveals a valuable lesson concerning Mary: Jesus does answer her pleas for others. The miracle of the wine at Cana testifies to this (see Jn 2:1-12).

What Is the Rosary? *[CCC 971, 2708]*

The church has many devotions to Mary, but the most popular is the Rosary, called by Pope Paul VI the "epitome of the whole gospel" (*Marialis Cultus*). The Rosary is a perfect blend of vocal prayers and meditation. The vocal prayers center on the recitation of a number of decades of Hail Marys, each decade introduced by the Lord's Prayer and concluded by a Glory Be. Introductory prayers to the Rosary include the Apostles' Creed, an initial Our Father, three Hail Marys, and a Glory Be. During the recitation of these vocal prayers, we meditate on certain events, or mysteries, from the life of Christ and Mary.

The complete Rosary consists of fifteen decades, though we customarily only recite five decades at a time. Rosary beads are used to help count the prayers.

The repetition of the Hail Marys helps to keep our minds from distractions as we meditate on the mysteries. Next to the Lord's Prayer, the Hail Mary is the most popular of all prayers among Catholics. The first part of the Hail Mary is rooted in the

New Testament; it combines the greetings of the angel (Lk 1:28) and Mary's cousin Elizabeth (Lk 1:42). The second part of this prayer requests Mary's intercession for us:

> Hail Mary, full of grace, the Lord is with thee;
> blessed art though among women and blessed is the fruit of thy womb, Jesus.
> Holy Mary, mother of God, pray for us sinners now and at the hour of our death. Amen.

These mysteries are divided into the following three categories:

Joyful Mysteries	Sorrowful Mysteries	Glorious Mysteries
1. The Annunciation	1. The Agony in the Garden	1. The Resurrection
2. The Visitation of Mary to Elizabeth	2. The Scourging at the Pillar	2. The Ascension
3. The Birth of Jesus	3. The Crowning With Thorns	3. The Descent of the Holy Spirit on the Apostles
4. The Presentation of Jesus in the Temple	4. The Carrying of the Cross	4. The Assumption of Mary Into Heaven
5. The Finding of Jesus in the Temple	5. The Crucifixion	5. The Crowning of Mary Queen of Heaven

What Are Some Other Marian Devotions? *[CCC 2679]*

Among the popular devotions to Mary are the Angelus, the First Saturday devotion, the Litany of the Blessed Mother, and various novenas.

The *Angelus* commemorates the Incarnation and is traditionally recited in the morning, at noon, and in the evening. It includes three short verses which recall the angel Gabriel's announcing to Mary that she was chosen to be the mother of the Lord and her humble acceptance. Three Hail Marys and a special prayer are also included. (You can find the Angelus as a Prayer Reflection on page 331.)

The *First Saturday devotion* originated as a result of Mary's appearances to the children at Fatima in Portugal in 1917. The devotion consists of the celebration of the sacrament of reconciliation, receiving holy communion on the first Saturday of five consecutive months, reciting five decades of the Rosary, and meditating on the mysteries of the Rosary for fifteen minutes. This practice is offered to God for the intention of the conversion of sinners and in reparation for sin.

A *litany* is prayer in the form of petitions with a response. The Litany of the Blessed Mother is found in most prayer books.

A *novena* is a devotion practiced over nine consecutive days (or over a period of nine weeks, with one day a week set aside for the devotion). A novena recalls the nine-day period of prayer spent by the apostles and disciples of Jesus in the upper room before the descent of the Holy Spirit. A popular novena to Mary is the novena in honor of Our Lady of Perpetual Help.

Concluding Reflections

Deep within us is an urgent longing for others to love, understand, and accept us as we are. We want union with others; we fear loneliness and isolation.

The Christian doctrine of the communion of saints teaches that the Christian is never alone. We are spiritually in union with all our brothers and sisters in the faith. The power and the love of the Lord bring us into the very unity of the Blessed Trinity. God loves us. Our Lord Jesus redeems us and continues to show his love by inviting us—both those of us alive on this earth and our brothers and sisters who have preceded us in death—into his family, a communion of love united by the power of the Spirit.

Prayer Reflection

The realization that God loves us in an incredibly wonderful way overwhelmed Mary. Her Magnificat is a powerful prayer of praise to a gracious God. All Christians can identify with Mary in this joyous song. God has done great things for us, inviting us into fellowship with the Blessed Trinity and the saints.

My soul proclaims the greatness of the Lord
and my spirit *rejoices in God my Savior;*
because *he has looked upon the humiliation of his servant.*
Yes, from now onwards all generations will call me blessed,
for the Almighty has done great things for me.
Holy is his name,
and *his faithful love extends age after age to those who fear him*
(Lk 1:46-49).

For Discussion

1. Who is your favorite saint? What do you know about your patron saint? What have you learned from their lives about how to respond to God?
2. What do the teachings about Mary reveal about her son Jesus? about the church?
3. What role does Mary play in your life?
4. Some people feel that Mary's life of obscurity and service is not a helpful model for today's active women. Do you agree? Why or why not? How might you counter that argument?
5. What can we learn about Christian living from what the gospels tell about Mary?

Further Reading

Leviticus 19 (the way to holiness)
Romans 6–8 (Christian freedom, holiness and spiritual life)

Chapter Eleven

Christian Destiny: The Last Things

We acknowledge one baptism for the forgiveness of sins.
We look for the resurrection of the dead and the life of the world
to come.
— from the Nicene Creed

Come, Lord Jesus!
— Revelation 22:20

In AD 627, the monk Paulinus visited King Edwin in northern England with the intent to convert him to Christianity. As Paulinus preached in a regal hall alighted with torches, an old earl interrupted. *"What happens after death? The life of man is like a little bird flying through this lighted hall, entering in at one door from the darkness outside, fluttering through the warmth and light, and passing through the farther door into the dark unknown beyond. Can your new religion solve this mystery for us? What will happen to us after death, in the dark, dim unknown?"*

The old nobleman knew the inevitability and apparent defeat of death which stares all humans in the face. But the gospel has joyous news. Because of Jesus' victory over sin and death, Christians can answer the earl's questions. The good news of Jesus proclaims: "Death does not have the last word. Life does!" St. Bernard of Clairvaux said it well: "Death [is] the gate of life." The good news of Christianity is that life has no end. Jesus taught:

"I am the resurrection.
Anyone who believes in me, even though that person dies, will live, and whoever lives and believes in me
will never die" (Jn 11:25-26).

Religion deals with the basic questions of life: Is there a God? What is the meaning of life? Are my sins forgiven? What is the meaning of death? Where and how will the world end? Is there life after death? This chapter will examine the church's teachings on these issues, topics in the area of **eschatology**. Eschatology is the study of the "last things"—death, judgment, Christ's second coming, heaven, hell, purgatory, the resurrection of the body, and life everlasting. But first, let us briefly consider the second to last clause of the Nicene Creed on baptism for the forgiveness of sin, a topic we will examine in greater detail in both Parts 2 and 3 of this book.

How Does the Church Continue Jesus' Ministry of Forgiveness? *[CCC 976-977; 984-985]*

At the heart of Jesus' ministry was his forgiveness of sin. Last century, Alice Carey wrote, "Nothing in this lost world bears the impress of the Son of God so surely as forgiveness." Imagine, for example, the impression Jesus made on the penitent woman who burst into Simon the Pharisee's house. Her rejoicing must have been great when Jesus said, "Your sins are forgiven" (Lk 7:48).

Also, consider the reaction of the paralytic who heard Jesus proclaim, "My child, your sins are forgiven" (Mk 2:5). When some Pharisees heard this announcement, they harshly criticized Jesus, mumbling that only God could forgive sin. To the astonishment of all, Jesus went on to cure the paralyzed man, thus revealing his divine identity and the source of his power to forgive sin.

Jesus proclaimed God's forgiveness for sinners even at his crucifixion. The Savior, though innocent, forgave his executioners:

> "Father, forgive them; they do not know what they are doing" (Lk 23:34).

Significantly, the Nicene Creed declares our belief in the forgiveness of sins after we affirm our faith in the one, holy, catholic, and apostolic church. Furthermore, the Apostles' Creed associates forgiveness of sin with faith in the Holy Spirit and in the communion of saints. Jesus extends to his church, through the bishops and priests, his power to pardon our sins. This power showed itself on Pentecost Sunday when the Holy Spirit descended on the apostles. Peter proclaimed:

> "You must repent . . . and every one of you must be baptized in the name of Jesus Christ for the forgiveness of your sins, and you will receive the gift of the Holy Spirit" (Acts 2:38).

The Acts of the Apostles reports that around three thousand did indeed repent and receive baptism and the forgiveness of sin on that glorious day.

The sacrament of baptism is the sign of new life that the Lord gives to the church. When new Christians receive baptism, they fully renounce the sin in their lives. (Or for infant baptism, the parents and godparents renounce sin for their child.) Baptism into Christ brings death to sin and a rebirth into the life of the Spirit. Baptism joins us to the Blessed Trinity, making us heirs to eternal life. Paul writes:

> "God sent his Son . . . to redeem . . . so we could receive adoption as sons. As you are sons, God has sent into our hearts the Spirit of his Son crying, 'Abba, Father'; and so you are no longer a slave, but a son; and if a son, then an heir, by God's own act" (Gal 4:4-7).

How Are Post-Baptismal Sins Forgiven? *[CCC 978-983; 986-987]*

Christ gave the church the power to forgive sin through the sacrament of baptism, but he also empowered it to forgive sins caused by our human weakness committed after baptism. The most serious kind of sin is **mortal** ("deadly") **sin**. A serious offense done with knowledge and consent, mortal sin destroys our relationship with God and the Christian community. However, if a person repents, the church offers forgiveness for this kind of sin in Christ's name through the sacrament of penance (also known as reconciliation and confession). The opportunity for forgiveness exists even up to the time of death.

In the sacrament of penance, the Lord left the church the "power of the keys," that is, the authority to remit sins committed after baptism. Jesus entrusted to the apostles and their successors this power to forgive sins. He said to Peter: "I will give you the keys of the kingdom of heaven: whatever you bind on earth will be bound in heaven; whatever you loose on earth will be loosed in heaven" (Mt 16:18-19). When we sin, we forget our identity as God's children and return to our former lives. When we sin, we must again renew our conversion and become reconciled with Christ and his church.

The sacrament of penance is often called the "second baptism;" it is a "laborious kind of baptism" (see *CCC* 980) in which the church proclaims once again Christ's forgiveness of the *contrite* sinner. Contrite sinners sincerely regret the evil they committed against God or others and firmly intend to avoid sin in the future. Repentant sinners also agree to make amends for any harm caused, as far as this is possible. John's gospel tells us how Jesus bestowed this authority to forgive sins on the apostles, a power that bishops and priests have today:

> Receive the Holy Spirit.
> If you forgive anyone's sins,
> they are forgiven;
> if you retain anyone's sins,
> they are retained (Jn 20:22-23).

What Does Our Faith Teach About Death? [CCC 1006-1010; 1016; 1018-1019]

Death, the separation of the eternal soul from the body, is the one inevitable event that faces everyone. It points to our common human destiny. The book of Ecclesiastes teaches that it is natural to die: "There is a season for everything . . . A time for giving birth, a time for dying" (3:1-2). Death might be natural, but most people fear it. Divine revelation tells us that death is a penalty for sin. St. Paul writes:

> It was through one man that sin came into the world and through sin death, and thus death has spread through the whole human race because everyone has sinned (Rom 5:12).

If sin had not infected the human race, we would be immune from bodily death.

To make sense out of death and our own future death, we must look to Jesus Christ. As a human being, Jesus himself was anxious about his own impending death. When he prayed in the garden of Gethsemane, he foresaw the terrible death that awaited him, and he petitioned his Father:

> "Abba (Father)! . . . For you everything is possible. Take this cup away from me. But let it be as you, not I, would have it" (Mk 14:36).

Jesus' "Let it be as you, not I, would have it" displayed his final act of total self-giving to the Father. His obedience transformed the curse of death into a great blessing for us. As his followers, we should imitate him. Though it is natural to fear dying, in faith we recite with Jesus, *"Father, into your hands I commit my spirit"* (Lk 23:46).

St. Athanasius agreed that people naturally fear death, but he also said that those who put their faith in the cross of Christ despise what they naturally fear. Why? Because Jesus is the resurrection and the life, the One who gives us eternal life.

How Is It Helpful to Contemplate Our Own Death? *[CCC 1011-1014]*

Thinking about our own death can help us resolve to live more purposeful and loving lives today, though we should not dwell on our death in fear. We die only once; there is no reincarnation after death. Thus, we should live each day as our last, as a great opportunity to show our love for God and neighbor. A famous philosopher once remarked, "When a man dies he clutches in his hands only that which he has given away in his lifetime." Christians believe if we imitate Jesus in his love of others, then we need not fear death. Jesus says to live as if we were wedding attendants awaiting the return of the Bridegroom (Mt 25:1-13). If we always live in preparation of Jesus' return, then we can control our fear death. In the words of St. John Vianney, "Life is given us that we may learn to die well, and we never think of it. To die well we must live well."

Let us never forget that Jesus Christ has rescued us from our natural fate:

> It is in the face of death that the riddle of human existence becomes most acute.
> . . . Although the mystery of death utterly beggars the imagination, the Church has been taught by divine revelation, and herself firmly teaches, that man has been created by God for a blissful purpose beyond the reach of earthly misery. In addition, that bodily death from which man would have been immune had he not sinned will be vanquished, according to the Christian faith, when man who was ruined by his own doing is restored to wholeness by an almighty and merciful Savior (The Church in the Modern World, 18).

Death is a profound mystery. But Christian faith reveals that Jesus Christ, our Savior, has conquered death. Jesus Christ lives! Jesus Christ wants us to befriend him in this life so we can live joyfully with him in eternity. This is the greatest news we could possibly want to know.

What Is the Christian Belief About Judgment? *[CCC 677-679]*

St. Paul gives this insight as to the Christian belief about judgment:

> For at the judgment seat of Christ we are all to be seen for what we are, so that each of us may receive what he has deserved in the body, matched to whatever he has done, good or bad (2 Cor 5:10).

The Biblical word for *judgment* is rich in imagery. It is often used in a positive way in the Hebrew scriptures. For example, God judged (delivered) David from his enemies, or God judged (defended) the poor, orphans, and widows. However, when the people refused to live up to the terms of the covenant, God's judgment was against them.

The New Testament understanding of judgment emphasizes the paradox of the present and future nature of God's kingdom. God's reign is already here, but has yet to come in all its fullness. We already share in Christ's resurrection, but we have yet to die physically. Jesus Christ is here living in our midst, but he has yet to come in his full glory. Christ has saved us, but our sins show that we are not yet perfect.

One way to consider the "day of judgment" is to think of it as our permanent decision to accept or reject Jesus Christ. But scripture reveals another judgment, at the end of time. It will be a final judgment when there will be final victory over evil.

What Is the Particular Judgment? [CCC 1021-1022; 1051]

The church also teaches that each person will immediately appear before God after death for a **particular judgment**. This judgment will lead to entrance into heaven (either immediately or after purification) or into eternal damnation. Jesus himself told us about this type of judgment in the parable of Lazarus and the rich man (Lk 16:19-31). The rich man indulged himself in this life and ignored the heart-breaking pleas of the starving Lazarus. His judgment after death led to the fiery torments of Hades (hell). Lazarus, on the other hand, went to a place of joy.

At death, our time of trial is over. The particular judgment will reveal us for what we are. We will see our lives as God sees them: either loving lives of service or lives of self-centeredness. The poet Dante Alighieri said this about the time of judgment:

> If you insist on having your own way, you will get it. Hell is the enjoyment of your own way forever. If you really want God's way with you, you will get it in Heaven.

If we live a good life based on love, we should not fear judgment. God's judgment is for us, not against us.

> "In all truth I tell you,
> whoever listens to my words,
> and believes in the one who sent me,
> has eternal life;
> without being brought to judgment
> such a person has passed from death to life" (Jn 5:24).

There will not be any surprises when we stand before the Lord's judgment seat. We know well enough if we are God-centered or self-centered. At the particular judgment Christ will judge us lovingly, mercifully, and justly. Jesus' judgment will simply be a declaration of what is the truth about our acceptance or rejection of him.

What Is the General Judgment? *[CCC 1038-1039; 1059]*

The **general** ("last") **judgment** will take place at the end of time. Then, God's saving plan will be clear to everyone who ever lived. Christ will fully reveal each person's true relationship before God, and the good one has done or not done in life and its results.

Matthew's gospel gives us a vivid image of a final judgment, when Christ will come again:

> "When the Son of Man comes in glory, escorted by the angels, then he will take his seat on his throne of glory. All nations will be assembled before him and he will separate people one from another as the shepherd separates sheep from goats" (Mt 25:31-32).

As judge, Jesus' goodness, justice, mercy, and peace will establish God's reign in all its glory. People will recognize the decisions they made in life, and everyone will acknowledge and marvel at the Lord's majesty.

The basis of this last or general judgment is simple: the love of God with our entire beings and our neighbor as ourselves.

> "For I was hungry and you gave me food; I was thirsty and you gave me drink; I was a stranger and you made me welcome; lacking clothes and you clothed me, sick and you visited me, in prison and you came to see me" (Mt 25:35-36).

What Is the Second Coming? *[CCC 1040-1041]*

The second to last verse in the Bible, Revelation 22:20, reads "Come, Lord Jesus." This expectant plea responds to Jesus' promise: "I am coming soon." All Christians look forward to the time of the Lord's return when God's justice will triumph over all the injustices committed by God's creatures, a time when God's love will triumph over death. The church teaches that human history will come to a close at some time in the future. Jesus will come again at the Parousia, a word which means "presence" or "arrival." When this takes place, everyone who ever lived will recognize Jesus as Lord of all. Christians do not fear this day.

The liturgical season of *Advent* (which means "coming") both prepares us for the second coming of Christ and reminds us of the birth of the Christ-child. The Christmas season celebrates the Lord who came to us. These church seasons remind us how Jesus is with us now. But they also remind us that even today we are in Advent, awaiting Christ's return at the end of time.

At the eucharist we proclaim: "Christ has died, Christ is risen, and Christ will come again." Like Advent and Christmas, the eucharist reminds us to look forward to the time when the Lord will come in all his glory. At that time, the entire universe will recognize him.

When Will Christ's Second Coming Occur? *[CCC 1042-1050; 1060]*

Only the Father knows the exact hour of the Son's return. Thus, we must always be ready, converting from our sins, and living Christ-like lives *right now*. The parable of the ten wedding attendants, five of whom were not ready for the master's unexpected return has an important lesson:

> "Stay awake, because you do not know either the day or the hour" (Mt 25:13).

Christ's second coming will mark the time when God's reign will be fully established on earth. God will renew and transform the entire universe. God's plan to bring all under Christ will be realized. The human unity God willed for us will come about. The new community formed in Christ will be free of sin and self-love. It will enjoy the **beatific vision** ("seeing God face to face") and a blissful union with God marked by happiness, peace, and mutual communion.

We have a foretaste of this time now because Jesus inaugurated God's reign in our midst. God's loving grace is freeing people right now, giving them life, saving them. And Christians help build Christ's kingdom through their work for peace, equal rights and human solidarity, respect for the dignity of others, and labors for the poor and defenseless.

God's kingdom is here, but we know that today many forces oppose God's saving will. God's reign has not taken root in the hearts of all. However, the virtue of hope enables us to look forward to the day when Christ's work *will* be complete. Christians look forward to this day as a joyful meeting with the risen Lord. Then, eternity and its promises of perfect happiness, joy, and peace will be ours—if we are ready to receive it.

"Look, I am standing at the door knocking. If one of you hears me calling and opens the door, I will come in to share a meal at that person's side" (Rev 3:20).

What Happens to Our Bodies After We Die? *[CCC 988-995; 1002-1004; 1015; 1052]*

At death our souls will separate from our bodies which will decay. Our souls will meet God at that time, but only when Christ comes again will God "grant incorruptible life to our bodies by re-uniting them with our souls, through the power of Jesus' Resurrection" (*CCC* 997). The resurrection of the dead will happen for everyone, both those who have lived good lives and merit eternal reward and those who have died separated from God and deserve punishment.

St. Paul uses a vivid image to describe when this will take place, at the Lord's second coming. When a trumpet blasts, God will take both living and dead up into the clouds "to meet the Lord in the air" (1 Thes 4:16-17).

> He who raised up the Lord Jesus will raise us up with Jesus in our turn, and bring us to himself—and you as well (2 Cor 4:14).

Our Christian belief in the resurrection of the body contrasts sharply with many other religions that teach some type of nebulous spiritual form of existence in the afterlife. Christian belief holds that the whole person—body and soul—will survive death.

God progressively revealed the belief in a bodily resurrection through salvation history, and Jesus taught it firmly. He linked faith in himself to belief in the resurrection: "I am the resurrection and the life" (Jn 11:25 *NAB*).

After death, we will share in Jesus' own resurrection and glory. Remarkably, in a certain way, we *already* share in the heavenly life of Christ through baptism. The eucharist especially nourishes us with Christ's life, enabling us to participate more fully in the body of Christ.

We shall rise like Christ, with him, and through him (*CCC* 995).

This doctrine of the resurrection of the body underscores the profound respect we should have for our own bodies and those of others. To be a *human* being is to have a *body* and soul which come from God and eventually return to God. The body is essential to being a person. To respect the human body, including those of the most defenseless among us (like unborn babies), means to show profound respect for the God who made us.

What Will the Resurrected Body Be Like? [CCC 997-1001; 1017]

This question has been pondered on by Christians of all ages. St. Paul offered this insight:

> Someone may ask, How are dead people raised, and what sort of body do they have when they come? How foolish! What you sow must die before it is given new life; and what you sow is not the body that is to be, but only a bare grain, of wheat I dare say, or some other kind; it is God who gives it the sort of body that he has chosen for it . . . .
> What is sown is perishable but what is raised is imperishable; what is sown is contemptible but what is raised is glorious; what is sown is weak, but what is raised is powerful; what is sown is a natural body, and what is raised is a spiritual body (1 Cor 15:35-37, 42-44).

The most important quality of the resurrected body is immortality; we will never die again. Paul lists other attributes that help describe the nature of the resurrected body: imperishable, glorious, powerful, and spiritual. Christian theology has interpreted these traits in the following way: We will never feel pain. Our bodies will shine brightly, reflecting the glory of the beatific vision, that is, "seeing God." Material creation will not hinder us; for example, we will be able to move about easily and swiftly. Finally, our spirits will control our glorified bodies.

Related to the resurrection of the body is our belief that God will transform material creation in Christ. We simply cannot imagine what God has in store for us. However, it makes sense that he has created a suitable environment where our resurrected, glorified bodies will thrive for eternity.

What Do Christians Believe About the Afterlife? [CCC 1033, 1035, 1730-1732]

Christians believe in an eternal life which we will spend in heaven or hell. The reward of heaven is eternal life spent in union with God and all those who share in God's life. Hell is eternal separation from God.

The existence of heaven and hell take very seriously the reality of human freedom. If we use our freedom properly, then we will choose our own eternal destiny— a joyous life with our loving, Triune God. If, on the other hand, we decide to model ourselves into heartless, unloving, selfish people, then God will respect our decision. When we choose self over God, then we have chosen hell. Our loving God respects our freedom and will give us what we want.

What Is Heaven? *[CCC 1023-1029; 1053]*

In heaven those who die in God's friendship and grace and are perfectly purified will celebrate eternal life. Heaven is the name for this superabundant life in communion with the loving Triune God, the Blessed Mother, the angels and saints. It is the community of all who are fully incorporated into Christ. Heaven will bring us supreme happiness beyond what we can imagine:

> [God] will wipe away all tears from their eyes; there will be no more death, and no more mourning or sadness or pain. The world of the past has gone (Rv 21:4).

Such life will infinitely fulfill our desires for truth, wisdom, goodness, beauty, peace, justice, companionship, understanding, and love.

Heaven will also bring *union* with God and all God's creations. Yet, we will maintain our individual identities as God's own unique daughter or son. The love of Jesus will transform us into unselfish images of the Father. Jesus prays fervently that this will happen to us:

> "May they all be one,
> just as, Father, you are in me and I am in you,
> so that they also may be in us" (Jn 17:21).

The awesome reality of heaven goes beyond human words. Scripture uses images to help convey its reality: life, paradise, light, the wedding feast, peace, the heavenly Jerusalem, and the like. Christian theology expresses heaven as **beatific vision**. This vision will enable us to "see" God face-to-face—intuitively, directly, intimately, plainly, and personally—as God actually is.

The joys of heaven are beyond what we can possibly describe:

> It is as scripture says: *What no eye has seen and no ear has heard, what the mind of man cannot visualize; all that God has prepared for those who love him* (1 Cor 2:9).

What Is Purgatory? *[CCC 1030-1032; 1054-1055]*

The church teaches the existence of purgatory, that is, the final purification of the elect before the final judgment.

This doctrine makes sense. When we die, we face God's infinite love. To embrace this all-loving God, we must let go of all imperfections and hesitations to love God perfectly. Purgatory is our passover from death to life. We pass through the fire of God's love which enables us to embrace completely the all-holy God with open hearts. Purgatory is necessary because, as the book of Revelation teaches, only a clean person can enter heaven.

Purgatory comes from the Latin word for "purification, cleansing." What needs cleansing are venial sins and any punishment due our sins which is present at death. This process of purification can also take place in this life as we continuously die to selfishness and rid ourselves of sin and self-pride. But experience teaches us that this purification is long and painful. To become other-centered, more loving, and Christ-like takes a lifetime of growing in holiness.

The church has not defined the exact nature of purgatory. And the church has not officially declared what kind of "place" purgatory is or "how long it lasts." Space and time images are just that—images that try to describe the mystery of eternal life.

This process of purification does involve some pain. For example, it will be painful to let go of *all* selfish attachments when we pass to a new life with our all-loving God. But those in purgatory are also joyful and peaceful because they know that they will one day be in union with God in heaven. Thus, purgatory involves a paradox: joy and peace while in a state of suffering, of purification. Traditionally the image of fire has helped us understand the nature of the suffering in purgatory. Perhaps, persons in purgatory "burn" with remorse because they are not yet one with God who is infinite goodness and love. This temporary separation from God due to our own actions on earth does bring suffering.

The best scriptural basis for the doctrine of purgatory is found in 2 Maccabees 12:41-45. This passage encourages those who are living to pray for the dead so they can be released from their sin. The church likewise teaches that the prayers of the living, especially in the eucharist, can help those in purgatory. The church also recommends almsgiving, indulgences, and works of penance to help those in purgatory. The doctrine of the communion of saints underscores our unity with all our Christian brothers and sisters. Our faith tells us that in God's goodness our prayers and good works mysteriously help lessen the pain of our brothers and sisters as they enter eternal life. And Jesus assures us that God hears the prayers we offer for others.

What Is Hell? *[CCC 1033-1037; 1056-1058]*

Hell is eternal separation from God. Its principal punishment is this separation because God created us to have life and happiness, realities we desperately thirst for which only God can fulfill.

In the words of the novelist George Bernanos, "Hell is not to love anymore." C. S. Lewis said, "Hell is a bad dream from which you never wake." The hell they describe exists as a doctrine of Christian faith. Jesus refers to Gehenna (hell) several times in his teaching. For example, in Mark's gospel Jesus warns against scandal:

> "It is better for you to enter into the kingdom of God with one eye, than to have two eyes and be thrown into hell where their worm will never die nor their fire be put out" (Mk 9:47-48).

The church affirms the existence of hell and its eternity, reserved for those who don't love God and have sinned against God, neighbor, or self. "Hell fire" is an image that tries to describe the basic horror of hell: love lost. It attempts to capture the state of a person who "burns" with self-hatred and abject loneliness because he or she has pridefully chosen self over God.

However, the central truth of hell's reality is that *it is an eternal life alienated from God and God's love.* This alienation extends to all interpersonal relationships. Christian theology has described this alienation as eternal separation from God and everything that it is good. The person who dies having turned away freely and deliberately from God's redeeming love has chosen to live a life turned in on oneself for all of eternity.

Hell is a reality because God respects human freedom, a freedom that can pridefully refuse God's grace, love, and mercy. The Lord continuously offers his grace and love. He invites us to join the divine family. But a person is free to reject that invitation through living a selfish, heartless, and unloving life. God respects that choice.

Although we know that one can choose self over God and thus merit eternal punishment, we do not know for sure who is in hell. We simply don't know who—in the depths of their consciences—have definitively rejected God. Jesus tells us not to judge others to avoid judgment ourselves. A significant work of Christian charity is to pray for others that they may accept Jesus and turn from their sinful ways.

Hell's existence challenges the Christian to turn to Jesus and to use our freedom in a loving way. We should never forget the good news that Christ Jesus will always forgive a repentant sinner.

Why Do We End Our Prayers with "Amen"?

[CCC 1061-1065]

"Amen" is a resounding, "Yes," an affirmation that punctuates our prayers and celebrations. It means, "so be it, "I agree," "it is firm." In Hebrew, *Amen* comes from the same root as the word for "believe." Thus, when we say "Amen," we are making an act of faith, proclaiming the truth of what we have prayed and celebrated.

It is a summary of our heartfelt conviction and expresses our solidarity with it. Saying "Amen" to the Nicene Creed restates our belief in God and all the other articles of the Creed.

Death is a kind of "Amen" to human life. For Christians who have "fought the good fight," death is a statement that readies us for eternity. If we lived struggling to do right, trying to love, repenting of our sins, trusting in Jesus—then our death is not something to fear. Rather, it punctuates the sentence of our lives. It enables us to present ourselves to God as the finished story of a loving disciple.

Concluding Reflections

Our Christian belief about the "last things" assures us that God has the last word. Our end in this life is but the birthday to an eternal life with the Lord. The doctrines of the resurrection of the body, judgment, and life everlasting teach that everything we do, or fail to do, has significance. If we choose Jesus, who is the AMEN of God's love for us, and stay close to him in this life, then we have the promise of Jesus:

> "In truth I tell you, there is no one who has left house, brothers, sisters, mother, father, children or land for my sake and for the sake of the gospel who will not receive a hundred times as much, houses, brothers, sisters, mothers, children and land — and persecutions too — now in this present time and, in the world to come, eternal life" (Mk 10:29-30).

Prayer Reflection

Think about your own death. Then, read with faith the following hope-filled words of St. Paul:

> And after this perishable nature has put on imperishability and this mortal nature has put on immortality, then will the words of scripture come true: Death is swallowed up in victory. Death, where is your victory? Death, where is your sting? The sting of death is sin, and the power of sin comes from the Law. Thank God, then, for giving us the victory through Jesus Christ, our Lord.

> So, my dear brothers, keep firm and immovable, always abounding in energy for the Lord's work, being sure that in the Lord none of your labors is wasted (1 Cor 15:54-57).

For Discussion

1. How do the Christian teachings about the "last things" give you hope that this life has ultimate meaning?
2. What poetic image could you use to describe our eternal life with God in heaven?
3. In what sense could this life be considered a kind of purgatory?
4. In what specific ways would your life change if you truly lived today as though it were your last?

Further Reading

Revelation 21–22 (the vision of a heavenly Jerusalem)

Part 2:

The Celebration of the Christian Mystery

The "economy of salvation" is a mystery of God's plan for all creation that all might be saved and that God's name will be glorified. St. Paul called the economy of salvation the "plan of the mystery." St. Augustine, as quoted in the *Catechism of the Catholic Church* (1067), adds:

> The wonderful works of God among the people of the Old Testament were but a prelude to the work of Christ the Lord in redeeming mankind and giving perfect glory to God. He accomplished this work principally by the Paschal mystery of his blessed Passion, Resurrection from the dead, and glorious Ascension, whereby 'dying he destroyed our death, rising he restored our life.' For it was from the side of Christ as he slept the sleep of death upon the cross that there came forth "the wondrous sacrament of the whole Church."

The *Catechism* continues:

> For this reason, the Church celebrates in the liturgy above all the Paschal mystery by which Christ accomplished the work of our salvation.

The chapters in Part 2 examine this mystery of our salvation as celebrated in the liturgy ("the work of the church") and the sacraments ("outward signs of God's grace instituted by Christ").

Chapter Twelve

Celebrating the Paschal Mystery Through Liturgy and the Sacraments

Whatever was visible in Our Redeemer has passed over into the Sacraments.
— St. Leo the Great

Chariots of Fire is a most inspiring movie that speaks of religious faith. This Academy Award winning film recounts the actual events leading up to the 1924 Olympic Games, including the story of Eric Liddell and his desire to balance running track with his goal to be a Christian missionary.

Liddell, a deeply religious young man, refused to race on Sunday, the day the preliminaries of the 100-meter were to be run. Despite enormous pressure, including newspaper charges that he was a traitor, he refused to go against his convictions and dishonor the Sabbath. He dropped out of the competition, switching to the 400-meter event instead, a race he had never tried before.

When it came time for Eric to run the first heat in the 400, an American competitor passed a note to him which read, "It says in the old book—'He that honors me, I will honor.' Good luck." Eric ran the race with this note clutched in his hand and, amazingly, won! His sincere conviction not to break God's law as he understood it, not to violate the Lord's day, was blessed by God. He became a hero to all persons of spiritual fiber.

Christians believe that God, the source of all blessings, should be worshipped on Sunday, the day of the Lord's resurrection. Eric believed his work on the Lord's day was to do the Lord's work. This chapter will discuss how and why we celebrate the liturgy, our participation in God's work of salvation. We will also look at how we celebrate Christ's Paschal Mystery through the seven sacraments. Celebrating the Paschal Mystery through the liturgy and the sacraments is absolutely central to Catholic identity and belief. To reflect on their meaning and to appreciate what they represent—God's presence to us in our ordinary life—is to grow in an understanding of what Catholics hold to be very precious.

What Is the Paschal Mystery? *[CCC 571, 674]*

The **Paschal Mystery** or Easter Mystery refers to Christ's saving actions through his blessed passion, death, resurrection, and ascension (or glorification). Through Jesus' death, our death was destroyed; through his resurrection, our life will be restored. What Jesus Christ has accomplished for us through the Paschal Mystery is the supreme act of God's love for us—our salvation and redemption. This dying-rising cycle is the very heart of the good news of Christ's gospel.

What Is Liturgy? *[CCC 1069; 1074-1075]*

The word **liturgy** traditionally meant a "public work" or "people's work." Today, it refers to the participation of God's people, through prayer and celebration, in "the work of God." God works for our salvation and redemption. Jesus Christ, our redeemer and high priest—the mediator between us and God—continues the work of our salvation through, in, and with the liturgy of the church.

In short, the liturgy of the church celebrates the Paschal Mystery through which the Lord saves us. The Lord continues his work of our redemption through it. Thus, the liturgy is the summit toward which the church directs its activity. It is the font from which the church's power flows. In liturgy, therefore, Christians are incorporated more fully into the mystery of Christ Jesus.

What Is the Relationship Between the Paschal Mystery and the Liturgy? *[CCC 1066-1068; 1070-1071; 1073]*

Historically, our salvation occurred once and for all. But sacramentally, by the power of the Holy Spirit who is the gift of God's love to us, Jesus makes his saving events present and real for us today. Through the liturgy of the word and sacrament, the Father's divine plan of love continues to touch us and form us into a community of love. Through the sacred action of the liturgy, we participate in Christ's own prayer to the Father in the Holy Spirit.

Thus, every liturgical action, but especially the celebration of the eucharist and the other sacraments, brings about an encounter between Christ and his church, God's people. The Holy Spirit gathers us into the body of Christ at liturgy to celebrate, to pray, to worship God, to proclaim the gospel, and to call us to live out the Paschal Mystery in our own lives. In liturgy we are sustained by the Word of God, nourished by the sacramental presence, and empowered by the Holy Spirit to be living signs of God's loving salvation to all we meet. We do this when we die to our own selfishness and rise to a new life of love of God, neighbor, and self.

What Do We Celebrate in the Liturgy? *[CCC 1076]*

In brief, the liturgy calls us to experience and celebrate our salvation. During this age of the church, the Lord manifests, makes present, and communicates the fruits of the Paschal Mystery until he comes again at the end of time. This is accomplished through the sacraments and the liturgy and is known as the "sacramental economy," that is, the system Christ uses to make the graces of his saving events present to us on earth. The liturgy celebrates this dispensation or communication of grace to us.

The gift of faith enables us to respond to Christ in the liturgy, getting us in touch with the Triune God of love who is the source of our eternal life, joy, and happiness. A major benefit of liturgical celebration is that we become more intimately united to the saints in heaven, joining them in their continual praising and adoration of God. In addition, the liturgy strengthens our bond of solidarity with other members of Christ's body here on earth.

What Is the Role of the Blessed Trinity in the Liturgy? *[CCC 1077-1112]*

The liturgy is the work of the Blessed Trinity. Through the liturgy the church blesses, praises, adores, and thanks *God the Father* as the source of all the blessings in creation and throughout salvation history. It is the Father's words and deeds that prepared the way for the Son. The Father has given us salvation through Christ and in the Spirit, enabling us to become members of the divine family. In the liturgy we remember and celebrate in praise and thanksgiving all the Father's gifts.

The *risen Lord Jesus* reaches out to us to dispense the graces of his Paschal Mystery through the sacraments—words and symbols that really bestow the graces they symbolize. Jesus promised to be with his church, a sign and instrument of his presence, by creating it as his body, and being present to it as its head. Through the liturgy, the risen Lord is truly present in the minister and in the worshipping community. He really speaks through the scriptures and dispenses his graces through the sacraments. Further, he joins us to the heavenly liturgy celebrated by the angels and saints, thus giving us a foretaste of our eternal destiny.

The *Holy Spirit* is the church's living memory. The Spirit prepares the assembly to encounter Christ by recalling God's work in the Old Testament. This is accomplished by praying the psalms, and by remembering the great events of salvation history, for example, the Exodus and Passover. Also, the Spirit "gives a spiritual understanding of the Word of God to those who read or hear it, according to the disposition of their hearts" (CCC 1101).

The remembering (of salvation history events) part of Mass is called the *anamnesis*.

By the power of the Holy Spirit, we can participate in the Lord's Paschal Mystery. This most dramatically takes place in the *epiclesis* (invocation prayer) at Mass. There the priest begs God the Father to send the Spirit to transform ordinary bread and wine into the Lord's body and blood, thus permitting us to unite with the Jesus who eternally offers himself to the Father.

Finally, the Holy Spirit is the principle of unity who joins us to Christ and to each other, thus empowering us to bring Jesus' love into the world.

What Does the Term "Sacrament" Mean? *[CCC 1115-1116; 1131]*

Previously, we mentioned how Vatican II described the church as a kind of sacrament of God's unity with his people. One definition of the term sacrament is "an efficacious symbol," that is, a special kind of sign that causes what it points to, that is what it represents.

This definition fits both Jesus and his church. Jesus not only signifies God's love for us, he *is* God's love. His teaching, his healings and other miracles, and his sacrifice on the cross all symbolize the love God has for us. But Jesus is more than just a sign of God's love; he is God-made-man, Love-made-flesh. Jesus is the living proof of God's care for his people. The mysteries of his life serve as the foundations of what he gives to us in the sacraments, through the ministers of the church.

The church is also a sacrament. It is an effective sign of salvation. The Holy Spirit gives life to the church. The risen Lord lives and works in the community of salvation which serves the cause of God's kingdom. Through the church we can meet Jesus. We can see him serving us in and through the church. We can hear him speak to us today when his word is proclaimed.

Jesus calls us through the church to be sacrament-people. Jesus invites us to be light to the world, beacons whose faithful lives of service point the way to him and his Father.

With this rich definition of a sacrament in mind, we can see how the seven sacraments are special actions of Christ entrusted to and working in the church. Sacraments are effective, symbolic actions that not only point to God's life but actually convey it to the members of the church. These Christ-instituted, efficacious signs of grace bring about the divine life to which they point. If we receive them properly, they bear fruit in us.

What Meaning Do the Sacraments Have for Our Lives?
[CCC 1118; 1121; 1128-1129; 1996-1999; 2002-2003; 2023]

The definition of sacrament underscores the meaning the sacraments have for our lives. For example:

* *The sacraments are signs.* Through words and actions we can experience and come to believe spiritual realities that exist beyond our senses. We can see water poured over an infant's head, feel the anointing of holy oils, taste the consecrated bread and wine, and hear the words of God's forgiveness or the exchange of marriage vows. We know that something important is happening behind these outward signs. We are celebrating Christ's presence; God's friendship with his people is entering our lives.

* *The sacraments are efficacious. Efficacious* means "capable of producing a desired effect." The sacraments are efficacious because Christ Jesus himself works through them. The power of the sacrament comes from God in the Holy Spirit, not by the righteousness or personal holiness of either the minister or recipients.

* *The sacraments convey grace.* All the sacraments convey *sanctifying grace,* that is, God's free and undeserved favor, and a participation in God's life. Sanctifying grace makes us holy and pleasing to God, adopted children of God, temples of the Holy Spirit, and heirs of eternal life. The sacrament of baptism brings us into God's family, and the sacrament of reconciliation restores God's life in those who have broken off their relationship with him. The other sacraments increase and intensify our friendship relationship with God. For believers, participating in the sacraments is necessary for salvation.

* *Each sacrament conveys sacramental graces,* that is, gifts proper to itself. Thus, the symbolic actions connected with baptism not only represent new life, but they actually cause a new life in union with God. They sanctify us and adopt us into God's family. Similarly, the eucharist not only signifies the sharing of a common meal, but actually and really

causes union with the risen Lord. Finally, the three sacraments of baptism, confirmation, and holy orders confer a **sacramental character** or "seal" that relates a Christian to Christ's priesthood according to a different state or function. These sacraments cannot be repeated because through them the Holy Spirit configures the Christian to Christ and the church in an indelible way.

- *Christ instituted the sacraments.* Jesus came to preach the good news and establish his Father's kingdom. He remains active through the church which continues his work in the world. With the guidance and power of the Holy Spirit, the church has recognized among its liturgical treasures and celebrations seven sacraments as special, unique signs whose purpose is to build up the kingdom of God. These signs are "by the church" in the sense that the church is Christ's sacrament in the world. They are also "for the church" because they help *make* the church, revealing and communicating to people the mystery of the Blessed Trinity's union of love with us through Christ.

- *Sacraments require proper dispositions on our part.* Of course, it stands to reason that for sacraments to bear fruit in us, we must receive them worthily. We must also respond in faith and cooperate with the gifts God gives to us through the sacraments. Through the sacraments, our Lord guarantees his friendship and help. We must respond to them and live the gift of God's life that is so generously offered to us.

What Are the Seven Sacraments? *[CCC 1113; 1119-1120; 1122; 1132]*

The Catholic church recognizes seven sacraments. The number 7 is symbolic of perfection or wholeness. We believe that the Lord has left the Christian community with these seven signs of love to touch us during the key moments of our lives and to empower us to be a priestly community. When we begin life, **baptism** unites us with the risen Lord and all our fellow Christians. As we mature and more fully begin to accept and live the Christian life, **confirmation** showers us with the strength of the Holy Spirit to live faithfully for the Lord. These two sacraments of initiation form Christians into a *priestly* people who can celebrate the liturgy. The **eucharist**, the summit of Christian worship, is a sacred meal that commemorates and re-enacts the Lord's sacrifice on the cross for our salvation. It nourishes our faith and both signifies and brings about our union with God.

When we are guilty of sin and in need of reconciliation and forgiveness, we experience the Lord's forgiving love in the sacrament of penance or **reconciliation**. And in times of serious illness, the

anointing of the sick gives us God's mercy, forgiveness, courage, and hope.

Jesus is with us as we live out our life's vocation. Those who are called to serve God's people as deacons, priests, or bishops are supported through the sacrament of **holy orders**. This sacrament creates the *ordained ministry* which serves the priesthood of the baptized. This ministerial priesthood is the sacramental bond linking the liturgical actions of today with those of the apostles, and ultimately to our Lord Jesus, the source and foundation of all the sacraments.

And, the sacrament of **matrimony** is an ongoing sign of God's love as it appears in the union of a couple who are committed to loving each other until death. Their union and their fidelity are signs of the Lord's union with us and his faithfulness to his church.

What Does a Sacrament Do for Us? *[CCC 1123-1124; 1130; 1133-1134]*

A sacrament makes visible the mystery of God's love for us. It is easy to see how this definition applies to Jesus Christ. He is the primary visible sign of invisible grace. In Christ Jesus, God has reconciled the world. The Father has spoken his Word in the visible form of Jesus. The incarnation of Jesus Christ is the primary sacrament of our salvation. His death on the cross made visible for all people the love God has for us.

In a similar way the church is sacramental because it continues Jesus' work of salvation. By announcing the good news of salvation and by building up a strong community of believers bound in love and service to others, the church makes visible the Lord who sacrificed his life so that people can have eternal life. The church's faith precedes and nourishes the faith of individual Christians who are called by the Lord to witness to him and to his message, to live a grace-filled life that attracts others to the gospel. They, too, have a sacramental vocation to be authentic signs of God's love.

The seven sacraments renew the mystery of God's love. They help us share in life everlasting even now while we await Christ's coming. They both strengthen and express our Christian faith. In the words of the Second Vatican Council:

> [Their purpose] is to sanctify men, to build up the body of Christ, and finally, to give worship to God. Because they are signs, they also instruct. They not only presuppose faith, but by words and objects they also nourish, strengthen, and express it (Constitution on the Sacred Liturgy, No. 59).

What Are the Scriptural Roots of the Sacraments? *[CCC 1114-1115]*

Each of the seven sacraments meets us in a key moment of our life. Each renews a key value from the life and ministry of Jesus. The following chart provides New Testament references which teach important insights about the seven sacraments and the values each sacrament contains.

Sacrament	Central Value	Scripture Reference
Baptism	new life; celebration of Christian community	Mt 28:19; Rom 6:3-11
Confirmation	strength and growth; celebration of gifts	Acts 8:14-17; Acts 19:1-6; 1 Cor 12:4-11
Eucharist	ongoing nourishment; celebration of unity	Lk 22:19-20; 1 Cor 11:17-34
Reconciliation	forgiveness; reunion	Lk 15; Jn 20:21-23; 2 Cor 2:5-11
Healing	physical, emotional, and spiritual health	Mk 1:32-34; Mk 6:13; Js 5:14-15
Matrimony	love; family life	Jn 2:1-12; Mt 19:4-6; Mk 10:11-12; Eph 5:21-33
Holy orders	service	2 Tm 1:6; Ti 1:5-9

Who Celebrates the Liturgy? *[CCC 1135-1144; 1187-1188]*

"Liturgy is the 'action' of the *whole Christ*" (CCC 1136). Thus, those in heaven who are in total union with Christ celebrate the heavenly liturgy. On earth, it is the church—the body of Christ with Jesus as its head—who celebrates the liturgy. Through baptism, we all become sharers in the priesthood of Christ. We thus have the privilege of joining the saints in heaven in offering worship to the loving Trinity.

Individual Christians have different roles in the liturgy. Those consecrated by holy orders to the special ministry of priesthood are empowered by the Holy Spirit to serve as celebrants. Others have different liturgical and pastoral ministries which flow from the common priesthood of the faithful. Examples include readers, commentators, servers, and choir members. Those performing these functions should do so according to the proper norms of the particular liturgical celebrations.

How Is Liturgy Celebrated? *[CCC 1145-1162; 1189-1192]*

Liturgies use signs—words, actions and gestures, and symbols—to celebrate Christ's Paschal Mystery of love and to communicate God's life to us. These signs come from creation (e.g., fire and water), human life (e.g., washing and anointing, breaking bread, and sharing a cup), the original Covenant (e.g., anointing, laying on of hands, Passover rituals), and Christ himself who used physical signs and ordinary words to proclaim God's kingdom (e.g., by anointing the sick or preaching parables).

Since Pentecost, the church has incorporated a host of signs, symbols, gestures, actions, and words into its liturgical life. These include Scripture reading, processions, holy water, kneeling, blessings, bread and wine, anointing with oil, candles, incense, standing and sitting, musical instruments, singing, homilies, and more.

The Liturgy of the Word has a privileged role to play because the scriptures and their explanations help instruct and unveil the profound meaning of the liturgical signs and actions. Music and singing also have an important function in liturgical celebrations. They express the beauty of our prayer, invite us to participate more fully, and add to the solemnity of our worship.

The setting for liturgy is also important. Liturgical celebrations use holy images—*icons*—to help focus our attention on God-made-man, Jesus. Statues, paintings, stained glass, and other sacred art present images of Jesus and those who have been transfigured into his likeness, including Mary, the saints, and angels for our contemplation.

When Is Liturgy Celebrated? *[CCC 1163-1173; 1193-1195]*

Sunday is the preeminent day to celebrate the liturgy. This is especially true of the eucharist which gathers us together to listen to God's word, makes present the Paschal Mystery, offers thanks to God who has saved us in Jesus, and gives us the Lord himself to receive in holy communion. The Lord's Day is also a time to celebrate family life and an opportunity to rest from work. The greatest Sunday celebration is Easter Sunday, the "feast of feasts," when we celebrate the Lord's resurrection, a day of victory over sin and death.

Additionally, over a year, the church unfolds in its liturgy the various mysteries of our redemption. These include the Incarnation of Jesus, his nativity, the major events in his teaching ministry, his passion, death, resurrection, ascension, the sending of the Holy Spirit on Pentecost, and the future anticipation of Jesus' second coming. By recalling these events, the church is making present anew the redemptive work of Christ, inspiring the faithful with the riches of the Lord's graceful presence.

The church calendar is outlined below:

Advent. Advent marks the beginning of the church year. Beginning around the end of November, it lasts about four weeks. It is a season of preparation for Christ's coming.

Christmas Season. This period begins with Christmas which celebrates the mystery of the Incarnation, God-made-man. Christmas proclaims *Emmanuel!*, "God is with us." This joyful season also celebrates the feast of the Holy Family, the Solemnity of Mary (January 1), and Jesus' epiphany or manifestation to the Magi. The season ends with the feast of the Lord's baptism.

Ordinary Time 1. Between the Christmas season and Lent, the church does not celebrate any particular aspect of the Christian mystery. Rather the church reads one of the gospels in sequence: Matthew (Cycle A), Mark (Cycle B), and Luke (Cycle C). (John's gospel is read during the Lenten and Easter season and for some of the ordinary time in Cycle B since Mark's gospel is short.) The good news proclaimed over a three-year cycle gives the Sunday Massgoer good exposure to the New Testament and much material for meditation.

Lenten Season. The word *Lent* comes from an Anglo-Saxon word for "spring." Beginning on Ash Wednesday, it is a season of penance in preparation for the solemn and joyful feast of Easter. Lent lasts six Sundays and 40 weekdays, concluding on Holy Thursday with the celebration of the Lord's Last Supper.

Historically Lent was the proximate period of preparation for catechumens ready for baptism. The *Rite of Christian Initiation for Adults* recaptures this historical thrust by preparing the *elect* for initiation. During Lent all baptized Christians are called on to contemplate and renew through penance and prayer their own baptismal commitment. This commitment implies walking the way of the cross to the glory of the Lord's resurrection.

Easter. Easter is at the very heart of the liturgical year and of Christian faith. It celebrates our redemption in Christ and his promise of everlasting life. The seasonal celebration consists of a Triduum (three days) from Thursday evening to Sunday night: Holy Thursday, Good Friday, and Holy Saturday. Easter is celebrated on the first Sunday after the first full moon of the spring equinox and is thus a moveable feast. This dating is tied in with the traditional date given for Jesus' crucifixion on the 14th day of Nisan (the date of the Passover in the year AD 30 on the Jewish lunar calendar).

Easter Season. This season of joy spans 50 days from Easter to Pentecost Sunday. Readings focus on the themes of death to sin, resurrection, and living a life of grace. The example of the early Christians in the Acts of the Apostles is often given as a model of Christians alive in the Lord. The last ten days of the Easter season celebrate the promise and gift of the Holy Spirit. Ascension Thursday occurs forty days after Easter; Pentecost, fifty days after Easter. Pentecost Sunday celebrates the descent of the Holy Spirit, the event in salvation history that inaugurated the Christian church.

Ordinary Time 2. Ordinary time resumes after the Easter season and proceeds to Advent and a new church year. Trinity Sunday is celebrated one week after Pentecost, and the feast of Corpus Christi ("Body of Christ") one week later. The following Sundays in ordinary time look to the teaching and ministry of Jesus. Toward the end of this period the readings turn to the end of time and Christ's second coming. The feast of Christ the King is the last Sunday of the church year.

Also worth noting is that the church honors Mary, Mother of God, with a special love, on many different occasions during the liturgical year. It is Mary who is linked inseparably with Christ's work and is an excellent example of the faithful disciple. Similarly, by memorializing the saints and martyrs, the church

> "proclaims the Paschal Mystery in those 'who have suffered and have been glorified. . . . She proposes them to the faithful as examples . . . '" (Sacrosanctum Concilium, 104 in CCC 1173).

Where Is the Liturgy Celebrated? *[CCC 1179-1181; 1186; 1197-1200; 1203-1209]*

Because all of creation is sacred, Christians can worship the Lord anywhere. As far as particular settings go, churches are built as houses of prayer, concrete signs of Christians gathering and living their faith in a particular geographical area. Tastefully constructed churches should encourage both prayer and recollection. When we enter a church to worship God, we cross a threshold that points to our entry into eternal life.

The liturgy of the church is celebrated worldwide in a variety of liturgical rites that reflect the diverse cultures from which they come. Today, the Catholic church approves of the following liturgical rites, all of which have equal dignity: Latin, Byzantine, Alexandrian or Coptic, Syriac, Armenian, Maronite, and Chaldean.

The liturgical life of a particular region helps reveal Christ to the people of that culture. The catholicity of the church embraces and purifies what is good in the diverse cultures. So, liturgical diversity is good as long as it does not harm the unity of the church which must be faithful to the apostolic Tradition. This Tradition, guaranteed by apostolic succession, grounds the unchangeable part of the liturgy instituted by Christ.

What Is the Liturgy of the Hours? *[CCC 1174-1178; 1196]*

The **liturgy of the hours**, or divine office, is a response to St. Paul's injunction to "pray constantly" (1 Thes 5:17). It contains psalms, hymns, scripture passages, responses, intercessory prayers, canticles, and other spiritual writings. The liturgy of the hours is part of the official, public prayer of the church. Recited seven times over the course of 24 hours, the liturgy of the hours recalls Christ's saving actions, prolongs the eucharistic celebration, and sanctifies the entire day. The church invites priests, those in religious life, and the rest of the faithful to partake in this constant praise of God, a joining in the priestly prayer of Christ.

What Are Sacramentals? *[CCC 1667-1679]*

Sacramentals resemble the sacraments. They are those objects, actions, prayers, and the like which help us become aware of Christ's presence. Sacramentals prepare us for the all-important signs of Christ's grace, the sacraments. The spiritual value of sacramentals depends on our personal faith and devotion, which is not true of the sacraments. The Lord works through the sacraments even when our faith is weak. Examples of sacramentals include the following:

- *Actions* (blessings; genuflections; the sign of the cross; bowing one's head at the name of Jesus; church processions)
- *Objects* (candles; holy water; statues and icons; holy pictures; blessed ashes; palms; rosaries; relics; incense; vestments; scapulars; church buildings; crosses; religious medals)
- *Places* (the Holy Land, Rome, Fatima, Lourdes, the National Shrine in Washington D.C., and other places of pilgrimage; chapels and retreat centers)
- *Prayers* (short prayers we say throughout the day; grace before and after meals)
- *Sacred Time* (holy days; feasts of saints; special days of prayer, fasting, and abstinence)

Concluding Reflections

The liturgy calls us to experience and celebrate our salvation. The liturgy is the work of the Blessed Trinity, the "action" of the "whole Christ," that is his body, the church.

Through the liturgy we participate in the Paschal Mystery. Every liturgical action, especially the celebration of the eucharist and other sacraments, brings about an encounter between Christ and his church.

The sacraments celebrate the mystery of God's presence and love in our midst. Part of this mystery is that each of us is also a true sign of God's love.

We need faith and sensitivity to see God working through ordinary, sacramental signs like water, bread, and wine. It also takes faith to realize that the Lord works through us. He has chosen us—ordinary people—to continue his work, to be his presence in the world.

Because Jesus acts through and is present in the sacraments, we can truly call them celebrations. Because the Lord lives in and works through us, we should fundamentally be joyful people. His promise to be with us through the Holy Spirit can help us see life as an adventure, as a journey where we are called to see God in everyone and do our part to spread the joy of the gospel.

Sacraments require openness, faith, and cooperation on our part. For us as individuals to be effective signs of God's love in the world, we too must be open to serving others. The proof that we are open is when we are willing to share our gifts, talents, time, and resources to help others, especially the needy.

Prayer Reflection

Every sincere disciple of Jesus strives to be his living symbol for others. A major theme of our prayer should be asking our Lord to teach us the way to serving him better. Perhaps the words of these two saints reflect the sentiments of our own heart.

> What have I done for Christ?
> What am I doing for Christ?
> What ought I do for Christ?
> —St. Ignatius of Loyola

> Day by day,
> day by day,
> O dear Lord,
> three things I pray:
> to see thee more clearly,
> love thee more dearly,
> follow thee more nearly,
> day by day.
> —St. Richard of Chicester

For Discussion

1. Share a time when a particular liturgy was really a celebration for you. What did you "get" out of these celebrations? What did you "give" to them?
2. In what ways are you a sacrament of God's grace?
3. How do the seven sacraments continue Christ's presence and work on earth?
4. What are the principal signs of God's love in your life?

Further Reading

Read the New Testament references given on page 172.

Chapter Thirteen

Two Sacraments of Initiation: Baptism and Confirmation

"Go, therefore, make disciples of all nations; baptize them in the name of the Father and of the Son and of the Holy Spirit, and teach them to observe all the commands I gave you."
— Matthew 28:19

Lord, send out your Spirit, and renew the face of the earth.
— from Psalm 104

The famous king and saint, Louis IX of France, knew that his life began when he was baptized. The saintly king used to sign his documents "Louis of Poissy," not, "Louis IX, King." His reason was that Poissy was the place of his baptism. He held it in higher regard than Rheims Cathedral, the site of his coronation. "It is . . . greater . . . to be a child of God than to be the ruler of a kingdom: this last I shall lose at death, but the other will be my passport to an everlasting destiny."[1]

This chapter will look at the sacraments of baptism and confirmation. Along with the eucharist (see Chapter 14), they are sacraments of initiation which lay the foundation of every Christian life (CCC 1265). Baptism—the gateway to the life in the Spirit—gives us new life; confirmation strengthens us to live Christ-like lives; and the eucharist is the food of eternal life (CCC 1212-1213). In short, these sacraments incorporate us into the Christian community and enable us to share in Jesus' work.

What Does the Word "Baptism" Mean? *[CCC 1214-1216; 1277]*

The sacrament of baptism derives its name from a Greek word that means to "plunge" or to "immerse" into water. Thus, its name highlights the new Christian's burial into Christ's death and resurrection into a new Christian life of grace.

Church tradition has also called baptism "the washing" or "regeneration" or "bath of enlightenment." These descriptions suggest a rebirth of the spirit and point to the necessity of receiving catechetical instruction about the mysteries of God's love to either before or after receiving the sacrament. Baptism also makes us children of light and empowers us to bring the light of Christ into the world. In brief, baptism is God's unearned gift to us that confers the grace and life of Christ.

What Are the Biblical Roots of Baptism? *[CCC 1217-1228; 1276]*

The Old Testament prefigures baptism in several ways. In the first Genesis account of creation, the Spirit overshadows the waters and brings life to the earth. In a similar way, today the Holy Spirit imparts new life at baptism. God used the Flood and Noah's ark to purify the earth and bring about a new beginning. Today, Christ gives new life to the Christian who emerges from the baptismal waters. During the Exodus, God's Chosen People gained liberty from the Egyptian slave masters when they crossed the Red Sea. Similarly, baptism frees us from the slavery of sin. Finally, when the Israelites crossed the Jordan River into Canaan, they entered the Promised Land. When we pass through the waters of baptism, Jesus promises us eternal life in heaven.

The prefiguring of the sacrament of baptism in salvation history is completed in the ministry of Jesus Christ. His own baptism, totally unnecessary for the Sinless One, reveals his remarkable humility and marks the beginning of his public life. The Savior's baptism looks forward to the sacrament he established and entrusted to his followers, for example, when he commanded his apostles to go out and preach the good news and to baptize in his name (Mt 28:19-20). Jesus also spoke of his suffering and Passion as a "baptism" which he had to undergo for our benefit. The water and blood that gushed from his side at the time of his death make it possible for us "to be born again of water and the Spirit."

The church has initiated new Christians through Baptism since the first Pentecost, when over three thousand were baptized. It is through our own baptism that we are united into Christ's death, burial, and resurrection.

How Did the Early Christians Prepare for Initiation? *[CCC 1229-1231]*

From apostolic times to our own day, Christian initiation involved a journey in several stages. Though historically the process varied in the time it took to complete, the following elements were always present: proclamation of the Word, acceptance of the gospel, conversion, profession of the faith, the baptism itself, the outpouring of the Holy Spirit through the laying on of hands, and reception of the eucharist.

Christianity was illegal in the first three centuries. Becoming a Christian was very serious business. It involved beginning a new life in Jesus Christ. It meant that a person had to renounce his or her former life, a life of sin. There was a possibility a convert would be *martyred*, or killed, for his or her faith either before or after being baptized.

Most converts to Christianity in the first century were adults. Thus it made sense to have a rather lengthy period of preparation—typically three years—before a person was fully initiated into the Christian community. To turn from a life of sin and embrace the life of love commanded by Jesus took sober thought, reflection, and formation. (When infant baptism became the norm in later centuries, a post-baptismal **catechesis** was established.)

The period of preparation was called the *catechumenate*. During this time, the **catechumens** in partnership with sponsors learned about the Christian faith and became disciplined to the Christian way of life through prayer, fasting, and self-denial. The key emphasis was on conversion to Christ.

The sacraments of initiation themselves were celebrated at the Easter vigil after a forty-day period of prayer and formal instruction in the faith during Lent. In this proximate period of preparation, the candidate learned the creed and the Lord's Prayer, the privileged prayer of Christians.

How Were the Sacraments of Initiation Celebrated in the Early Church? *[CCC 1232-1233]*

The initiation rite itself consisted of the sacraments we recognize today as baptism, confirmation, and eucharist. Both the candidates and the Christian community prayed and fasted to prepare spiritually for this occasion. The bishop was the main celebrant of the sacraments. He questioned the candidates to see if they were ready to live out the Christian commitment. The candidates demonstrated their assent by renouncing Satan and a life of sin. The bishop then sealed the candidates with oil before they entered the water.

Assisted by deacons or deaconesses, the candidates were stripped of their clothes, entered the water, and were immersed three times. After each immersion they were asked the Trinitarian questions: "Do you believe in the Father? Do you believe in the Son? Do you believe in the Holy Spirit?"

After emerging from the water, the five senses of the candidates were anointed with chrism and the Holy Spirit was invoked to fill the new Christians with his power. (Today we recognize this second anointing as the sacrament of confirmation.) Candidates were given new white garments to signify the new life of Christ; they were also handed candles which were lit from the Easter candle to symbolize their vocation to be the light of Christ. After the new Christians were introduced to the assembly, common prayers were recited, a sign of peace was exchanged, and the eucharist was celebrated. At this eucharistic celebration the new Christians received their first holy communion.

This ancient way of initiating adults into the Christian community has been revived today through the *Rite of Christian Initiation of Adults (RCIA)*.

What Is the "Rite of Christian Initiation of Adults (RCIA)"? *[CCC 1247-1249]*

The four periods and three stages of the RCIA process are outlined and briefly described below.

Period 1: Precatechumenate. The journey to Christian initiation begins with a period of inquiry. Attracted by God to examine the Christian faith community, the inquirers share life experiences with Catholics, reflect on the scriptural word of God, seek knowledge about the Catholic religion and its relationship to Christianity, and have the opportunity to learn about Jesus Christ, at least in a preliminary way.

Stage 1: Rite of the Catechumenate. Through a rite of welcome, the seekers ask for acceptance into the Catholic faith community, and they are joyfully accepted into the church as candidates for Christian initiation. They become known as catechumens, persons who promise to take instructions in the Catholic faith and live a Christian life.

Period 2: Catechumenate. After the initial celebration of welcoming in which the catechumens renounce sin and take on a new Christian name, they study the Christian faith more deeply (sometimes under the guidance of a Christian sponsor, a caring role model for how a Christian lives). During this period, which may last for months or even years, the catechumens grow familiar with the Christian way of life, study the Christian scriptures and participate fully in the Liturgy of the Word, and begin to take an active role in the life of the church community. Through study, community participation, service, and prayer, the catechumens can properly be called "Christians-on-the-way" toward a full commitment to Jesus Christ and his body, the church.

Stage 2: Rite of Election. After the lengthy period of instruction and testing of the catechumens' resolve to follow the way to Jesus, the church calls them forward to a deeper stage of spiritual preparation. On the first Sunday of Lent the "elect" gather at their parish and are called forward to take the final steps toward Christian initiation. Later in the day they travel to the cathedral where all the catechumens from around the diocese are enrolled as the elect who will be baptized on the Easter vigil and fully received into the Christian community.

Period 3: Enlightenment. When the bishop enrolls the elect, he challenges them to prepare themselves for baptism and full reception into the community by prayer and fasting during the Lenten season. This period of proximate preparation for full initiation into the church is known as the Enlightenment. It coincides with Lent, that time in the liturgical year when all believers are to prepare themselves in a special way for the celebration of Christ's Paschal Mystery.

During the Sundays of Lent there are special rituals and prayers for the elect. Reflection on the Sunday readings, especially from John's gospel, helps the baptismal candidates choose Jesus and his kingdom over the way of Satan and darkness. The elect also learn the Christian creed and the Lord's Prayer, the basic summary of Christian beliefs and the prayer of all those who follow Christ.

Stage 3: Rite of Initiation. The rite of initiation typically takes place during the Easter vigil liturgy. At this service the elect are baptized, confirmed, and take holy communion for the first time as full members of Christ's body. The rite of baptism includes a special litany, the blessing of the water, the baptism itself, clothing in a white garment, and the presentation of a candle lit from the paschal candle. Confirmation includes simple words of prayer, the imposition of hands, and the anointing with the blessed oils knows as *chrism*. We can easily see how the RCIA parallels the practice of the early church.

Period 4: Mystagogia. During the weeks following Easter, the new Christians meet to reflect on the meaning of the recent events in their lives as Christians. They are supported by the community through a post baptismal catechesis, that is, a deeper study into the mysteries of the faith. The term *mysteries* refers to those signs of God's love which are present in the church's sacramental life and in the lives of Christians who are united to the Lord.

Pentecost Sunday concludes the catechumenate and begins the lifelong pilgrimage of a fully initiated Christian. By this time the new members of the church have selected some service activity which will contribute to the building of Christ's body. They now have the full responsibility of a follower of Jesus.

Why Does the Church Baptize Infants? *[CCC 1250-1255]*

The RCIA acknowledges the connection between faith and baptism. The community must always be ready to help those who need Christ and to help nurture the faith of all the baptized *after* baptism. This is true in a special way for children who are baptized in the faith of the church.

Infant baptism is a time-honored tradition in the church. *Its firm practice manifests Christ's sheer gift of salvation and grace which is extended to all,* even infants. When parents present their children for baptism, they profess their willingness to raise them with gospel faith. Assisting them are godparents who must be firm believers, able and willing to help the new Christian on his or her faith journey. In addition, the entire church community is also responsible to help develop and safeguard the gift of God's life given in baptism.

How Does the Church Celebrate Baptism for Infants? *[CCC 1234-1240; 1244-1245; 1256; 1278; 1282; 1284]*

Ideally, baptism is celebrated at the Easter vigil or on Easter Sunday, but also on other Sundays ("little Easters") of the year. It is quite appropriate to celebrate baptism at a Sunday liturgy. But it should always be celebrated in an assembly of Christian believers.

The ceremony begins with a greeting from the ordained minister (bishop, priest, or deacon), the ordinary minister of the sacrament of baptism. The minister reminds the parents and godparents of their duty to raise the child in a Christian home. He then welcomes the child and marks the child as belonging to Christ by making the *sign of the cross* on his or her forehead, and inviting parents and godparents to do the same.

Next, the minister *proclaims God's word,* the purpose of which is to elicit a faith response. This is followed by *prayers of exorcism* to demonstrate how baptism frees one from sin and the power of Satan. The minister then *anoints* the child with the oil of catechumens, proclaiming that the child is to be joined to Christ, the Anointed One. He then blesses the baptismal water and leads the parents, godparents, and the Christians assembled to profess their faith and renew their baptismal vows on their own behalf and on behalf of the child.

After the parents and godparents affirm that they desire baptism for their child, the *essential rite* follows. The minister pours water on the head of the child three times (or immerses the child in water three times) and pronounces the words:

> "N., I baptize you in the name of the Father, and of the Son, and of the Holy Spirit."

Following the baptism the child's forehead is anointed with sacred *chrism* (perfumed oil), signifying the giving of the Holy Spirit. A *white garment* is placed on the child, and a *candle* lit from the paschal candle is held by one of the parents or godparents. The celebrant touches the ears and mouth of the child and prays that the child will hear the gospel and proclaim God's word. All assembled recite the Our Father after which the celebrant concludes the ceremony by blessing the mother, then the father, and finally the entire congregation.

All of these baptism rituals may be incorporated into the full context of Mass. Incidentally,

> "in case of necessity, any person, even someone not baptized, can baptize, if he . . . [intends] what the Church does when she baptizes . . . [and applies] the Trinitarian baptismal formula" (CCC 1256).

The newly baptized has now entered God's family and has the privilege of reciting the great Christian prayer—the Our Father—and receiving the Lord in holy communion. The Latin church reserves admission to the eucharist to those who have obtained the age of reason. The Eastern churches, however, allow the newly baptized and confirmed—even infants—to receive holy communion. Historically, these churches have emphasized the inner unity of all three sacraments of initiation, thus conferring them all at the same time.

What Are the Principal Symbols of Baptism and What Do They Signify? *[CCC 1241-1243]*

The principal symbols of baptism signify the following:

Water. Besides cleansing, water symbolizes destruction and death. Baptismal water means the death of an old life to sin. Water also means life; without it, we would die. Jesus reminded Nicodemus that he was living water, the source of all life. In baptism we are reborn into a new life with Jesus Christ. Original sin is washed away, and we inherit eternal life as adopted children of God. We must strive continually to live our baptism.

Oil. Oil heals and protects. It was also used to anoint kings and queens. The anointing with oil in baptism reminds us that the Lord extends salvation to us and sends his Spirit to protect and strengthen us. The root meaning of *Christ* is "anointed one." The oil of baptism (known as chrism) symbolizes that we have been "Christed," that we share in the life of Jesus Christ. We become his followers, a kingly people. We become the anointed of the Anointed One. The new identity brings new responsibilities. Adopted daughters and sons of a loving Father share in Jesus' mission of preaching the good news of God's kingdom and in the healing ministry of serving others and working toward the unity of a wounded human community.

White garment and *candle*. In the early church Christians customarily put on new white robes when they emerged from the baptismal pool, representing rising with Christ. Today a white cloth serves a similar symbolic function, that is, "being clothed in Christ" (Gal 3:27). Wearing a symbol of purity, festivity, and a new identity signifies a willingness on behalf of the baptized to live a new life in union with the Lord.

The candle, lit from the Easter candle, signifies how Christ has enlightened Christians, making them light of the world.

Is Baptism Necessary for Salvation? *[CCC 1257-1261; 1281; 1283]*

The church teaches that some form of baptism in Jesus Christ is necessary for salvation. This teaching is rooted in Jesus' response to the Pharisee Nicodemus:

> "In all truth I tell you,
> no one can enter the kingdom of God
> without being born through water and the Spirit" (Jn 3:3).

Traditionally the Catholic church has taught there are three forms of baptism: baptism of water (through the sacrament of baptism), baptism of blood (the death of martyrs who died for their faith before being baptized), and baptism of desire. Baptism of desire applies to catechumens who die before receiving baptism but whose conversion, explicit desire for the sacrament, and charity assure them of the salvation the sacrament conveys. Baptism of desire also refers to those who were not granted the gift of faith but whose lives show that they would have accepted Jesus Christ had they been given the chance to know him.

The church entrusts unbaptized children to God's infinite and mysterious mercy which desires the salvation of all. Jesus himself was tender toward children (Mk 10:14). We should recall that God's ways are not our ways. But since divine revelation is silent on this question of unbaptized infants, the church teaches that parents should take care to baptize their babies into the Catholic faith without unnecessary delay. Total union with God in heaven is such a great gift that we should do everything within our power to share it with our loved ones.

What Are the Effects of Baptism? *[CCC 1262-1271; 1279]*

By God's grace the sacrament of baptism accomplishes the following in those who receive it:

- Baptism forgives both original and personal sin and remits all punishment due to sin. However, some consequences of sin remain, for example, suffering, weakness of character, inclination to sin (traditionally called *concupiscence*), and death.

- Baptism remakes us into a new creation, imparting in us life in Christ. It makes us children of God and temples of the Holy Spirit.

- Baptism confers sanctifying grace, the grace of justification, enabling us to believe, to hope, and to love. It also gives us the Holy Spirit and the Spirit's gifts which enable us to grow in holiness and goodness.

- Baptism initiates and incorporates us into Christ's body, the church. It empowers us to share in Christ's priestly ministry of worship and service. Baptism joins us to all Christians, even to those who are not yet fully united to the Catholic church.

Who Can Be Baptized? *[CCC 1272-1274; 1280]*

Only those who have not been baptized before can be baptized. Another effect of baptism is the sealing of a Christian with an indelible spiritual character, marking us as belonging to Christ. For this reason baptism cannot be repeated. The Catholic church accepts as valid baptisms from most other Christian denominations. The baptismal character consecrates us for Christian worship and seals us to the Lord and eternal life. If a Christian remains true to his or her baptismal demands until death, the Lord has promised the beatific vision in a resurrected body united to the Blessed Trinity and all God's loved ones.

What Is the Sacrament of Confirmation? [CCC 1285; 1302-1305; 1316-1317]

Confirmation completes the sacramental grace of baptism. It is the second of the three sacraments of initiation. Confirmation gives us the full outpouring of the Holy Spirit, enabling us as God's children more readily to cry out, "Abba! Father!" Confirmation also binds us more closely to the church and unites us more firmly to Christ. It increases the gifts of the Holy Spirit in us, enriching us with the Spirit's special strength. It also empowers us to spread and defend the Christian faith by word and deed.

Like baptism, confirmation imprints an indelible spiritual mark on the soul, and so can be received only once. This sacramental character is the sign that Christ has marked a Christian with the seal of the Holy Spirit, empowering him or her to witness to the Lord. This character brings to completion the common priesthood of the faithful received in baptism.

What Are Some Biblical and Historical Roots of Confirmation? [CCC 1286-1292; 1318]

The biblical roots of confirmation extend to the time of the Old Testament prophets who promised that the Spirit would rest on the coming Savior. The Spirit did indeed descend on Jesus at his baptism, signaling that he was the awaited Messiah, the Son of God. Jesus' life was intimately connected to the Spirit. He was conceived by the Spirit, and he conducted his ministry of teaching and healing in union with the Spirit. Further, several times Jesus promised to send the Holy Spirit. He fulfilled this promise on Easter and especially on Pentecost Sunday when the Holy Spirit came on the apostles in power. Immediately, the apostles began to proclaim the gospel of Jesus, baptize in his name, and lay on hands to convey the gift of the Holy Spirit.

The church recognizes *the laying on of hands* by the apostles as the essential rite and origin of the sacrament of confirmation. Another essential rite—an anointing with perfumed oil (chrism)—underscores the name "Christian" which means "anointed," deriving ultimately from Christ himself who was "anointed with the Holy Spirit."

As discussed above, in the early church baptism and confirmation were part of the adult initiation process that climaxed at the Easter vigil liturgy. After the lengthy period of preparation the candidate was baptized, anointed by the bishop (confirmed), and received the eucharist for the first time. In these early years children probably joined their parents in the initiation process. Whole households became Christian together.

As Christianity grew, infant baptisms multiplied, rural parishes increased, and dioceses grew to large size. As a result, it became increasingly difficult for the bishop to be present at every baptism in every parish of his diocese. Permission was given for the priests to baptize, but the bishop wished to retain some role in the initiation process.

Thus, in the Western church, there gradually grew the custom of the bishop anointing, laying on hands, praying for the power of the Spirit, and "confirming" the baptismal commitment of Christians baptized as infants. This practice in the Western church signifies the Christian's communion with the bishop as the guarantor and servant of church unity, catholicity, and apostolicity. Because of the size of his diocese and the numbers involved, this confirmation ceremony took place at some later, more convenient time. By the thirteenth century church leaders saw a need for youngsters to learn about their baptismal commitment. Confirmation became the logical event for catechetical instructions in the faith.

Thus, until and including recent times in the Western church, the confirmation of those baptized as infants was administered by the bishop some time after the age of reason.

However, the Eastern churches have maintained the ancient tradition by emphasizing the unity of Christian initiation. The administering priest immediately confirms the new Christian after baptism and then allows the child to receive first eucharist. Interestingly, though, the connection with the local bishop is also maintained. The priest who confirms must do so only with "myron" (or chrism) blessed by a bishop, thus signifying the special ecclesial bond resulting from confirmation.

Who Is the Minister of Confirmation? *[CCC 1297; 1312-1314]*

As noted above, the bishops were the original ministers of the sacrament of confirmation. In the Latin rite, the bishop continues to be the ordinary minister of confirmation, though for grave reason (including the danger of impending death), he can delegate priests to do so. Also, when adults are baptized, or Christians who were baptized in other Christian denominations are fully received into communion with the church, the priest who baptizes or receives them also confirms them.

In the Eastern churches, the priest who baptizes also confirms, but he does so with the chrism consecrated by the bishop. The consecration of the sacred chrism by the bishop at the Chrism Mass on Holy Thursday is an important liturgical action that precedes the celebration of confirmation in both traditions.

How Does the Church Celebrate Confirmation? *[CCC 1298-1301; 1320-1321]*

Confirmation in the Latin rite typically occurs within celebration of the eucharist, thus stressing the unity among the sacraments of initiation. The liturgy of confirmation begins with a renewal of baptismal promises and a profession of faith by those to be confirmed (*confirmands*). This renewal also connects confirmation with baptism, so that all three sacraments of initiation are united in this one liturgy.

The bishop then extends his hands over the confirmands (individually or as a group) and invokes the outpouring of the Holy Spirit. Then the *essential rite* follows: The minister anoints the forehead of the confirmand with sacred chrism (in the Eastern churches, the other sense-organs as well), lays on his hand, and recites the words: "Be sealed with the gift of the Holy Spirit." (In the Eastern churches, the minister says, "The seal of the gift that is the Holy Spirit.")

A sign of peace concludes the rite, demonstrating union with the bishop and the church.

What Do the Signs of Confirmation Symbolize? *[CCC 1293-1296]*

Confirmation involves *anointing with oil* that *imprints a spiritual seal*. Anointing with oil has rich biblical meaning, representing joy and abundance; cleanliness and limbering; healing; and the radiance of health, beauty, and strength. The sacraments incorporate this symbolism often. For example, the pre-baptismal anointing with the oil of catechumens signifies cleansing and strengthening. Anointing the sick with oil points to healing and compassion. Anointing after baptism in confirmation or holy orders represents consecration.

The anointing with chrism at confirmation consecrates one totally to Christ. It signifies a full sharing in the mission of Jesus. Given the fullness of the Spirit, the confirmed may now exude in word and deed "the aroma of Christ."

This anointing marks the Christian with the seal of the Holy Spirit. A seal designates a person as belonging to another, in this case to Christ Jesus as he belonged to his Father. Confirmation marks the Christian as totally belonging to Christ, to be his servant of the gospel forever.

Who Should Receive Confirmation? *[CCC 1306-1311; 1319]*

Every baptized and non-confirmed Christian should be confirmed; otherwise, the process of Christian initiation would be incomplete. In the Latin tradition, "the age of discretion" is the proper time for confirmation. (But in danger of death, even children should be confirmed.) The candidate for confirmation must profess the faith, be in the state of grace, intend to receive the sacrament, and be ready to serve as a disciple and witness to the Lord Jesus Christ.

Preparation for confirmation should include a period of catechesis on the Holy Spirit and the meaning of the Spirit's gifts. This preparation time should also help awaken in the confirmands a sense of belonging to the universal church and to the local parish. It should help them reflect on the privilege of using their gifts and talents for the Lord.

Prayer and recourse to the sacrament of reconciliation should be part of the preparation for this sacrament. In addition, the confirmands should choose a sponsor, most appropriately one of their baptismal godparents.

Concluding Reflections

The church has practiced infant baptism from time immemorial. Today's rite rightly emphasizes the important role parents have to enkindle and nurture the faith in their children. To underscore this responsibility, parish adult education programs help new parents understand the meaning of baptism. They also stress the privilege parents have to be the primary religious educators of their children.

In recent decades, confirmation has been understood and recognized as the sacrament of maturity. Baptism and confirmation are, of course, gifts of God's love to us that convey the gift of the Holy Spirit. We do not earn them. However, because the Latin rite celebrates confirmation at a later age, confirmands can better appreciate the demands of Christian faith. We all need the Holy Spirit and the Spirit's gifts to live a courageous life of witness in today's secular world.

The gifts of the Spirit—wisdom, understanding, knowledge, counsel, fortitude, piety, and fear of the Lord (see Is 11:2)—take root in us and grow as we mature into Christian adults. The Lord calls those of us confirmed in the faith to work for peace and social justice, to speak out for innocent life, to act honestly, and to share our faith. Through acts of kindness and love we live our Christian vocation and use the gifts of the Holy Spirit given to us for others.

The next chapter is completely devoted to a study of the eucharist, the third sacrament of initiation. The body and blood of our Lord is the spiritual food we need to realize our baptismal and confirmation commitments to be other Christs in the world.

Prayer Reflection

The sacraments of initiation celebrate the life of becoming a Christian. Reflect on the scriptural passages which teach of our common Christian vocation.

Baptism: Who we are—persons who share the *identity* of Jesus Christ (members of his body, the church).

> But now that faith has come we are no longer under a slave looking after us; for all of you are the children of God, through faith, in Christ Jesus, since every one of you that has been baptized has been clothed in Christ. There can be neither Jew nor Greek, there can be neither slave nor freeman, there can be neither male nor female—for you are all one in Christ Jesus (Gal 3:25-28).

Confirmation: What we do—persons who are empowered by the Holy Spirit to share the *mission* of Jesus Christ.

> "But I say this to you who are listening: Love your enemies, do good to those who hate you, bless those who curse you, pray for those who treat you badly. . . .
> "Be compassionate just as your Father is compassionate. Do not judge, and you will not be judged; do not condemn, and you will not be condemned; forgive and you will be forgiven. Give, and there will be gifts for you" (Lk 6:27-28; 36-38).

Eucharist: Where we are going—persons sharing the *destiny* of Jesus Christ, our Lord and Savior.

> "Anyone who does eat my flesh and drink my blood
> has eternal life,
> and I shall raise that person up on the last day.
> For my flesh is real food
> and my blood is real drink.
> Whoever eats my flesh and drinks my blood
> lives in me
> and I live in that person.
> As the living Father sent me
> and I draw life from the Father,
> so whoever eats me will also draw life from me" (Jn 6:54-57).

For Discussion

1. Explain how the baptism of infants can be a meaningful event for the adult Christian community.
2. What does it mean when we say that Christians are initiated into the death and resurrection of Jesus? How can Christians live this mystery in a practical way?
3. At what age do you think those who were baptized as infants should be confirmed? Why?
4. Discuss evidences of the presence of the Holy Spirit in your own life. For example, when have you put into action one of the seven gifts of the Holy Spirit?

Further Reading

Ezekiel 36:24-28 (clean water, new heart)
Isaiah 61:1-9 (the Spirit of the Lord)
John 3:1-8 (Jesus with Nicodemus)
John 4:5-14 (waters of eternal life)
Galatians 5:16-25 (life in the Spirit)

Chapter Fourteen

The Eucharist

"In all truth I tell you
if you do not eat the flesh of the Son of man
and drink his blood,
you have no life in you.
Anyone who does eat my flesh and drink my blood
has eternal life,
and I shall raise that person up on the last day."
— John 6:53-54

Reception of the eucharist completes our initiation as full members of Christ's body. More, all the other sacraments and apostolic ministries of the church are bound up with and oriented to the eucharist. In the words of the *Dogmatic Constitution on the Church*, the eucharist is "the source and summit of the Christian life" (11). It signifies and really causes our union with the Blessed Trinity, and it is the source of union among the people of God. The eucharist, a sublime mystery of God's love, unites us to Christ's sacrifice on the cross, a sacrifice of praise and thanksgiving to the Father. Through this wondrous gift, the Lord continues to pour out his saving graces on the members of his body, the church (see *CCC* 1322-1327; 407).

The saints understand well the power of the eucharist and its importance for Catholic life. Consider the following words:

> Holy communion is the shortest and safest way to heaven. There are others: innocence, but that is for little children; penance, but we are afraid of it; generous endurance of the trials of life, but when they come we weep and ask to be spared. The surest, easiest, shortest way is the Eucharist.[1] — St. Pius X

> Our Lord does not come down from Heaven every day to lie in a golden ciborium. He comes to find another heaven which is infinitely dearer to Him—the Heaven of our souls.[2] — St. Thérèse of Lisieux

> Whoever turns to it [the eucharist] frequently and devoutly so effectively builds up his soul's health that it is almost impossible for him to be poisoned by evil affection of any kind.[3] — St. Francis de Sales

This chapter will take a closer look at this sacrament, a foretaste of our eternal life and a participation in the heavenly liturgy of praise of our Triune God of love.

What Are Some Names for the Eucharist? [CCC 1328-1332]

The eucharist is a mystery of love, rich in its many-faceted aspects. Its various names reveal some of its wealth of meaning. The term *eucharist* itself comes from the Greek for "thanksgiving." In the eucharist, we express gratitude for God's many gifts and graces, most notably for *creation*; *redemption* through our Lord and Savior, Jesus Christ; and *sanctification*.

We call this sacrament the *Lord's Supper* to recall Jesus' Last Supper with his apostles on Holy Thursday and to look forward to the wedding feast of the Lamb in the heavenly Jerusalem. The church's earliest term for the eucharist was *breaking of the bread* (cf. Acts 2:42), bringing to mind Jesus' celebration of the Passover meal in anticipation of breaking himself for us so we might have eternal life. Scripture also tells us that the early Christians recognized the risen Lord in the "breaking of the bread" (Lk 24:35).

The eucharist is also the *memorial* of the Lord's passion and resurrection. It is the *holy sacrifice* that makes present Christ's own sacrifice on the cross for us and includes the sacrificial offering of the church.

This sacrament goes by the name *eucharistic assembly* to highlight how we celebrate it in the midst of the assembled faithful who are the visible expression of the church. It is also the *holy and divine liturgy*, the very heart of the church's liturgical life and "the *Most Blessed Sacrament*, because it is the Sacrament of sacraments" (CCC 1330). (In addition, we designate the consecrated eucharistic species, the bread which has become Christ's body and is reserved in the tabernacle, by this name.)

The eucharist is also *Holy Communion* because it unites us to Christ Jesus and forms us into his body, the church. Finally, we call the eucharist the *Holy Mass*. This term derives from the sending forth of the faithful at the dismissal rite (in Latin, "Ite missa est"). We are to become the eucharist for others, the Christ we receive in this most Blessed Sacrament.

What Are the Biblical Roots of Eucharist? *[CCC 1333-1344]*

The church believes that in the eucharist bread and wine are changed into the body and blood of Jesus Christ. In reflecting on salvation history, the church sees a foreshadowing of this outpouring of divine love in the offering of bread and wine by the priest Melchizedek (see Gn 14:18). In addition, the unleavened bread of the Passover celebration commemorating the Exodus, God's gift of manna in the desert, and the cup of blessing of the Passover meal prefigure the eucharist.

The eucharistic language and actions are also present in two gospel miracle stories: the multiplication of the loaves and the transformation of water into wine at Cana. The superabundance of the miracle of the loaves points to the outpouring of grace in the eucharist. And the festive wine points to the heavenly feast of the Father's kingdom.

Jesus declared the importance of eating his body and drinking his blood, a hard teaching that caused some disciples to leave him. This announcement was an invitation to believe in him as the source of eternal life, to believe that to receive the eucharist is to receive the Lord himself.

The Lord established the sacrament of eucharist at the Last Supper in the context of the Jewish feast of Passover. During this meal, he took unleavened bread, blessed and broke it, and gave it to his apostles, saying, "Take and eat. This is my Body, which will be broken for you. Do this in memory of me."

Similarly, Jesus took the third Passover cup of wine after the meal, a joyful sharing among friends, and proclaimed, "Take and drink. This is the Cup of my Blood, the Blood of the new and eternal covenant, which will be shed for you. Do this in memory of me."

Jesus instituted the eucharist as a memorial of his death and resurrection, and he commanded his apostles to celebrate it until his return in glory. The church has been faithful to his mandate from its first days, breaking bread on Sunday to commemorate Jesus' resurrection on Easter. The church will never cease doing so until our Lord comes again in the fullness of time.

How Is the Eucharist a Ritual? *[CCC 1099, 1324-1327]*

Rituals like the traditions surrounding Thanksgiving meals or family gatherings at Christmas help celebrate and give meaning to life. Similarly, the eucharistic liturgy is a ritual that celebrates and gives meaning to our life in Christ. It does so by renewing the New Covenant in Jesus Christ, that is, by memorializing his sacrifice. This profound ritual has past, present, and future dimensions. For example, it enables us to enter into the Lord's Passover by celebrating, recalling, and re-enacting the *past* of our salvation—the life, death, resurrection, and glorification of our Savior. Also, by virtue of the liturgical action, the eucharist helps us celebrate the Paschal Mystery of Christ's Passover which is happening *right now*. The fruits of Christ's sacrifice are sanctifying us in the present. Finally, the eucharist directs us to the *future* of the church and our ultimate human destiny—a risen life with the Lord in heaven.

How Does the Eucharist Represent Christ's Sacrifice on the Cross? *[CCC 1356-1373; 1409-1410]*

Sacrifice comes from a Latin word which means "to make holy" or "to do something holy." Holiness refers to sharing in God's life, being, and love. But only God can make us holy; only God can share the divine life with us.

Catholics believe that the Mass is a sacrifice instituted by our Lord at the Last Supper. It represents the sacrifice of Christ on the cross. The shedding of the Lord's blood at Calvary was the supreme sign of the love he has for us. In representing the sacrifice of Calvary, the Mass is the action that makes us holy and pleasing to God. It does so in three ways.

First, the eucharistic sacrifice praises and thanks the Father for all God's countless gifts of creation and the sublime gift of salvation. In this sacrifice of self-giving love, Jesus is the high priest and the victim who offers himself through the celebrant and the assembled Christian community in praise, thanksgiving, petition, and atonement.

Second, the eucharist re-presents (makes present) Christ's sacrifice on the cross, memorializing and applying its fruits to the members of Christ's body. The Christ who is offered at the eucharist in an unbloody manner is the very same Christ who died for our sins.

The church is intimately involved in this sacrificial offering because the church is the body of Christ joined to him as the head. Thus, the sacrifice of the Mass is also the sacrifice of the Christian faithful, involving their adoration, prayers, sufferings, and works. Moreover, it is the sacrifice of the *whole* church: the pope who is the sign and servant of church unity, the bishop of the local diocese, the ministers of the eucharist, and all the church faithful still living and those who have won the prize of heaven. Furthermore, this sacrifice is offered for the faithful departed still undergoing purification. The church offers the sacrifice of the Mass so the light and peace of Christ might fully embrace them.

Third, the eucharist celebrates the presence of Christ by the power of his word and spirit. It is true that the Lord is present to us in many ways: in his scriptural word; in the prayer of Christians; in small groups gathered in the Lord's name; in the poor, sick, and imprisoned; in the sacraments which Christ himself authored; in the sacrifice of the Mass; in the priest celebrant. And, the Lord is uniquely present in the eucharistic species, the consecrated bread and wine which are the body and blood of Christ.

What Is Meant by the "Real Presence" of Christ in the Eucharist? *[CCC 1374-1381; 1413; 1418]*

The Holy Spirit's gift of faith enables Catholics to believe the awesome truth that in the eucharist "the body and blood, together with the soul and divinity, of our Lord Jesus Christ and, therefore, *the whole Christ is truly, really, and substantially* contained" (CCC 1374, quoting the teaching of the Council of Trent).

This presence of Christ in the consecrated species of bread and wine is called the "real presence." This does not mean that our Lord is not present in other ways; rather, it emphasizes his fullest presence in the eucharist. It is in the eucharist that Jesus Christ—God and man—makes himself wholly and entirely present to us, that is, *substantially* present.

Exactly how Jesus is present in the consecrated bread and wine is a mystery. The term **transubstantiation** expresses that at the consecration of the Mass the reality (the substance) of the bread and wine change into the reality of Jesus—his risen, glorified body and blood. The Lord is present whole and entire in each species from the moment of consecration for as long as the eucharistic species subsist (see CCC 1377). To receive Jesus in the "species" of the bread or the "species" of the wine is to receive the whole Christ since he is totally present in both species.

Catholics believe that it is a singular privilege to receive our Lord in holy communion. We cannot be more closely united to Christ and to one another than in our reception of the eucharist.

Because our Lord's presence endures in the sacred species, in Catholic churches the Blessed Sacrament is reserved in the **tabernacle**, a safe-like and secure receptacle usually located in a chapel or side altar. A traditional devotion to our Lord is to visit and adore him in the Blessed Sacrament. Genuflection, kneeling, and bowing our heads proclaim our faith in and love for the Lord in the Blessed Sacrament.

What Are the Essential Signs of Eucharist? *[CCC 1412]*

Wheat bread and grape wine are the *essential* signs of the eucharistic sacrifice. In the liturgy of the eucharist, the priest consecrates bread and wine by invoking the blessing of the Holy Spirit. He does so with the words of Jesus himself: "This is my body which has been given up for you. . . . This is the cup of my blood. . . ."

Jesus recited these words at the Last Supper, choosing a Passover *meal* setting to initiate the events of salvation. Meal symbolism, in fact, helps us understand some of the rich meaning in Jesus' actions. First, meals are intimate, a symbol of *companionship*, a word that means "breaking bread together." Eating a meal together is a universal symbol of friendship and love. Sharing the same food and drink signifies unity of heart, spirit, and mind. It helps create and celebrate memories. Shared meals are one of life's peak moments. The shared meal of the eucharistic sacrifice is the peak moment of the church.

At the Last Supper, Jesus transformed the *unleavened bread* of the Passover meal into his body. Bread symbolizes life. Similarly, the eucharistic bread—the body of Christ—is the food necessary for spiritual survival. Jesus, the Bread of Life, has rescued us from sin and death, as Yahweh rescued the Jews in the desert. It is the food we need to help us on our own earthly pilgrimage.

Jesus also transformed *wine* into his blood. Wine, a drink that gladdens people's hearts (Ps 104:13-15), symbolizes both joy and life itself. Jesus changed the wine into his blood, the blood of his new sacrifice, his death on a cross. Jesus' sacrifice gave us eternal life and union with the Father. The eucharist gives us a foretaste of the joy of a superabundant life the Lord has won for us. When we drink the cup of salvation, we participate in the great saving deeds of Jesus.

Finally, the eucharistic meal symbolism recalls the scriptural image of the heavenly banquet that signifies the ideal human condition at the end of time. Jesus himself used the banquet symbol in parables to announce the good news. He also ate with various outcasts to prove in action the coming of God's reign among us. Thus, the eucharist prefigures the heavenly banquet where God will unite us once and for all with our brothers and sisters.

How Does the Church Celebrate Eucharist? *[CCC 1345-1355; 1408]*

The eucharistic liturgy has kept a basic structure through the centuries. It consists of two major parts—the liturgy of the word and the liturgy of the eucharist. The liturgy of the word finds its roots in the ancient Jewish synagogue service, which gathered people to pray, read, and learn from God's word. The liturgy of the eucharist reflects the Jewish Temple service with its emphasis on gathering people to pray and to offer sacrifice. The liturgy of the eucharist also has roots in the Jewish Passover meal.

After the gathering of God's people, the eucharistic celebration includes the proclamation of the word (with readings, homily, and general intercessions); the presentation of bread and wine; the thanksgiving to God for all God's gifts, especially the Son; the prayer of consecration; and holy communion. All these elements in both the liturgy of the word and the liturgy of the eucharist form "one single act of worship." The order of a typical Sunday Mass follows.

Introductory Rites
1. *Entrance and Greeting.* The Mass begins with everyone standing and singing an appropriate song. The focus is on the *lectionary*, the book containing God's word held high for all to see. The priest, acting in the person of Christ, processes to the altar along with the other liturgical ministers. They all bow. The priest then kisses the altar as a sign of respect and affection for Jesus. The lector places the lectionary at the lectern, the place for doing the readings.
2. *Penitential rite.* In the Sermon on the Mount, Jesus taught that we should worship God with a pure heart. We should forgive those who have hurt us and ask for their forgiveness if we have harmed them. In this rite the priest and people acknowledge their sinfulness and ask for God's forgiveness.
3. *Gloria.* The "Glory to God" is then sung or recited in praise and thanksgiving to the Triune God.
4. *Prayer of the Day.* The Introductory rites end with a prayer of petition on behalf of the community, which recalls the mystery of salvation proper to the day or feast.

Liturgy of the Word
1. *The First Reading and Responsorial Psalm.* The first reading usually comes from the Old Testament. Thus, the word God spoke to our ancestors in the faith continues to form us today. The response, either sung or recited, comes from one of the Psalms and expresses our willingness to take God's word to heart.
2. *Second Reading and Alleluia or Acclamation.* The second reading typically comes from one of St. Paul's letters and usually deals with a problem facing followers of Jesus. The Alleluia verse is our resounding "yes" to God who meets us in the word.

3. *Gospel Reading.* The key reading of the liturgy of the word comes from a gospel, thus linking us with our Christian heritage and with Jesus, our Lord. We show our reverence for the gospel by standing and signing ourselves with a small cross on the forehead, lips, and heart. This symbolically states our commitment to make God's word come alive in what we think, in what we say, and in our lives of loving service.

4. *Homily.* The priest or deacon explores the theme of the readings in the homily to help us gain new insights on how to live the Christian life.

5. *The Creed.* The congregation professes its faith by reciting the Nicene Creed, a summary of our Catholic beliefs. Expression of our common belief binds us more closely as a community.

6. *General Intercessions.* Here we pray with confidence that the Lord will take care of our needs and those of our world.

Liturgy of the Eucharist

1. *The Offering.* The liturgy of the eucharist begins with representatives of the community carrying bread and wine to the altar and the altar being prepared. These symbols represent God's goodness to us which we now offer back to God. A time-honored custom has been the bringing of gifts to share with the poor along with the gifts of bread and wine. This *collection* draws its inspiration from Jesus himself who loved the poor in a special way. A regular monetary collection is also taken to support the parish and its ministries.

2. *The Eucharistic Prayer.* The eucharistic prayer is the heart of the eucharistic liturgy (also called the **canon of the Mass**). It begins with the *preface*, an introductory prayer that reminds us of our duty to thank the Father through Jesus Christ in the Holy Spirit. The entire congregation assents to the Preface by singing or reciting the great hymn of praise, the Sanctus, or "Holy, Holy, Holy."

The church has four Eucharistic prayers. Each of these prayers:

- invokes the power of the Holy Spirit (the *epiclesis*);

- has an *institution narrative* that recounts the words of institution proclaimed by Jesus at the Last Supper, remembers and acknowledges Christ's saving deeds (*anamnesis*), and offers the sacrifice of Jesus to the Father;

- petitions God for peace and various intentions of the whole community;

- concludes with the Great Amen where the whole community responds in a agreement with all that was spoken before with a resounding "yes!"

3. *Communion Rite.* The congregation prepares to receive the living Lord by reciting the Lord's Prayer and sharing a sign of peace. These words and gestures reinforce the truth of our faith that Jesus Christ, by the power of the Holy Spirit, has joined us into one body. We pray together the Agnus Dei ("Lamb of God"), recognizing our own sinfulness and need for Christ's healing touch.

The priest breaks the one bread, a symbol of unity, so all may share in the same body. The faithful approach the altar for God's heavenly gift to us—the risen Lord in holy communion. This is the food of salvation where we become one in the Lord so we can be one in loving others.

The communion rite closes with a concluding prayer.

Concluding Rite
The Mass concludes when the bishop, priest, or deacon blesses and dismisses the people. The words of the dismissal rite remind us what God has given us—peace—and what we must do in turn—love others and serve the Lord.

The priest and other liturgical ministers recess while the congregation sings an apt song.

Who Is the Proper Celebrant at Eucharist? *[CCC 1411]*

"Only validly ordained priests can preside at the Eucharist and consecrate the bread and wine so that they become the Body and Blood of the Lord" (CCC 1411).

How Often Should Catholics Receive Holy Communion? *[CCC 1382-1390; 1415; 1417]*

The Lord's invitation to receive him in holy communion is indeed a great privilege. The church *encourages* us to receive this most Blessed Sacrament every time we participate in a eucharistic liturgy. However, we must receive holy communion worthily, that is, we be must in the state of sanctifying grace. Therefore, if we are aware of mortal sin, we must first receive the sacrament of reconciliation. St. Paul warns us:

> Whenever you eat this bread, then, and drink this cup, you are proclaiming the Lord's death until he comes. Therefore anyone who eats the bread or drinks the cup of the Lord unworthily is answerable for the body and blood of the Lord.
> Everyone is to examine himself and only then eat of the bread or drink from the cup, because a person who eats and drinks without recognizing the body is eating and drinking his own condemnation (1 Cor 11:26-29).

Before receiving holy communion, we humbly prepare ourselves by keeping the appropriate fast (one hour from food or drink), showing in our clothing and demeanor at Mass our reverence for the Lord in the Blessed Sacrament, and expressing our unworthiness in the words of the centurion, "Lord, I am not worthy" (see Lk 7:1-10).

Church law obliges Catholics to go to Mass on Sundays and holy days. The purpose of this "Sunday obligation" finds its roots in Jesus' mandate to break bread in his name. Weekly Mass attendance joins us to our brother and Savior Jesus and to one another in worship of the Father. A positive approach to this obligation includes an attitude of asking what we can bring to the liturgy, "the people's work."

Finally, prepared by the sacrament of penance, the church obliges Catholics to receive holy communion at least *once a year*, if possible during the Easter season.

Jesus' sacrifice makes it possible for us to receive him as food that gives true life. The Lord invites us to come to his banquet table and receive him in holy communion. When we do receive the Lord either under the species of bread or wine, we receive the whole Christ. However, the sign of the eucharistic meal is more complete when we receive him under both kinds.

What Are Some Effects of Receiving Holy Communion?
[CCC 1391-1397; 1414; 1416]

All of the sacraments point to what they bring about and bring about what they point to. As a sacrament of initiation, the eucharist makes us full participating members of the church. In fact, the eucharist is the sacrament of Christian community, bringing about as its primary effect the intimate union with Christ Jesus. In the other sacraments, we receive the graces of Christ. In the eucharist we receive Christ himself, whole and entire, God and man, not only as individuals but as a worshipping community.

The eucharist is the heart of Catholic life, the source, center, and summit of the whole life of the church. It is the prime sacrament, the one from which all others come and the one to which the others point. We call this sacrament "blessed," a biblical word that means a communication of God's life to us. "*Blessed* Sacrament" is an apt name for holy communion, especially when we consider some blessings bestowed on us when we receive it.

- The eucharist is a sacrifice. The church offers it as a reparation for the sins of the living and the dead. By means of it, we obtain spiritual and temporal benefits from God.

- The eucharist brings about spiritual life and nourishment. St. Thomas Aquinas tells us that the eucharist does for the spiritual life what food does for bodily life. It sustains and restores us, helps us grow, and brings us joy.

- The eucharist cleanses us from *past* sins by wiping away venial sin. It preserves us from *future* mortal sins and gives us the graces to repent of mortal sin. (However, the sacrament of penance is the proper sacrament to gain forgiveness of mortal sin. The eucharist is the sacrament for those who are in the state of sanctifying grace, in full communion with the church.)

- The eucharist increases the theological virtues of faith, hope, and love and strengthens the gifts and fruits of the Holy Spirit.

- The eucharist gives us spiritual energy for our earthly pilgrimage, grants us a foretaste of heaven, and unites us with the church triumphant—the Blessed Mother and the saints in heaven.

- In sum, the eucharist puts us in touch with the saving effects of the Paschal Mystery, the eternal life that Jesus' sacrifice has won for us.

Can Non-Catholics Receive Holy Communion? *[CCC 1398-1401]*

The eucharist is *the* sacrament of faith, unity, and love. Catholics believe in the real presence of Jesus in the eucharist. Holy communion celebrates our unity in the Lord and with each member of the church. It would be false for someone to join in this symbol of unity if he or she is not one in faith with us.

The *Directory of Ecumenism* (55) has strict guidelines for intercommunion. For Christians not in full communion with the Catholic church to receive holy communion, they must:

- believe the same as Catholics do about the eucharist

- be in a state of "urgent necessity" (examples: during persecution, in prisons)

- be unable to have recourse to their own ministers

- request the sacrament on their *own* initiative, not at the prompting of a Catholic.

Only the bishop of the local diocese has the authority to judge if intercommunion can take place.

Finally, anyone—Catholic or not—must have the right disposition to receive the eucharist. This means that we should be in the state of grace, that is, free of any conscious mortal sins that separate us from the Blessed Lord. Because the eucharist is a banquet of love, everyone who receives it should do so worthily.

It is also important to remember that the church does not allow Catholics to participate in a communion service at a Protestant church. Because of our different beliefs—slight or great—we do not want to imply that we agree with what another church holds about the eucharist.

An urgent task for all Christians is to pray for unity among the members of the body of Christ.

Concluding Reflections

In the person of Jesus Christ, both God and humanity are joined. Jesus is God's love incarnate. But Jesus is also the perfect human being, our representative before God. Through him, humanity both receives and responds to the offer of God's love. The human Jesus was totally open, receptive, obedient, and responsive to his heavenly Father—even to death. Unlike the first representative of the human race, Adam, Jesus Christ allowed himself to be put totally in the hands of his Father. By surrendering himself in obedience to his Father's will, Jesus sacrificed for us. He made us holy; he made it possible for us to share God's life. He did this when he loved us completely, pouring out his blood for our sake.

When we offer the sacrifice of the Mass, we continue to be made holy by accepting and living the example of our brother and savior Jesus Christ. His freely accepted death shows us that love is the way to holiness. When we remember, re-enact, and attempt to live his sacrifice—his way of love—God changes us into more loving people.

The Mass eloquently reminds us that communal worship must never be focused on itself. When we "break bread" in the name of Jesus, we are celebrating our brotherhood and sisterhood and receiving the source of our life, the Lord Jesus. In this sacred meal, he reminds us to take him out into the world, a world that desperately needs his love. We must be broken for others just as he was broken for us. Christian worship that does not translate into service for others is not true worship. Jesus said:

> "It is not anyone who says to me, 'Lord, Lord,' who will enter the kingdom of Heaven, but the person who does the will of my Father in heaven" (Mt 7:21).

The eucharist reminds us that because we have received the body of Christ we must *become* the body of Christ. We are the Lord's hands that touch and care for the sick, old and infirm; his feet that walk to meet and befriend the lonely; his understanding eyes that reveal compassion to the hurting and lost in our midst; his voice of power and righteousness to speak out for the marginalized in the cause of justice.

Prayer Reflection

"I am the bread of life,
No one who comes to me will ever hunger;
no one who believes in me will ever thirst . . ."
"I am the living bread which has come down from heaven.
Anyone who eats this bread will live for ever;
and the bread that I shall give
is my flesh, for the life of the world" (Jn 6:35, 51).

For Discussion

1. A friend has told you that she stopped going to Mass because she was bored with the repetitious ritual. What could you say to her to help her reconsider joining her Christian brothers and sisters at the Lord's table?
2. "The eucharist both creates and celebrates Christian community." Explain.
3. How does the eucharist challenge you to greater Christian responsibility?

Further Reading

Exodus 16 (Yahweh saves Israel by sending manna)
Luke 22:14-20 (institution of the eucharist)
1 Corinthians 11:17-34 (proper celebration of the eucharist)

Chapter Fifteen

The Sacraments of Healing: Reconciliation and Anointing of the Sick

Receive the Holy Spirit.
If you forgive anyone's sins,
they are forgiven;
if you retain anyone's sins,
they are retained.
       — John 20:22-23

> The prayer of faith will save the sick person and the Lord will raise him up again; and if he has committed any sins, he will be forgiven.
>   — James 5:15

Accepting blame is a sign of maturity. To be human means that at times we will make mistakes and commit sins. However, owning up to them quickly and candidly is another matter.

Through this short note, a business owner shows how to acknowledge being wrong and admitting it frankly and without excuses. The note read:

> "Dear Mr. Jones:
> "You're right. We're wrong. We're sorry.
> Sincerely yours. . . ."

How refreshing to see a person take blame and not squirm out of responsibility. Similarly, in the spiritual life, how good it is for sincerely contrite persons to confess forthrightly their sins and make amends to God. Doing so makes them pleasing to God, neighbors, and self. Doing so has a healing effect on the soul.

This chapter looks at the sacraments of reconciliation and the anointing of the sick, two wonderful opportunities Catholics have to be touched by Christ's healing presence and to be unburdened of their sins.

Jesus knows both our spiritual and physical sicknesses, and he has come to restore us to health. He is the Divine Physician.

> "It is not those that are well who need the doctor, but the sick. I have come to call not the upright but sinners to repentance" (Lk 5:31-32).

What Are Some Names for the Sacrament of Reconciliation? [CCC 1422-1429; 1486]

Two powerful effects of baptism are forgiveness of sin and the adoption of the baptized into God's family. Further, the Holy Spirit given in the sacraments of baptism and confirmation and the reception of the Lord in the eucharist make us holy. However, the new life we receive through the sacraments of initiation does not take away our weakened human nature. Our inclination to sin (traditionally termed *concupiscence*) remains, requiring a lifelong struggle to conversion.

A major help in this struggle to heed Jesus' command to repent and to believe in the gospel is the sacrament of conversion, also termed penance, confession, forgiveness, and reconciliation.

We call it the *sacrament of conversion* because it makes sacramentally present Jesus' call to repent. This, in fact, is the first step for sinners to take in returning to the loving Father who awaits with open arms. This sacrament calls Catholics as individuals and as a community to turn to God's infinite mercy and walk the path of renewal.

We call it the *sacrament of penance* to emphasize that a life of conversion involves doing penance and making satisfaction for sins we have committed.

We call it the *sacrament of confession* because an essential element of the sacrament is to tell our sins to the priest. Through this sacrament we also "confess," that is, acknowledge and praise God for the bounteous mercy God extends to us.

We call it the *sacrament of forgiveness* to underscore that through the priest's absolution God imparts pardon and peace.

Finally, we call it the *sacrament of reconciliation* because God's love empowers us to become reconciled, to become one again, with those we have harmed through our sins.

What Does Conversion Involve? *[CCC 1430-1438; 1490]*

The words *conversion* and *repentance* are synonymous. In the gospel, when Jesus calls for his followers to convert and to embrace the gospel, he is talking about interior conversion, that is interior repentance. This interior conversion is first a gift from the Holy Spirit who gives us the grace to return to the Lord, to have the courage to begin anew. Interior conversion involves reorienting our lives, returning to God, rooting out sin in our lives, and hating the evil we have committed. It also involves deeply wanting to change our lives, firmly intending to sin no more, and trusting fervently in God's infinite mercy and grace. A wonderful help for Christians to help reorient their lives is to look at Christ Jesus suffering on the cross for our sins.

Interior conversion manifests itself in external actions of penance. Scripture and Tradition have always stressed the importance of fasting, prayer, and almsgiving—three acts that express conversion in relation to self, to God, and to others. Other traditional ways to express interior conversion include efforts to make peace, prayer for one's neighbors, the intercession of the saints, and works of charity.

Conversion is accomplished by efforts at reconciliation, concern for the poor, works of justice, frequent examination of conscience, recourse to spiritual direction, accepting suffering and by taking up whatever cross may come one's way in imitation of Jesus. The eucharist, reading the Bible, frequent prayer, and participating in the church's seasons and days of penance (for example, Lent) all nourish a spirit of conversion in Christians trying to conform themselves to Christ Jesus.

Who Can Forgive Sin? *[CCC 1440-1445; 1487-1489]*

For believers, sin is a great evil because of what it does to the sinner, the church, and the world. The sinner needs God's grace to convert. Sin offends God's honor and love; it results in a break in our union with God. Sin also ruptures communion with the church, of which each member is a living part.

Jesus, the Son of God, forgave sins often in his earthly ministry. His ready acceptance of sinners—for example, when he ate with them—showed that his forgiveness of sinners reestablished them into the community.

Jesus continues his ministry of reconciliation today through his body, the church. He commissioned the whole church through its life and prayer to continue his ministry of reconciliation, that is, to be a sign and instrument of the forgiveness and reconciliation accomplished by his death and resurrection. Furthermore, he gave the power of absolution to the apostles and their successors. Today, bishops and priests serve the official ministry of reconciliation for Jesus.

By giving the apostles his authority to forgive sins in his name, Jesus also gave them the power to reconcile sinners with the church. We find in Matthew's gospel the key scriptural passage where the Lord empowers Peter and the other apostles to forgive sin in his name.

> "I will give you the keys of the kingdom of Heaven: whatever you bind on earth will be bound in heaven; whatever you loose on earth will be loosed in heaven" (Mt 16:19).

"Bind and loose" mean that whoever is excluded from or included anew in communion with the church is excluded or included anew with God. For Christians, *reconciliation with the church and reconciliation with God are inseparable.*

How Has the Sacrament of Reconciliation Been Celebrated in History? *[CCC 1446-1448; 1491]*

The practice of the sacrament of reconciliation has varied through the different eras of church history. For example, in the first centuries it was used to reconcile those sinners who were guilty of grave sins like idolatry, murder, and adultery. The sacrament was tied to rigorous public penances, sometimes lasting years. In certain regions, the faithful were only allowed to receive it once a lifetime. Sinners entered an order of penitents to underscore the seriousness of their sins.

During the seventh century, Irish monks introduced into Europe a second form of the sacrament. It took the form of private, individual, and devotional confession to a priest. It did not require public or long penitential works before becoming reconciled with God's people. This private, individual confession could be repeated often, thus opening the way to devotional confessions, even of venial sins. This form of the sacrament is the one we know today.

Regardless of how the church celebrated the sacrament of reconciliation through the centuries, its fundamental structure always consisted of two essential elements. First are the *acts of the penitent* whom the Holy Spirit leads to **repentance**: contrition, confession, and satisfaction. Second is *God's action* through bishops and priests who forgive sin in Jesus' name, determine the manner of satisfaction, and pray for and do penance with the penitent.

What Is Absolution? *[CCC 1449]*

Through the formula of **absolution**, the bishop or priest proclaims God's forgiveness of the sinner. Absolution means "to pronounce clear of blame or guilt." The formula for absolution in the Latin rite reads as follows:

> God, the Father of mercies,
> through the death and the resurrection of his Son
> has reconciled the world to himself
> and sent the Holy Spirit among us
> for the forgiveness of sins;
> through the ministry of the Church
> may God give you pardon and peace,
> and I absolve you from your sins
> in the name of the Father, and of the Son,
> and of the Holy Spirit.[1]

What Acts Are Required of the Penitent? *[CCC 1450-1460; 1492-1494]*

The sacrament of reconciliation requires that repentant sinners be contrite and confess and make satisfaction for their sins.

Contrition is genuine sorrow for one's sins, a detesting of them, and a firm resolve not to sin again. *Perfect* contrition is sorrow that comes from love of God. It forgives venial sin and even mortal sin if a person intends to receive the sacrament of reconciliation as soon as possible. *Imperfect* contrition is also a gift from God. It arises from a fear of eternal damnation or from thinking about the ugliness of one's sins. Although imperfect contrition does not forgive mortal sin, it does ready a person to celebrate the sacrament of reconciliation.

Confession of sin is the second required act of penitents. Before that takes place, however, penitents should examine their consciences in light of God's word, especially the Ten Commandments, the Sermon on the Mount, and the apostolic letters. With the help of the Holy Spirit, an honest examination of conscience will disclose the presence of sin in our lives and will move us to want to seek forgiveness and repair any harm we have caused by our sin.

Confession is good for the soul. It helps us confront and take responsibility for our sins. Saying them aloud to God's representative is a concrete sign that we have owned up to them and are honestly sorry for them and ready to do something about them. The church obliges us to confess all mortal sins of which we are consciously aware. We must do this at least once a year or before receiving holy communion—which requires us to be in the state of grace. Although the church does not mandate the confession of venial sins, doing so has many benefits. It strengthens conscience formation, empowers us to fight our evil inclinations, allows the Divine Physician to heal us, and enables us to grow in the spiritual life, especially by extending God's mercy to others.

Absolution forgives our sins, but it does not repair or make *satisfaction* for the harm our sins have caused. Doing satisfaction, also called *penance*, is part of the reparation sinners need to do. Sincere contrition proves itself in repairing any harm our sins caused, for example, by returning stolen goods or restoring a person's damaged reputation caused by slander. It also includes the saying of prayers, works of mercy or service, acts of self-denial, and the like. The priest tailors the penance to the spiritual needs of the penitent.

Who Is the Minister of the Sacrament of Reconciliation? [CCC 1461-1467; 1495]

Holy orders empowers bishops and priests with the Christ-given authority to forgive sins in the sacrament of reconciliation. Priests exercise their ministry after receiving their commission from their bishop or religious superior.

The confessor's role is to represent Christ and announce the words of absolution on behalf of the church. When the priest holds his hands over the penitent's head and recites the words, "I absolve you from your sins in the name of the Father, and of the Son, and of the Holy Spirit," Christ himself is giving us the sign we need to know that God forgives us. Jesus loves us as individuals; as unique individuals we need to hear the Lord speaking directly to us.

While standing in the place of Christ, the Good Shepherd, confessors should exhibit qualities of compassion, patience, and priestly competence in this sacrament of mercy. They serve as a special sign of God's forgiving love when they do penance and pray for the faithful who approach them for reconciliation. Under severe ecclesiastical penalties, confessors are bound to keep absolute secrecy about any sins revealed in confession. This "sacramental seal" guarantees the total respect due penitents who bare their souls in this sacrament.

How Is the Sacrament of Reconciliation Celebrated? [CCC 1480-1484; 1497]

The ritual celebration of the sacrament of forgiveness is both beautiful and meaningful. Ordinarily, the confessor warmly greets and blesses the penitent and then reads a short scripture passage that proclaims God's forgiving love. Next, the penitent confesses his or her sins, mentioning all mortal sins committed since the last confession, and prays an act of contrition. The priest then assigns a suitable penance before pronouncing the words of absolution. The liturgy concludes with a prayer of praise and thanksgiving followed by the dismissal and a blessing by the priest.

Confession to a priest either face-to-face or anonymously behind a screen is an ordinary fact of church life. For example, it is celebrated in most parishes every Saturday and whenever requested. During certain liturgical seasons like Lent, however, many parishes have communal celebrations of the sacrament of reconciliation, thus highlighting the liturgical nature of penance. These services include scripture readings, a common examination of conscience, a homily, the Lord's Prayer, and hymns and music. These communal celebrations also allow time for individual confessions of sins to a priest. Therefore, many priests may participate in a communal reconciliation service.

On occasions of grave necessity, a priest may give a general absolution after a common prayer of confession of sin by those assembled. However, those in mortal sin must intend to confess their sins in individual confession as soon as possible.

For Catholics, individual and integral confession followed by absolution is the ordinary way of reconciliation with God and the church. It is the means Jesus has chosen to proclaim his loving forgiveness to sinners in a personal way.

What Does the Sacrament of Reconciliation Accomplish? [CCC 1468-1470; 1496]

The sacrament of reconciliation results in forgiveness of sins and reconciliation with God and the church. It also provides peace of conscience and spiritual comfort and strengthens us to live the Christian life. In addition, it partially takes away some of the temporal punishment due to sin and totally remits the eternal punishment resulting from mortal sin.

Finally, because we submit ourselves to God's mercy, this sacrament anticipates our final judgment when we meet the Lord at death. It helps us to repent and teaches us penance and faith in God's loving mercy. By God's grace, these virtues will help us pass from death to an eternal life of joy in heaven.

What Are Indulgences? [CCC 1471-1479; 1498]

Church teaching links the sacrament of reconciliation to the doctrine and practice of indulgences. An *indulgence* remits either partially or fully temporal punishment due to sins already forgiven.

The church declares that certain prescribed prayers or actions have special value because they share in the spiritual merits gained by Jesus Christ and in the good works of the saints. This spiritual treasury of graces shared among its members underscores the concern and love that various members of Christ's body have for each other.

The teaching concerning indulgences acknowledges that sin has two effects. Serious sin breaks off our relationship with God, thus depriving us of eternal life. We need the healing effect of the sacrament of reconciliation to forgive this sin and restore our heavenly inheritance. Although sins are forgiven in this sacrament, every sin also results in unhealthy attachments. These "attachments" need to be purified either here on earth or in purgatory before we are free to embrace the all-holy One in heaven. (This purging process is the temporal punishment we must undergo to become totally loving and open to the Lord.)

Prayer, acts of penance, works of charity and mercy, bearing our daily crosses—all these help purge the remnant selfishness. The church provides additional help by offering us indulgences, that is, by sharing the spiritual treasury built up by Christ and the saints (especially our Blessed Mother). Through this sharing of love between the members of Christ's body, the holiness of one profits others. The church has the authority to grant these indulgences through the "binding and loosing" power granted by Jesus.

We may also show concern for those in purgatory by gaining indulgences for them. By saying prayers and performing actions approved by the church, we can help our departed brothers and sisters gain indulgences, thus remitting some of the temporal punishment due for the sins they committed in their earthly life.

What Are the Biblical Roots for the Sacrament of the Anointing of the Sick? [CCC 1499-1510; 1526]

Anyone who has ever experienced or witnessed illness knows how it makes a person helpless and vulnerable. Sickness sometimes leads to self-absorption and even anger against God. It also brings into stark relief human mortality. Yet in our need and misery, illness can also turn us to God through prayer and conversion. The Hebrew scriptures saw the mystery of sickness intertwined with sin and evil. God's Chosen People also looked to a time when God would wipe away sin and bring to health and wholeness all those who are ill.

Jesus Christ healed the sick in his own public ministry, especially through the laying on of hands. For example, Jesus cured the blind, made lame people walk, cleansed lepers, and brought the dead back to life. Through his cures he showed special love to the suffering by healing their spiritual, psychological, and physical hurts. Jesus was specially responsive to people who exhibited faith in him as the sign of God's love.

Jesus charged his disciples to continue his message and mission of healing. Thus, the early church celebrated and proclaimed the good news of salvation by continuing Jesus' healing ministry. The apostles preached repentance, cast out demons, and anointed and healed the sick.

Today, the Lord continues "to touch" and to heal the sick and suffering. He does so through the prayers of the church and through the sacraments, especially the eucharist which has a healing effect, and the distinct rite for the sick, the sacrament of the anointing of the sick. The biblical roots of this latter sacrament are found in the letter of James:

> Any one of you who is ill should send for the elders of the church, and they must anoint the sick person with oil in the name of the Lord and pray over him. The prayer of faith will save the sick person and the Lord will raise him up again; and if he has committed any sins, he will be forgiven. So confess your sins to one another, and pray for one another to be cured; the heartfelt prayer of someone upright works very powerfully (Jas 5:14-16).

How Did the Anointing of the Sick Develop Through History? [CCC 1511-1512; 1514-1515; 1528-1529]

As noted in the letter of James, the apostolic church prayed for, anointed, and healed the sick in Jesus' name. Also, the Acts of the Apostles recounts many healings accomplished through prayer, anointing, and the laying on of hands (see, for example, Acts 9:34 and Acts 28:8). St. Paul also reports how the Holy Spirit gave some disciples the gift of healing to show forth the power of the risen Lord (1 Cor 12:9, 28, 30). Historians conclude that anointing and praying for the sick were commonplace in the early church.

By the ninth century the clergy became the ordinary ministers of this sacrament and by the Middle Ages the sacramental action of anointing was reserved, for all practical purposes, for those who were dying. The name for the sacrament became **extreme unction**, that is, the "last anointing" before death. Penance and the reception of a final eucharist (known as *viaticum*—"food for the way") preceded the sacramental anointing. The medieval practice of anointing *only* those near death continued until recent times. However, we should note that through these centuries the liturgy always begged God to heal the sick and dying person, if this would be conducive to his or her salvation.

The liturgical reforms of the Second Vatican Council again stress the ancient practice of this sacrament as the anointing of the *sick*. The sacrament is for those suffering from serious illness, for the elderly, for those facing major surgery, as well as for the dying. The sick person may repeat the sacrament if, after recovery, he or she falls ill again or if the original condition worsens.

How Is the Sacrament of the Anointing of the Sick Celebrated Today? [CCC 1513; 1517-1519; 1524-1525; 1531]

Today's ritual includes the following essential elements: the priest lays hands on the sick; he prays for them in the faith of the church; and he anoints their forehead and hands (in the Roman rite) or other body parts (in the Eastern rite) with blessed oil (ideally blessed previously by a bishop).

The anointing of the sick is both a liturgical and communal celebration. Celebrating it within the eucharist is fitting. Where appropriate, the sacrament of reconciliation can be celebrated first, followed by the anointing within the eucharist. Certainly, for the dying person, "viaticum" (holy communion) should be the last sacrament administered. Just as baptism, confirmation, and the eucharist initiate us into the Christian community, so reconciliation, anointing of the sick, and the eucharist prepare us for heaven. They complete our earthly pilgrimage.

Today's rite recognizes the importance of the *laying on of hands*. It is a biblical sign of Jesus' touch and the outpouring of the Spirit of strength, love, and forgiveness. The prayer of the priest over the sick person invokes the grace of the Spirit:

> Through this holy anointing may the Lord in his love and mercy help you with the grace of the Holy Spirit. May the Lord who frees you from sin save you and raise you up.[2]

In the Latin rite, the priest recites this prayer while *anointing the forehead and hands of the sick person with the blessed oil*. Anointing symbolizes healing, strengthening, and special dedication to God.

Who Is the Minister of the Sacrament of the Anointing of the Sick? *[CCC 1516; 1530]*

Priests or bishops are the ministers of the sacrament of the anointing of the sick. Note, though, that the sacrament includes the prayerful support of the Christian community (the family, friends, and parish community of the sick person). Communal anointings during the Mass, for example, sensitize the parish to respond lovingly to the needs of the sick among is membership.

The sick person also has a crucial role. Today's rite underscores the need for the sick person to overcome the alienation caused by sickness and suffering. It helps and challenges the sick person to grow to wholeness through the illness, to identify with the sufferings of Jesus Christ, and enter more fully into the Paschal Mystery. The rite also urges the person to assume a more active role, for example, by requesting the sacrament himself or herself rather than having someone else do it.

What Are the Effects of the Anointing of the Sick? *[CCC 1520-1523; 1527; 1532]*

The sacrament of anointing has several effects:

- It wipes away sin and its remnants if a person has not been able to obtain forgiveness through the sacrament of reconciliation.

- It brings about spiritual healing by fortifying the sick and dying during their suffering. The Holy Spirit gives the sick or dying person comfort, peace, and courage.

- It restores physical healing when this will help the person in his or her condition before God.

- It unites the anointed person more closely to Christ's redemptive passion. By associating with the Lord's passion, the sick contribute through their suffering to their own good and the welfare of all God's people.

Finally, the person who receives this sacrament and viaticum shortly before death has the nourishment necessary for the passover from this life to eternity with the Triune God.

Concluding Reflections

An oft-quoted line from the 70s movie *Love Story* was "Love is never having to say you're sorry." This observation is simply not true. To express sorrow verbally to a loved one is often the catalyst for healing relationships. We need to say we are sorry when we have sinned against someone.

We also need to hear, "You are forgiven." These words speak of true love. This is why the sacrament of reconciliation is truly a sign of the good news of God's love. This sacrament affords us the opportunity to express our sorrow and, more important, to be assured of God's forgiveness and love.

The Lord continues his healing ministry in the sacrament of reconciliation and the sacrament of the anointing of the sick. Through both of these signs, the Lord also challenges us—we who are forgiven and healed by his love—to be signs of reconciliation and healing to others.

Sacraments are not magic. Rather, they are actions of the Lord working through his body, the church. We are the church. The Lord taught us best. We must infect others with the good news of salvation. Because we have been forgiven, we have the duty to be signs of forgiveness to others. "Forgive us our trespasses as we forgive those who trespass against us."

Prayer Reflection

Place yourself in the presence of God. Feel his love for you. Ask the Holy Spirit to help you review your day. What good things happened to you? Where and when were you a true sign of God's love?

Then turn to those times when you might have missed the mark. What words, thoughts and actions were self-centered? What attitudes were unworthy of a child of God? What did you fail to do that you should have done?

When finished with your examination of conscience, turn to the Lord and repeatedly pray the "Jesus Prayer":

> Lord, Jesus Christ, Son of the Living God, have mercy on me, a sinner.

For Discussion

1. What in your life needs the healing touch of the Lord?
2. Why is it so important for us to forgive ourselves?
3. Explain how reconciliation is related to the forgiveness of sin.
4. How can you personally contribute to the healing ministry of Jesus Christ?

Further Reading

Ezekiel 18:20-32 (the converted sinner finds life)
Joel 2:12-19 (a call to repent)
Luke 7:36-50 (Jesus and a repentant sinner)
Matthew 9:9-13 (Jesus and sinners)

Chapter Sixteen

Sacraments at the Service of Communion: Holy Orders and Matrimony

"You know that among the gentiles those they call their rulers lord it over them, and their great men make their authority felt. Among you this is not to happen. No; anyone who wants to become great among you must be your servant, and anyone who wants to be first among you must be slave to all."
— Mark 10:41-44

This is why a man leaves his father and mother and becomes attached to his wife, and they become one flesh.
— Genesis 2:24

In the novel *Atticus*, a Colorado widower, Atticus Cody, leaves his ranch for Mexico to reclaim what he thinks is the body of his reckless, wayward son. This son, Scott, had gone to a village there to live among expatriates and practice his craft as an artist. The suspense story revolves around Scott's apparent suicide, allegedly committed in a drunken frenzy. But Atticus would not accept the obvious—that the body whose face had been obliterated by a gunshot wound was that of his son. He doggedly pursued his instincts until he solved a mystery that related symbolically to the name of the village—Resurrección.

This mystery novel retells in its own way Jesus' parable of the prodigal son. The "lost" son does come back to life. However, he is not the focus of the story. The father is. Atticus—like the father in Jesus' parable—madly loves his son and goes to great lengths to show it.

This chapter will look at two sacraments of love—holy orders and matrimony, what the *Catechism of the Catholic Church* calls "the sacraments at the service of communion" (1533). Christian life is about loving and serving as Jesus taught and did.

For example, those called to serve God and the Christian community as bishops, priests, and deacons have Christ's invitation to love God's people with an unfailing "fatherly" love, rooted in their own dedication to the Lord and his gospel. They are to mirror the generous, unconditional love of the father who refuses to give up on his son. Similarly, a man and a woman called to permanent, total love in the covenant of marriage have the Christ-given vocation to be signs of unconditional love to each other and to their children. Their motherly and fatherly love dedicated to serving their children and their love for each other draw strength from the Lord who abides in their hearts and homes.

What Is the Common Vocation of All Christians? [CCC 1533; 1544-1545]

The sacraments of initiation call all Christians to holiness, to be witnesses and servants of Christ's gospel. They give the graces we need to live Christ-like lives for others. Baptism and confirmation, moreover, initiate each of us into the common priesthood of the faithful. By definition a **priest** is an intermediary between God and people. Jesus, of course, is the mediator *par excellence*, the one mediator between God and us. When we are joined to Jesus in baptism we share in his priestly function, that is, we are his servants helping in his work of salvation. The Lord commissions all members of his body to preach the good news of salvation. We do this through prayer, loving service of others, healing and reconciliation, acts of justice and mercy shown to the poor and oppressed, and through any work on behalf of God's kingdom.

What Is the Function of the Ordained Ministry? [CCC 1546-1547]

Although all baptized Christians are called to ministry and to share in the priesthood of Jesus Christ, there is a need in the Christian community for certain members of the Lord's body to "minister to the ministers." The Christian community is also an organization; it needs order, fixed structures, clearly defined duties, and visible leaders to organize the massive efforts necessary to carry on Christ's mandate to preach and to live the gospel to the very ends of the earth. *Ordained ministers* serve in one of the structured ministries of the church; they are entrusted with leading the church through a special ministry of service to the Christian community and by extension to the whole world. The ministerial priesthood is essentially different from the common priesthood of the faithful. Its main function is to help unfold the baptismal graces of all Christians.

What Is the Sacrament of Holy Orders? *[CCC 1536-1538; 1548-1553; 1591-1592]*

It is through the sacrament of holy orders that Christ Jesus continues the ministry he entrusted to the apostles. Through the service of ordained ministers, especially that of bishops and priests, Christ himself becomes visibly present to the church as its head and high priest of his redemptive sacrifice. Furthermore, the ministerial priesthood also acts in the name of the whole church when worshipping God on behalf of the church.

By means of ordination the Lord consecrates certain men to one of three degrees of a sacred order: episcopacy (bishops), presbyterate (priests), and diaconate (deacons). The sacrament of holy orders confers a gift of the Holy Spirit that allows those ordained to exercise a "sacred power" on behalf of Christ for his church.

The Second Vatican Council teaches that the priesthood of the faithful and the ministerial priesthood (ordained ministers) are interrelated. Each of them participates in a special way in the Lord's own priesthood.

The ministerial priest, by the sacred power he enjoys, molds and rules the priestly people. Acting in the person of Christ, he brings about the eucharistic sacrifice, and offers it to God in the name of all the people. For their part, the faithful join in the offering of the eucharist by virtue of their royal priesthood. They likewise exercise that priesthood by receiving the sacraments, by prayer and thanksgiving, by the witness of a holy life, and by self-denial and active charity (*Church in the Modern World*, 10).

Bishops, priests, and deacons must proclaim and teach God's word to all people, lead the Christian community in worship, and guide and rule God's people by imitating Jesus' model of humble service.

What Are the Biblical Roots of the Sacrament of Holy Orders? *[CCC 1539-1545; 1550; 1554; 1590; 1593]*

The Jewish people, God's Chosen People, was "a kingdom of priests, a holy nation" (Ex 19:6). Yet, God chose the tribe of Levi to serve the nation at liturgical services. Besides the Levites, the priesthood of Aaron and Melchizedek and the institution of seventy elders prefigure the ordained ministry of the New Covenant.

The sacrifices and prayers offered by the priests of the original covenant could not bring about salvation. That was left to Jesus Christ, our savior, whose unique sacrifice accomplished our redemption once and for all. The eucharist makes present Jesus' saving sacrifice, and holy orders makes present the Lord's priesthood. Because Christ is present through the priesthood of ordained men, we can be assured of his graces coming to us through the sacraments. However, this does not mean that ordained ministers are free from all weakness, error, or sin. They remain human. But the ordained must strive to live their lofty vocation of serving God's people in imitation of Christ the humble servant.

Various New Testament passages attest to the sacrament of holy orders. For example, St. Paul wrote to his disciple Timothy about the laying on of hands of ordination (2 Tm 1:6) and about the office of bishop being a worthy way to serve God's people (1 Tm 3:1). Paul also directed his collaborator Titus to ordain priests to assist the church in Crete (Titus 1:5).

What Is the Special Role of Bishops? *[CCC 1555-1561; 1594]*

A **bishop** receives the fullness of the sacrament of holy orders, what church tradition has termed the "high priesthood." Consecration to the episcopal office confers the Christ-given responsibility to teach, to rule, and to sanctify. In addition, episcopal consecration impresses a sacred character, enabling bishops—successors of the apostles—to take Christ's place and represent him in his roles of teacher, shepherd, and priest.

In today's church, the pope must approve the ordination of bishops, who may be consecrated only by other bishops. This practice stresses the collegial nature of the order of bishops and their union with the bishop of Rome.

Each bishop is in charge of a local church (diocese) and is its visible head. In addition, with the college of bishops, he bears responsibility for the care and service of the universal church under the authority of the pope.

What Is the Special Role of Priests? *[CCC 1562-1568; 1595]*

Think of priests as co-workers with the bishops, their helpers and extensions in preaching the gospel, pastoring God's people, and leading the community in worship. Like the bishops to whom they are joined and under whom they serve, priests are empowered by the Holy Spirit with a sacramental character to act in the person of Christ. They do this most fully when they celebrate the eucharist, acting in the person of Christ to make the graces of his loving sacrifice present for all the faithful.

Priests represent their bishops to the local community and are bound to them in an intimate sacramental fellowship.

What Is the Special Role of Deacons? *[CCC 1569-1571; 1596]*

A **deacon** is ordained to service, not to the priesthood. Receiving their commission to serve from their bishop, deacons receive a sacramental character from their ordination, a character that configures them to Christ Jesus who came "to serve not be served."

In the Roman Catholic church, married men may be ordained to the "permanent diaconate." Deacons assist bishops and priests at liturgies, by distributing holy communion at Mass and to the sick, by proclaiming and preaching the gospel, by blessing marriages and presiding at funerals, and by engaging in a variety of other service activities for the body of Christ.

How Do the Various Roles and Ministries of Bishops, Priests, and Deacons Compare? *[CCC 1554-1571]*

The following chart compares and contrasts the various roles and ministries of the ordained orders.

BISHOP	PRIEST	DEACON
Word comes from *episkopoi* which means "overseer"	Word comes from *presbyteroi* who were "elders" in the early church and who presided over the eucharist	Word comes from *diakonoi* which means "servers"
Successor to the apostles; in union with the pope—the bishop of Rome—and other bishops; is responsible for the welfare of the whole church	Helps the bishop; is his extension into the diocese	Today, a "revived" order which can include married and single men of more mature age as well as celibate young men
Spiritual "father" of the local church/diocese	Presides at eucharist; leads the people and serves the Lord in representing the sacrifice of the cross	Ordained by a bishop; serves him and the people of God by baptizing, anointing the sick, distributing communion, teaching, conducting marriages and funerals, administering "sacramentals," doing works of charity, and perhaps doing church administrative work
Minister of all sacraments; the only one who can administer holy orders and is the normal minister of confirmation	Preaches and teaches God's word, calling on God's blessing for the people	
	Is an active agent for building the Christian community	

How Is Holy Orders Celebrated? *[CCC 1572-1574; 1597]*

Holy orders takes place within a eucharist presided over by a bishop or bishops. Representatives from all the faithful from the diocese should be present at this celebration, since it is from them that ordained ministers are called to serve the Christian community and all people everywhere. Ideally, ordination should take place on a Sunday in the cathedral of the diocese.

The essential sign of ordination for a bishop, priest, or deacon is the bishop's laying on of hands on the head of the ordinand followed by a prayer of consecration asking the Holy Spirit to shower the special graces needed for the particular ordained ministry.

To illustrate a particular celebration of holy orders, consider the ordination of priests. The candidates are called forth by name after the liturgy of the word. They are asked whether they wish to serve God's people. Each candidate responds, "I am ready and willing." The bishop elicits confirmation that the candidates are worthy to serve, and the people of God show their approval by applauding and responding "Thanks be to God."

The bishop then questions the candidates about their willingness to share in his care for God's people, in celebrating the sacraments, in preaching God's word, and in a life dedicated to God's kingdom. He asks if they are willing to obey their bishop.

Finally, ordination takes place. The bishop (and other presbyters present) lay their hands on the candidates while the bishop leads prayer. The hands of the newly ordained priests are anointed and the symbols of their office are conferred (vestments, chalice containing water and wine, a paten on which rests the bread to be consecrated). The sign of peace is exchanged. The liturgy continues with the newly ordained concelebrating with the bishop and their fellow priests.

Who May Ordain and Be Ordained? *[CCC 1552; 1575-1578; 1598; 1600]*

Christ chose his apostles to continue his work after his resurrection. The bishops are the successors of the apostles, and it is their privilege to perpetuate the "apostolic line" by ordaining other bishops and their helpers, priests and deacons. Thus, validly ordained bishops are the only ones empowered by Christ to confer the three degrees of holy orders.

Church teaching maintains that only a baptized man (male) can validly be ordained in the Catholic church. The church teaches that it *cannot* ordain women to the priesthood. Jesus, who chose only male apostles, did not ordain women, though he stressed their dignity against many repressive laws of his own day. Jesus did not even choose Mary—his mother and the greatest saint—to serve as an apostle, bishop, or priest. The apostles, those closest to Jesus during his earthly ministry, imitated Jesus when they chose only male collaborators to succeed them in their ministry.

Church teaching stresses that sacramental signs—both persons and objects—should represent what they signify by natural resemblance. The priest is a perceptible sign, "another Christ." He represents the Lord when he presents to God the prayer of the church, especially the eucharistic sacrifice. Because Christ was a male, the priest must be a male.

The church teaches that these reasons reflect Christ's intention concerning ordination. To clear up confusion, Pope John Paul II told the world's bishops in a "definitive statement" (*On Reserving Priestly Ordination to Men Alone* [*Ordinatio Sacerdotalis*]) that the church has no authority to ordain women to the priesthood. This decision is not sexist, as some people charge. Rather, it results from the church's sincere effort to follow Christ's teaching.

Priesthood is a gift that Jesus Christ gives to his church. It is not a *right* that anyone deserves, but a call by God to serve the church in a particular way. Many other ministries are open to women and men. Through baptism, we become members of Christ's body, sharing a basic dignity as God's adopted daughters and sons. The Holy Spirit showers us with many gifts, especially the gift of love which enables us to live and serve as Christ's brothers and sisters.

Why Does Church Law Require Priestly Celibacy? *[CCC 1579-1580; 1599]*

Church law requires priests and bishops (but not deacons) of the Latin Catholic church not to marry. This is known as priestly **celibacy**. Priests and bishops undertake this discipline freely to express their wholehearted commitment to serve both God and God's people. The following four reasons are generally offered for this practice.

St. Paul noted that celibacy gives a person more freedom to serve Christ. Not having a family to worry about, a priest is both more free to serve others and more able to attach himself wholeheartedly to the Lord. Second, giving up a family is a concrete witness to the sacrifices in the name of the gospel asked by Jesus of some of his followers:

> "And everyone who has left houses, brothers, sisters, father, mother, children or land for the sake of my name will receive a hundred times as much, and also inherit eternal life" (Mt 19:29).

Third, and perhaps most important, by living as a loving celibate person, a priest is in reality pointing to eternal life when there will be no marriage. His life is a witness, in the middle of the ordinary affairs and concerns of the world, that we are all destined for union with God.

Finally, there is the witness of Jesus himself who did not marry so that he could be totally involved in doing God's will in serving others.

The Eastern churches have permitted a different discipline, allowing married men to be ordained as deacons *and* priests, though bishops are chosen from among celibates.

What Are the Effects of the Sacrament of Holy Orders? [CCC 1581-1589]

Holy orders, like baptism and confirmation, confers an indelible spiritual character that configures those ordained to Christ and enables them to act for the Lord in his triple office of priest, prophet, and king.

In addition, the Holy Spirit gives bishops the graces necessary to guide properly and defend their churches with prudence and strength, and with the love necessary to reach out in a special way to the poor, sick, and needy. The graces of this sacrament also impel bishops to proclaim the gospel to everyone, to live upright and exemplary lives, and to embrace the eucharist as the primary way to identify with Jesus.

The Spirit showers priests with the gifts to proclaim the gospel truthfully, to offer spiritual gifts and sacrifices, and to draw others to the faith through preaching, baptism, and example.

The Spirit imparts to deacons the graces for the service of the liturgy, gospel, and various works of charity. Holy orders dedicates deacons to serve God's people under the direction of bishops and in cooperation with priests.

Holy orders does not automatically guarantee the personal holiness of those ordained. It is Christ who accomplishes salvation through his ordained ministers. Their unworthiness cannot prevent him from acting. Christ's ordained ministers must dedicate their lives to ongoing conversion, to union with the Lord Jesus. They do so by exercising the virtues, especially love, humility, fidelity, obedience, devotion to the eucharist, and a forgiving heart toward people.

What Is the Sacrament of Matrimony? [CCC 1601; 1660]

In the sacrament of matrimony a baptized man and woman vow their love in an exclusive, permanent, sexual partnership. This union is marked by love, respect, care and concern, and a commitment to share responsibility in the raising of a family if God should bless them with children.

Christian marriage is an extraordinary sign of God working through and in the ordinary. Christ Jesus has raised marriage to the dignity of a sacrament. Simply put, a good marriage is not simply a *civil contract* between two persons; rather, it is a holy covenant involving three persons. The couple is joined on their life's journey by Jesus Christ who promises to bless, sustain, and rejoice in their union.

What Does the Old Testament Say About Marriage? *[CCC 1602-1608]*

The vocation of marriage is written in the very nature of men and women who are created by a God of infinite love. Original sin, however, taints God's intent for the harmonious loving between men and women. Thus, men and women must seek God's grace to achieve the loving unity God intends for them.

Through the period of the original Covenant, there was a gradual growth in understanding of the meaning of marriage. In early times polygamy was tolerated; husbands could freely divorce their wives (who were often treated as property); and a married man could have sexual relations with an unmarried woman and not be accused of adultery. By the time the book of Genesis was written, however, God revealed to the Jewish people two profound truths about the *purposes* of marriage. First, marriage is a share in God's creative act of bringing new life into the world. Second, marriage is meant to enhance, celebrate, and increase the love between the wife and husband.

Genesis tells us that Yahweh established marriage and sex and declared that they are good and are meant for the procreation of human life.

> God created man in the image of himself,
> in the image of God he created him,
> male and female he created them.
> God blessed them, saying to them, "Be fruitful, multiply, fill the earth and subdue it." . . .
> God saw all that he had made, and indeed it was very good (Gn 1:27-28, 31).

Genesis also reveals the other major purpose of marriage: companionship between friends who share the same life and love:

> This one at last is bone of my bones and flesh of my flesh! She is to be called Woman, because she was taken from Man. That is

why a man leaves his father and mother and becomes attached to his wife, and they become one flesh (Gn 2:23-24).

God fully intends a permanent, exclusive, monogamous relationship between man and woman who have been created in the divine image.

How Does Marriage Mirror God's Love for Us? *[CCC 1609-1611]*

Divine mercy would not allow God to forsake humans tainted by sin. Although pain in childbirth and the need to toil by "the sweat of your brow" were two effects of original sin, God uses marriage to help man and woman "to overcome self-absorption, egoism, pursuit of one's own pleasure, and to open oneself to the other, to mutual aid and to self-giving" (CCC 1609).

The prophets use marriage as an image to describe Yahweh's great love for his people, Israel.

I shall betroth you to myself for ever,
I shall betroth you in uprightness and justice,
and faithful love and tenderness (Hos 2:21)

The prophet Malachi forcefully states the ideal:

Yahweh stands as witness between you and the wife of your youth, with whom you have broken faith, even though she was your partner and your wife by covenant. Did he not create a single being, having flesh and the breath of life? (Mal 2:14-15).

Proverbs paints a picture of an ideal wife: "She is clothed in strength and dignity" (Prv 31:25). The books of Ruth and Tobit highlight the fidelity and tenderness of spouses. The Song of Songs describes love between a bride and a bridegroom. Because God has blessed marriage, affectionate, erotic love between a man and woman is something good and holy and joyful.

What Does the New Testament Reveal About Marriage? *[CCC 1613-1616; 1659]*

The New Testament reveals further important insights into the nature of marriage. Jesus' attendance at the wedding feast of Cana underscores the goodness and naturalness of marriage. When Jesus teaches about marriage, he reaffirms the original intention of his Father—that marriage should be a permanent, exclusive love relationship:

"Everyone who divorces his wife and marries another is guilty of adultery, and the man who marries a woman divorced by her husband commits adultery" (Lk 16:18).

Jesus shows his profound respect for human dignity when he teaches that looking at a woman lustfully is the equivalent of committing adultery (Mt 5:27-28). Motives and interior attitudes are important to him.

The early church also regarded marriage highly. St. Paul, for example, supplies a key teaching on marriage:

> In the same way, husbands must love their wives as they love their own bodies; for a man to love his wife is for him to love himself. A man never hates his own body, but he feeds it and looks after it; and that is the way Christ treats the Church, because we are parts of his Body. . . . This mystery has great significance, but I am applying it to Christ and the Church (Eph 5:28-32).

The union of a husband and wife is like the union of Christ with his church. St. Paul calls this reality a *mystery* (a word translated by St. Augustine as "sacrament"). Christian marriage is an external sign of Christ's love. Marriage is a covenant, a total lifelong commitment that mirrors Christ's love for his church.

How Is Marriage a Covenant? *[CCC 1612; 1617; 1661]*

The church teaches us that the sacrament of marriage mirrors God's covenant of love with his people. By giving us his Son, the Father loves us freely and faithfully keeps his promises to us. Jesus—the greatest sign of God's love—draws us into community, showers us with unexpected gifts, relates to us as unique individuals, and invites us to grow in love by serving others.

In the covenant of Christian marriage, a husband and wife freely bind themselves together for life. Theirs is an open-ended commitment to love exclusively. No time conditions or any other conditions are put on their relationship. In sickness or health, in poverty or wealth, in good times and in bad times, the couple promises to be faithful. A marriage covenant commitment mirrors God's unconditional love for his people. If a man and woman insist on certain conditions when getting married, they are simply engaged in a legal contract.

In Christian marriage love is freely given and faithfully weathers the trials that come its way. Christian marriage is life-giving because through it God gives the married couple the privilege of procreating life.

It is full of surprises, providing countless opportunities to grow in holiness.

It is a concrete way to live the Christian life of love and service in the context of family living.

It is a place to receive the Lord who showers the couple with the graces to love each other with the very love he has for the church. These graces perfect the human love of the spouses, strengthen their indissoluble unity, and sanctify them on their journey to eternal life.

How Is the Sacrament of Matrimony Celebrated? *[CCC 1621-1624; 1663]*

In the Latin rite, the spouses are the ministers of the sacrament. They mutually confer the sacrament on one another by expressing their consent to be married. The sacrament of Christian marriage usually takes place during a eucharistic celebration. By having a wedding with Mass, the couple celebrates their spousal love as a reflection of the sacrificial love that the Lord has for the couple and the church. Also, because the marriage ceremony should be valid, worthy, and fruitful, the church highly recommends that the couple prepare for it by confessing their sins in the sacrament of reconciliation beforehand.

The wedding liturgy includes an entrance procession, greeting, prayers, readings, and homily. After this, the priest questions the couple concerning their freedom in choosing marriage, their desire to be faithful, and their willingness to have and rear children. The bridal couple then exchanges vows in the presence of the priest, two witnesses, and the assembled Christian community. The groom and bride join hands and in turn verbalize their consent. They promise to be true in good times and bad, in sickness and in health, and to love and honor each other until death.

As the church's official witness, the priest blesses the rings and asks the couple to exchange them as symbols of fidelity and unending love. The liturgy of the eucharist proceeds as usual with the nuptial blessing given after the Lord's Prayer.

When a man and woman exchange their vows, the church witnesses, blesses, and celebrates their covenant promises. However, the sacrament of marriage is not just a one-day affair; it unfolds over the years as the husband and wife live out their mutual relationship with each other and the Lord. The risen Lord promises to be with the couple to sustain them on their life journey. He sanctifies sexual love, a most powerful sign of total, exclusive, intimate sharing. He sustains the couple in the ordinary give-and-take of family life. He empowers them to be signs of love to each other, their children, and to all their friends and acquaintances. Through their daily love and fidelity, they will meet the Lord who lives within them by the power of the Holy Spirit. The celebration of Christian marriage is "till death do us part."

What Are the Requirements for a Valid Marriage? *[CCC 1625-1631; 1662]*

To celebrate the sacrament of marriage validly, the couple must be of mature age, unmarried, not closely related by blood or marriage, and freely consent to marry. Freedom of consent means that neither party is under constraint nor impeded by any natural or church law.

The exchange of consent is the indispensable element that makes the marriage valid. This consent, in which the parties freely give themselves to each other, must be free of coercion or grave external fear. If freedom is lacking, then the marriage never really exists.

Consent means that a couple commits themselves to a lifelong covenant of love. Furthermore, the spouses must be capable of sharing sexually since sexual intercourse is a sign of mutual love and union, the full expression of the mutual love between husband and wife. Finally, the couple must be open to the possibility of raising a family if God blesses the marriage with children.

In the Latin rite, the ministers of the sacrament of Christian marriage are the bride and bridegroom themselves. Because marriage is an ecclesial reality, church law requires that a Catholic couple exchange their vows before a priest and two other witnesses. Exchanging vows publicly helps the spouses remain faithful to their commitments.

How Does a Couple Prepare for Marriage? *[CCC 1632-1637]*

Marriage is important not only to the couple but to the church and society as a whole. For this reason, the church puts a great emphasis on suitable marriage preparations. The witness of loving parents and families is critical, but so are the catechetical efforts of pastors and the parish community.

Preparation for a Christian marriage in most dioceses includes a policy that the engaged couple participate in a marriage preparation conference, retreat, or workshop. These church-sponsored "classes" give the couple an opportunity to learn about what the sacramental commitment entails from a priest and members of the community, including couples who are living the sacrament. During the period of preparation, a priest or other parish minister will continue to meet with the couple to prepare them for the serious commitment they are about to make. Topics examined in these meetings include communication skills, parenting issues, the role of a faith life in marriage, and plans for the actual ceremony.

When a Catholic marries a non-Catholic Christian (a mixed marriage), special attention is paid the situation by the couple and the pastor. When a Catholic marries a non-baptized person (disparity of denomination), an express dispensation must be granted for the marriage to be valid. The Catholic partner promises to continue to live his or her Catholic faith and have his or her children baptized and raised in the Catholic faith. The non-Catholic partner is made aware of this pledge, but is not required to make any promises. Both partners must know and not exclude the essential purposes and qualities of marriage.

The banns (announcements) of marriage are usually printed in the parish bulletin for three consecutive weeks before the wedding ceremony. The reason for the publication and reading of the banns is to notify the Christian community of the impending celebration and to give informed parties the opportunity to come forward if they know any reason the sacrament of marriage should not take place.

When one of the parties is a non-Catholic, special permission can be obtained from the local bishop and pastor for a minister of another faith to participate in the marriage ceremony. In extraordinary circumstances a dispensation might be given for a minister of another faith to witness the exchange of vows.

What Is an Annulment? [CCC 1629]

An **annulment** is an official declaration of the Catholic church that what appeared to be a valid Christian marriage in fact was not. A couple may have entered the marriage psychologically immature or lacking true understanding of the demands a marriage covenant makes. One or both partners might not have given free, true consent to the marriage. Perhaps one or both partners intended never to have children. Possibly one or both partners were incapable of sexual relations.

A "failed" marriage may never have been a true Christian marriage to begin with. In these cases the couple should submit their situation to the diocesan marriage tribunal (court) for examination and judgment. If it can be shown that the marriage was not valid from the beginning, then the individuals involved are free to enter a true Christian marriage in the future.

What Are the Principal Effects of the Sacrament of Matrimony? *[CCC 1638-1642]*

Christ's love sanctifies the love of the husband and wife in the sacrament of marriage. Once the marriage is consummated, an irrevocable, perpetual, and exclusive bond results between the spouses who freely consented to become lifelong partners. Their relationship is covenantal, not simply contractual, in which the Lord showers his graces to perfect their love and strengthen their unity. A major fruit of their life in common is the welcoming of any children God may send them. Their life together, along with their efforts to rear and educate their children in a family setting, is the primary means for a married couple to attain holiness.

What Are the Essential Qualities of a Christian Marriage? *[CCC 1643-1645; 1652-1654; 1664]*

Christian marriage involves a total commitment of a couple's bodies, feelings, affections, hearts, wills, and spirits. It results in a deep unity of body, heart, and soul. As a result, marriage demands indissolubility, fidelity, and openness to fertility. Practices contrary to these essential goods include polygamy, which destroys the exclusivity of marriage and undermines the dignity of the man and woman; **divorce**, which ends up separating what God has joined together; and refusal of fertility, which deflects marriage from its greatest gift—children.

Married love is a great gift from God. Sexual sharing in a marriage is a profound means of love and commitment between a man and a woman. Its purpose in God's plan is twofold: *unitive*, that is, to bond a man and woman together as partners for life; and *procreative*, that is, to share in God's creative activity of bringing new life into the world. Children are the crowning gifts of marriage, contributing to the good of the mother and father. Marriage and the family are the exemplars of God's gift of life and are at the service of life.

Why Is Christian Marriage a Permanent Commitment? *[CCC 1646-1651; 1665]*

The example of permanent marriage commitment is a prime way to bring Christ into the world. This is concretely true for the children who result from the marriage. Children first encounter the love and knowledge of God from their parents and are, in fact, living symbols of their parents' love. Children need the stable, reassuring love of a solid marriage to develop healthy attitudes to life and to God.

But a faithful marriage is a powerful sign to those outside of the immediate family as well. Just as God's love is unconditional and forever, so the Christian husband and wife strive for this ideal in their lives together. Their fidelity and exclusive love is an extraordinary sign to the world of God's fidelity and undying love for his people.

Jesus himself underscored the permanence of the marriage bond:

> "Have you not read that the Creator from the beginning *made them male and female* and that he said: *This is why a man leaves his father and mother and becomes attached to his wife, and the two become one flesh?* They are no longer two, therefore, but one flesh. So then, what God has united, human beings must not divide" (Mt 19:4-6).

Thus the Catholic church does not permit divorce and remarriage because Jesus forbade it. The covenant made between two validly married Catholics can only be dissolved by the death of one of the partners. In extraordinary circumstances a couple may separate for the good of the children and the individuals involved. Though the civil authority may dissolve the legal aspects of a valid marriage (called in civil law a divorce), the state has no authority to dissolve a true Christian marriage—its true sacramental nature.

According to church teaching, a legally separated Catholic (divorced under civil law) may not remarry while his or her spouse is alive. This teaching is consistent with the Lord's teaching, "Everyone who divorces his wife and marries another is guilty of adultery" (Lk 16:18). Christ calls his disciples to high standards. Moreover, he gives them the graces to live his commands. The church encourages a person who is suffering from a broken marriage to continue to celebrate the sacraments and remain close to the Christian community. The Lord promises in a special way to bless those who suffer most. Fellow Christians should support hurting brothers and sisters, pray for them, and follow the teaching of the Lord by not judging them.

What Does the Church Say About Family Living? *[CCC 1655-1658; 1666]*

To be sure, the church today clearly considers Christian marriage and family living a primary means to holiness. The family is, in fact, the "domestic church," a center of living faith. According to the Second Vatican Council document, *Constitution on the Church in the Modern World:*

The Christian family, which springs from marriage as a reflection of the loving covenant uniting Christ with the Church, and as a participation in that covenant, will manifest to all men the Savior's living presence in the world, and the genuine nature of the Church. This the family will do by the mutual love of the spouses, by their generous fruitfulness, their solidarity and faithfulness, and by the loving way in which all members of the family work together (48).

These lofty ideals require a Catholic couple to make their family the number one priority in their lives. Married couples know from experience that they have to construct their marriage on trust, forgiveness, and a genuine desire to make it a real sign of love. They take seriously their commitment to remain faithful until death separates them. Because of the stresses in our fast-paced, materialistic society, wise couples know the value of prayer, developing a personal relationship with the Lord, and staying close to him in the eucharist. Today's church supports marriages through various retreat programs like Marriage Encounter, parish renewals, enrichment programs, and seminars.

Finally, the church also remembers in its pastoral care childless couples and single people. Those who cannot have children for whatever reason can still enjoy a married life full of love and meaning. Those with a call to the single life should always find a family of love and support in the parish community.

Concluding Reflections

Christian ministry is the urgent work of the church today. No Catholic can "pass the buck" when it comes to service. Vatican II rightly pointed out that the laity has always had a special vocation of engaging in temporal affairs and ordering them according to God's plan (*Church in the Modern World*, 31). General Christian ministry includes work on behalf of peace and justice, resolution of social, political and economic conflicts, work on behalf of the poor, the oppressed, all the "little ones." We serve Christ when we bring the gospel to the marketplace. But Vatican II also reminds us that:

As sharers in the role of Christ the Priest, the Prophet, and the King, the laity have an active part to play in the life and activity of the Church (Decree on the Apostolate to the Laity, 10).

Married couples minister in a special way to each other and to their children as they help form the "domestic church." The sacrament of matrimony celebrates the great vocation to love as Christ loves and to serve each other in the context of family living.

The ordained ministry is a special vocation of service. Those who generously respond to this vocation are a sign to all God's people of the presence of the kingdom. We live in an age when the ordained ministry and the religious life are especially countercultural. All Catholics have the duty to support and encourage our bishops, priests, and deacons. Furthermore, we can encourage our young people to consider the possibility that God might be calling them to the religious life. Praying for religious vocations and for generous hearts among God's people is itself an important ministry in today's church.

Prayer Reflection

The petitions in this much-beloved Prayer for Peace attributed to St. Francis Assisi apply in a special way to those whose lives are dedicated to serving God in holy orders or Christian marriage.

> Lord, make me an instrument of your peace.
> Where there is hatred, let me sow love;
> where there is injury, pardon;
> where there is doubt, faith;
> where there is despair, hope;
> where there is darkness, light;
> where there is sadness, joy.
> O Divine Master, grant that I may not seek so much
> to be consoled as to console;
> to be understood, as to understand,
> to be loved, as to love.
> For it is in giving that we receive,
> it is in pardoning that we are pardoned,
> and it is in dying that we are born to eternal life.

For Discussion

1. What common characteristics would you like to see in all Christian ministers?
2. How is Christian ministry related to holy orders?
3. What can you do in a concrete way to further vocations to the priesthood and religious life and to support those who are serving in the ordained ministry?
4. What advice would you give a couple contemplating marriage?

5. Why is fidelity a key virtue in marriage? How does it mirror God's covenant love? How does the church's teaching in regard to sexual morality support this virtue?

Further Reading

Jeremiah 1 (the call of the prophet)
Acts 9:1-16 (the call of Paul)
Matthew 25:31-46 (Christian service)
Song of Songs
1 Peter 3:1-9 (harmonious family living)

Part 3:

Life in Christ

Living a Christian life means living in Christ himself. As Christ always did what was pleasing to the Father, so too are we his disciples, called to point our lives in the direction of God in order to seek the perfection Christ craves for us.

Christian morality, then, is to live a "life in Christ." As the *Catechism of the Catholic Church* reminds us:

> The way of Christ "leads to life"; a contrary way "leads to destruction." The Gospel parable of the two ways remains ever present in the catechesis of the Church; it shows the importance of moral decisions for our salvation: "There are two ways, the one of life, the other of death; but between the two, there is a great difference" (1696).

Part 3 examines some foundational themes of Christian morality—the dignity of the human person; the role of the Holy Spirit who lives within as a sure guide; the function of grace in the Christian life; the Beatitudes; sin and forgiveness; the human and theological virtues; the centrality of love of God, neighbor, and self; and the support of the Christian community as a help to grow and develop as moral beings (CCC 1691-1697).

Christian morality helps us live as imitators of our brother and savior, Jesus Christ. Its principles instruct us on how to conform our thoughts, words, and actions to him who is our example. Jesus is the first and last point of reference for Christian morality; he is "the way and the truth and the life" (Jn 14:6 *NAB*, cf. CCC 1698). Christian morality is simply being who we are as God's children and brothers and sisters to the Lord. In the words of St. Paul, "Life to me . . . is Christ" (Phil 1:21).

Chapter Seventeen

Foundations of Catholic Morality

After all, brothers, you were called to be free; do not use your freedom as an opening for self-indulgence, but be servants to one another in love, since the whole of the Law is summarized in the one commandment: You must love your neighbor as yourself. If you go snapping at one another and tearing one another to pieces, take care: you will be eaten up by one another.
— Galatians 5:13-15

There is a story told about a searcher who was seeking out spiritual wisdom. He heard about a renowned spiritual Master; he approached one of the Master's disciples:

"What miracles has your Master worked?" he said . . . "Well, there are miracles and miracles. In your land it is regarded as a miracle if God does someone's will. In our country it is regarded as a miracle if someone does the will of God."[1]

Christians should live in the land of miracles of the second type: doing the will of God. Doing God's will is the source of personal holiness and happiness.

Christianity is more than a set of beliefs; it is a way of living. Christian faith must result in a life of loving service or it is an empty faith. This chapter explores some of the basic concepts of Catholic morality and issues in Christian living.

What Is Christian Morality? [*CCC 1731-1738*]

Christian morality is *responsibility in love*. First, it is a *response* to God's freely given love and the gift of salvation offered to us through Jesus Christ. However, salvation is a gift that we cannot earn. We can only accept it and live our lives according to God's will.

God, however, respects our freedom. He does not thrust salvation on us as though we were mere puppets. God extends divine love to us, but we are free to respond or not. Christian morality comes to the forefront when people say "yes" to God, when they freely respond to his love by loving in return. The essence of Christian morality is, simply, love. Reflect on the words of Jesus:

> "You must love the Lord your God with all your heart, with all your soul, and with all your mind. This is the greatest and the first commandment. The second resembles it: You must love your neighbor as yourself" (Mt 22:37-39).

Second, Christian morality is the *ability* to respond to God, the ability to love, the ability to say yes to God. This is also a gift, also freely bestowed on us. It is part of what it means to be a human being.

What Does It Mean to Be Human? *[CCC 1699-1715]*

Humans are made in God's image and likeness, conformed to Christ Jesus who is "the image of the invisible God." Because God makes us in the divine image, we are beings of incomparable worth, endowed with a human soul with its two magnificent powers—intellect and free will. Humans are the only beings on earth that God created for our own sakes, destining us from the very moment of conception for eternal beatitude, that is, happiness.

The human intellect enables us to recognize and understand God's command to do good and avoid evil. Free will enables us to choose good with the guidance of our conscience and to obey God's law of love. In seeking and loving truth and goodness, we humans find our perfection and happiness.

In a perfect world, our intellects and wills would be wholly attuned to God's will. However, original sin has weakened us, inclining us to commit evil by making bad judgments and by choosing lesser goods. Jesus has freed us from Satan and sin, giving us a new life in the Holy Spirit. Baptism and faith in Jesus as our Lord and Guide make us the children of God. This adoption into God's family imparts in us Christ's life, enables us to live morally, and merits for us an eternal reward in heaven.

What Is the Purpose of Human Existence? *[CCC 1718-1724; 1728-1729]*

We are created by God out of total love so that we can come to know, to love, and to serve God in this life on earth and to be eternally happy with God in heaven. God made us to be happy and to partake of divine nature, that is, to enter into the glory of Christ and the Trinitarian life.

The happiness or "beatitude" God intends for us is pure gift. It goes by various names—the coming of God's kingdom, the vision of God, entering into the joy of the Lord, entering into God's rest. God has implanted in our hearts a keen desire for happiness. This desire draws us to the Lord who alone can help us attain it.

To find the happiness for which we were made requires pure and decisive moral choices on our part. The Ten Commandments, the teaching of the apostles, and the Sermon on the Mount (especially the Beatitudes) are sure and steady norms to help us to our ultimate goal of union with God. With the Holy Spirit's grace and Christ-centered living, we can attain the happiness (beatitude) for which we were created.

What Are the Beatitudes? *[CCC 1716; 1725-1727]*

The Beatitudes summarize the morality followers of Jesus should strive to live in response to both God and neighbor. They introduce and capsulize the essence of New Testament morality found in the Sermon on the Mount (Mt 5–7).

Jesus did not give a detailed list of rules and regulations. Rather, he taught attitudes of being (listed below) that his followers should have in relationship to other people and to God.

How blessed are the poor in spirit:
the kingdom of Heaven is theirs.
Blessed are *the gentle:*
they shall have the earth as inheritance.
Blessed are those who mourn:
they shall be comforted.
Blessed are those who hunger and thirst for uprightness:
they shall have their fill.
Blessed are the merciful:
they shall have mercy shown them.
Blessed are the pure in heart:
they shall see God.
Blessed are the peacemakers:
they shall be recognized as children of God.
Blessed are those who are persecuted in the cause of uprightness:
the kingdom of Heaven is theirs (Mt 5:3-10).

The Beatitudes fulfill the promises which God made to Abraham and show us the way to achieve the desire for happiness God implanted in our hearts. They teach how to attain, with God's grace, the gift of eternal destiny as sons and daughters of a loving Triune God whose life we are gratuitously called to share.

How Can We Understand the Beatitudes? *[CCC 1716-1717]*

The Beatitudes are at the heart of Jesus' preaching (CCC 1716). They can be understood as follows:

How blessed are the poor in spirit: the kingdom of heaven is theirs. Jesus showed that God's reign had broken into human history by his proclamation of the gospel to the poor. In a special way, he loved and associated with the downtrodden, the poor, the unfortunate. He wants us to do so, too.

Jesus is not praising the condition of poverty but an attitude of vulnerability, openness, and trust before God the provider of all. Poverty of spirit translates into humility which recognizes that everything we have—our lives, intelligence, education, possessions—are gifts from a loving God. We show our gratitude when we share what God has given us. Generosity is a true sign that we recognize that God is our source and our destiny. We give back to God when we give to others.

Blessed are the gentle: they shall have the earth as inheritance. The biblical notion of "meek and gentle" means "unassuming, tolerant, and patient." Jesus exemplified well this virtue by accepting everyone with compassion and gentility.

God is patient with us in our sinfulness. We imitate Jesus' example when we accept the dignity of others and when we suffer with them in their human weaknesses. Gentle persons humbly work to solve problems without hatred, rancor, ill-will, or violence.

Blessed are those who mourn: they shall be comforted. A complacent society lets immorality seduce it into thinking that everything is OK. If, however, we take to heart the message of this beatitude, then we will surely lament that not all is well in the world. Our hearts and spirits ache for the sins of the world and for our own sins, too. The Lord promises, though, that in the midst of our difficulties and our mourning, consolation will eventually be ours.

Blessed are those who hunger and thirst for uprightness: they shall have their fill. St. Augustine wrote, "Our hearts were made for you, O Lord, and they are restless until they rest in you." In this beatitude, Jesus is praising those who realize that only God and God's uprightness (or righteousness) can fulfill us. We are created to seek divine justice, a good relationship with God. We seek the Father's holiness and the nurturing sustenance of Christ's patient and forgiving friendship.

Catholics especially appreciate the eucharist as a concrete way to grow in holiness and righteousness.

Blessed are the merciful: they shall have mercy shown them. In the Lord's Prayer we ask God to forgive us as we forgive others. The Father loves us without our ever deserving it. He compassionately forgives our sins and accepts us into the divine family as adopted children. In return, he asks us to extend mercy, love, and forgiveness to one another. When we forgive those who have hurt us, even our enemies, we show that God is loving and merciful and cares for us all.

Blessed are the pure in heart: they shall see God. The pure or clean in heart have a single-hearted commitment to God. This beatitude tells us that nothing should distract us from God. Job, family, friends, reputation are all good, but they should play a secondary role in our lives. Seeking and accomplishing God's will are the primary duties of a disciple of Jesus Christ.

Blessed are the peacemakers: they shall be recognized as children of God. Lives lived in love and peace are the twin signs of being God's adopted children. Christians must neither seek nor cause conflict. Moreover, they have the duty to unite those who are in strife, disharmony, or opposition by helping them realize our common brotherhood and sisterhood with Jesus Christ. Jesus was a peacemaker, and we should be, too.

Blessed are those who are persecuted in the cause of uprightness: the kingdom of heaven is theirs. There is no greater sign of our union with our Lord than being willing to suffer for him. Jesus' words and deeds brought him misunderstanding and abuse. To be Christian means to be willing to stand up for our convictions, even if this means rejection, abuse, or martyrdom. The reward which Jesus promises his sincere disciples is nothing less than heaven and the eternal happiness it brings.

How Does Human Freedom Relate to Responsibility? *[CCC 1730-1748]*

God created us in the divine image and endowed us with an intellect and free will. Freedom is a power that flows from our capacities to think and to choose. It enables us to act or not to act, that is, to perform deliberate actions for which we are responsible. If we exercise our freedom in conformity with God's law, we are doing good and becoming truly free. If we turn away from God's will, we abuse our gift of freedom and become slaves to sin.

We are responsible for our actions to the degree that they are voluntary. Imputability (blameworthiness) for actions can be lessened or negated by ignorance, inattention, force, fear, habit, inordinate attachments, or other psychological and social factors.

We exercise our freedom in relationships to others. As beings of incomparable worth and dignity, we have an inalienable right to exercise our freedom, especially in religious and moral matters. Civil authorities have the duty to recognize and protect this fundamental human right within the limits of the common good and public order.

True freedom is not license to do or say whatever we want. As limited beings, humans have misused and misdirected their freedom. Our first parents made a bad choice to turn from God; their original sin has infected human history ever since. Choosing self over God or others, making power or money or sex or a similar lesser "good" into a "god"—these have caused great harm to individuals and to the human family. Such choices make us the slaves to sin.

The antidote to the slavery of sin is the cross of Christ which has set us truly free. To help us choose wisely, the risen Lord has given us abundant graces and the gift of the Holy Spirit. These gifts are the source of strength we need to attain inner freedom, the kind of freedom that helps us choose God, who is supremely good and the true source of human happiness.

How Is the Morality of Human Actions Evaluated? *[CCC 1749-1761]*

We can judge whether an action is good or evil by reflecting on the three *sources* of morality: the object chosen, the intention (or end), and the circumstances.

The *object* is the "matter" of the human act, the "what" we do. An example of a good act would be volunteering our time at a hospice; an example of an evil act would be tearing down another's reputation. Objective norms of morality determine if an act is good or evil, whether it is for a person's ultimate good or not, whether it conforms to God's will or goes against it. Our reason and conscience help us discover the truth of these norms. Certain actions, like blasphemy, perjury, murder, and adultery, are always seriously wrong because they always involve moral evil, a disorder of the will. Neither good motives for performing such actions nor circumstances surrounding them can *ever* justify them.

Rooted in an act of the will, the *intention* is one's purpose or motive for acting. It answers the question "why" one does a particular act. One's intention can be involved in a series of actions or several motives can be involved in the same act. A key principle of Catholic morality centers on the role of intention: *A good intention can never make an intrinsically evil action good. The end does not justify the means.* For example, killing an innocent human being by having an abortion to protect the woman's reputation is seriously wrong. The good motive (saving a reputation) can never justify the evil act (abortion). Furthermore, a bad intention can turn a good act into an evil one. An example is the giving of money to the poor (almsgiving) for the sole reason of being commended or praised (pride).

Circumstances are secondary elements of a moral act—the how, who, when, where of the act. They can contribute to the goodness or the evil of an act. For example the more money stolen, the greater the evil. Circumstances can also lessen or heighten a person's blameworthiness for a particular act. However, they cannot change an evil act into a good one. Thus, neglecting to help a person in need is un-Christian and evil. But if fear kept one from doing so, the person's culpability could be diminished.

An excellent principle of Christian morality is expressed this way: *For an act to be morally good, the object, end (purpose), and circumstance must* **all** *be good. What* one does (the object) must be good; at the same time, *why* (the intention) one does it and the circumstances of the act must also be good. It is wrong to judge the morality of an action based only on one's motivation or on the context and circumstances. *We can never do evil so good can come from it.*

> The primary and decisive element for moral judgment is the object of the human act, which establishes whether it is capable of being ordered to the good and to the ultimate end, which is God (Pope John Paul II, Splendor of Truth, 79).

How Can Emotions Affect the Choices We Make? *[CCC 1762-1775]*

In traditional Catholic morality, emotions are referred to as the **passions**, that is, feelings that incline us to act or not to act towards something we feel or imagine to be good or evil. Love and hatred, desire and fear, joy and sadness, and anger are all examples of these passions. These feelings are morally neutral, neither good nor bad. Passions derive their moral quality based on how our reason and will govern them. Thus, they become morally good when they help us do a good act; they become evil if they lead us into an evil act. For example, anger at an unjust situation that causes one to get involved in politics in order to correct it is good. But anger that leads one to a violent action is evil and against the good of humans.

Strong feelings have no inherent connection to one's holiness. However, they can be taken up by the virtues to help us do good or perverted by vices that lead us away from God.

What Is Conscience? *[CCC 1776-1782; 1795-1797]*

Conscience is a practical judgment of reason enabling us to discern whether an action or attitude is good or evil. It is an ability to discover God's will for us. In the depths of our conscience, we are alone with God whose voice echoes in our hearts. The right to follow one's conscience is fundamental, especially in religious matters.

Another way to view conscience is that within us there is an inner dialogue with God who calls us to be the persons we are intended to be—his children. To hear God's voice requires a certain degree of *interiority*, a quality of quieting down and examining our lives before God.

Conscience includes the ability to perceive the principles of morality, their application to the given circumstances by discerning reasons and goods, and the judgment about the morality of concrete acts ready to be performed or already performed. Because of our conscience, we can assume responsibility for our actions. And when we sin, our conscience calls us to repent and return to the Lord.

There are two key principles to keep in mind when dealing with judging right and wrong. First, we must properly form our consciences. Second, we must follow our consciences.

> In the depths of his conscience, man detects a law which he does not impose upon himself, but which holds him to obedience. Always summoning him to love good and do it and to avoid evil, the voice of conscience can when necessary speak to his heart more specifically: do this, shun that. For man has in his heart a law written by God. To obey it is the very dignity of man: according to it he will be judged (Pastoral Constitution on the Church in the Modern World, 16).

Must We Always Follow Our Consciences? *[CCC 1790-1794; 1799-1801]*

We must always obey the certain judgment of our conscience. To deliberately act against it is to sin. This duty to obey our conscience underscores the necessity of properly forming it. This is because all of us can make mistakes when we are left to ourselves. Many factors can help cloud a conscience and make it difficult to distinguish right from wrong. It is possible to have an erroneous conscience.

Ignorance, simply not knowing or being told the right thing to do or the wrong thing to avoid, can cause us to make false judgments. Sometimes we are not responsible for ignorance (called invincible ignorance) and consequently are not morally blameworthy for a

mistaken judgment. Other times we are responsible for not knowing because we made little effort to find out what is true and good
or we allowed ourselves to be blinded by the habit of sin. *Emotions*
can cloud our conscience. We may be tempted to do things because
they feel good, but feeling good does not necessarily mean the actions are right. Being blinded to passions can help to contribute to
an erroneous conscience. *Conformity* to what others are doing or following their bad example can also muddy our decisions. Just
because everyone else is doing something does not make it right.
Other possible sources of error in forming an upright conscience
could include ignorance of Jesus and his teaching, a belief that the
individual is supreme and does not need the guidance of anyone
else in making moral decisions, a lack of love or repentance, and a
refusal to follow the teaching of the church's magisterium.

A sincere Christian will take steps to find out the right thing to
do, to clear up doubts before making a decision, and to correct a
badly formed conscience. He or she will also avoid those situations
where experience has taught that strong emotions have a tendency
to destroy the freedom to choose the good thing. The mature Christian knows that doing the right thing often means standing against
the crowd. Finally, true faith grounded in Christ's love enlightens a
good and true conscience.

How Do We Form Our Consciences? *[CCC 1783-1789; 1798; 1802]*

A Christian conscience is both truthful and true. Consequently,
it brings peace. Its formation is a lifelong task. Its education will be
in harmony with reason and will center on the person of Jesus and
the gospel. It will be attentive to the authoritative teaching of the
church, sensitive to the guidance of the Holy Spirit, attuned to the
Spirit's gifts, and will seek the advice of others.

Some steps we can take and the questions we can ask ourselves
to help our conscience to grow and to be attuned to God's will include the following:

1. *Find the facts. What* is the issue? *Who* is involved? *Where? When?
   How?*
2. *Examine your motives. Why* do you want to do this? Pure intentions were very important in the teaching of Jesus.
3. *Think of the possible effects.* How will this action (or non-action)
   affect you? others? society as a whole? What would happen if
   everyone did this?
4. *Consider alternatives.* Is there another way to act? Use your
   imagination to find alternatives.

5. **What does the law have to say?** Law is not opposed to conscience. In fact, it greatly helps to form it. Conscience is the subjective norm or morality; law is the objective norm. The kinds of laws that need to be considered are:

    Natural Law. God's law written into the nature of things, the way things are made. Prohibitions against murder, the recognition of the dignity of the individual, and honesty in dealing with others are examples of the natural law.

    Civil Law. Particular applications of natural law for a given society. In the United States, everyone drives on the right side of the road (civil law) to avoid killing (natural law). In England, motorists drive on the left side of the road. In both cases, the civil law is meant to apply the natural law for the protection of human life.

    Divine Law. Law revealed by God. The Sermon on the Mount and the Ten Commandments are classic examples of divine law, as is the law to love God, neighbor, and self.

    Church Law. Particular applications of divine law for the Christian community. The church teaches that we must worship God weekly at the Sunday liturgy, for example. This law is a particular application of the third commandment—Remember to keep holy the Sabbath—for Catholics. The laws or precepts of the church are listed on pages 280-282.

6. **What is the reasonable thing to do?** Because we are people with minds, we must use them in figuring out the right thing to do. Ask yourself what the reasonable decision is.

7. **What does your own experience and that of other people say about the issue?** Because we are social beings with a history, we must check out other responses to similar problems. If possible, seek out the wisdom of others.

8. **What would Jesus have done?** How does this action measure up to Jesus' yardstick of love? What does the New Testament have to say? Jesus is the absolute norm of Christian morality. He is the one perfect human response to God. Seek out his will and his teaching before making a decision. For example, Jesus would have us **always** follow these three rules:

    *   The Golden Rule: "So always treat others as you would like them to treat you" (Mt 7:12).
    *   Never do an evil that good may come from it. The end does not justify the means.
    *   Love always respects one's neighbor and his or her conscience.

9. **What is the teaching of the church?** We believe that the Holy Spirit resides in the church and helps guide us in right behavior.

Jesus continues to teach through the pope and the bishops united with him. Thus, sincere Catholics consider it a serious obligation to consult magisterial teaching on moral issues as well as to learn from competent theologians and other teachers in the church.

10. *Pray for guidance.* The Lord will help you if you ask.
11. *Admit that you sometimes sin and might be wrong.* As St. Paul said, one effect of original sin is that we do not always do the good we wish to do and we do the evil we wish to avoid.
12. *After all of this, follow your conscience.* Going against your conscience is always wrong. "Everyone who knows what is the right thing to do and does not do it commits a sin" (Jas 4:17).

How Do the Virtues Help Us Live a Moral Life? *[CCC 1803-1804; 1833-1834]*

A **virtue** is a power or habit that enables us to translate our Christian ideals into everyday life. It is a firm disposition to do good. Virtues help us perform actions with facility and competence. Human virtues govern our actions, help us control our passions, and guide our actions in light of faith and reason. We acquire moral virtues by effort, through repeated good acts. They help us draw closer to God.

The goal of the Christian life is to let the Lord live in and work through us. The human virtues, especially the cardinal virtues, and the theological virtues enable us to become like God.

What Are the Cardinal Virtues? *[CCC 1805-1811; 1835-1839]*

The four **cardinal** (or "hinge") **virtues** are the source of all other virtues, that is, good habits. They guide our intellects and wills, enabling us to live Christian and moral lives. The cardinal virtues are *prudence*, the ability to discern proper moral behavior and the means to achieve it; *justice* which gives God and others their due; *fortitude*, which is the courage and strength to do good, especially in the face of difficulties, temptations, and fear; and *temperance* which moderates our appetites for pleasure, secures the balance in created goods, and helps us control our instincts and desires in a Christ-like way.

What Are the Theological Virtues? *[CCC 1812-1829; 1840-1844]*

The infused virtues of faith, hope, and charity—the **theological virtues**—relate us to God. The Triune God is their origin, motive, and object. They serve as the foundation of the Christian moral life.

Faith enables us to believe in God who is truth itself and in all that God has revealed to us through scripture and the church. Further, faith enables us to enter into a personal relationship with God, for example, by accepting Jesus, the good news of salvation, and the profound mystery of the Triune God. A Christian must not only believe, but translate faith into action, profess it, and spread it to others.

Hope enables us to trust in God's promise of salvation. Hope permits us to desire heaven and to be assured, with God's grace, that we can achieve it. Hope keeps us from despair and self-centeredness. It empowers us to work for God's kingdom here on earth, especially by extending God's justice to the defenseless, those Jesus associated with in a special way. Christian hope is rooted in the Lord's own preaching of the Beatitudes and is sustained through prayer.

Charity, or *agape*-love, is the basis of Christian life. Both a virtue and a gift, active love for God and neighbor is essential for Christians (1 Cor 13:1-3). God is love; Jesus comes to us out of love; the Holy Spirit is a Spirit of love who makes us holy by giving us the power to love.

Charity is love of God above all else for God's own sake and the love of neighbor as oneself for love of God.

Jesus gave his disciples the command to love: "Love one another as I have loved you" (Jn 15:12). This law is the basic moral law for Christians.

Love is the greatest of all the virtues, making us God's children. It gives form and shape to all the virtues, binding them together in perfect harmony. It empowers us to relate joyfully, mercifully, and peacefully to others as our brothers and sisters.

What Are the Gifts and Fruits of the Holy Spirit? *[CCC 1829-1830; 1845]*

We are not alone in trying to live virtuously. The Holy Spirit sustains our efforts by giving us seven gifts: *wisdom, understanding, counsel, fortitude, knowledge, piety, and fear of the Lord* (Is 11:2). Furthermore, when we allow the Spirit's love to live within us, certain fruits are produced in us. Traditionally, these "fruits" are *charity, joy, peace, patience, kindness, goodness, generosity, gentleness, faithfulness, modesty, self-control, and chastity* (cf. Gal 5:22-23). The purpose of these gifts and fruits is to help us live like Jesus Christ, our Lord and Savior.

What Is Sin? *[CCC 1846-1853; 1870-1873]*

Sin is an offense against reason, truth, and right conscience; it is failure in genuine love for God and neighbor caused by a perverse attachment to certain goods. It wounds the nature of man and injures human solidarity (CCC 1849).

When we sin, we choose self over God, revolting against God in an act of disobedience. The passion narratives in the gospels illustrate well the many forms of sin: unbelief, hatred that leads to murder, mockery, cowardice, cruelty, betrayal, denial, flight from the truth.

In brief, sin is a failure to love ourselves, others, and God resulting in a breach in covenant love. The heart of the gospel is that Jesus Christ came to extend God's forgiveness to sinners. Without a healthy concept of sin, people tend to see little need for Jesus, the one who frees us from sin. Christians do not harp on sin out of a morbid attraction to evil; bad news is not the Christian message. Rather, we talk of sin to stress the good news that God forgives us and in the person of Jesus has rescued us from its effects. To receive Christ's mercy means that we must admit our sins.

There are many ways to classify sins, for example, those directed against God, neighbor, or self. A traditional grouping lists sins of the spirit and sins of the flesh. Another classification labels sins as those of thought, word, deed, or omission. Yet another categorization distinguishes between original sin and personal sin. And sin can be categorized according to its gravity, determined principally by the moral object. Thus, we speak of mortal sin and venial sin.

What Is Original Sin? *[CCC 390, 397; 416-417]*

Original sin refers to that condition of disharmony into which all humans are born. This condition is inherited.

> It is human nature so fallen, stripped of the grace that clothed it, injured in its own natural powers and subjected to the dominion of death (Pope Paul VI, *Credo of the People of God*, 16).

Universal human experience confirms the Catholic teaching that we are born into a sinful state. The evil we see around us, the anger we have within us toward others and ourselves, the good resolutions we so often break are all evidence of the sin which is part of humanity's condition.

What Is Personal Sin? *[CCC 1854]*

Personal (or "actual") **sin** is any free and deliberate action, word, thought, or desire that turns us away from God's law of love. It can be seen as a weakening (venial sin) or killing (mortal sin) of our relationship with our loving God.

What Is Mortal Sin? *[CCC 1855-1861; 1874]*

Mortal sin is serious sin. Mortal sin includes attitudes, desires, or actions (or failures to act) that kill our relation to God and others (including our fellow Christians). Mortal sin destroys love in the human heart by gravely violating God's law. No disciple of Jesus takes it lightly. To sin mortally, the sin must include:

* *grave matter* For example, murder, adultery, and apostasy are serious, gravely wrong actions.

* *sufficient reflection* This means that we know full well that what we propose to do is seriously wrong, that is, is sinful and opposed to God's law, but we do it anyhow.

* *full consent of the will* This means that we do the action with freedom and not under the influence of limiting factors like force, fear, or blinding passion. Sin committed with malice, by deliberately choosing evil, is the worst kind of sin.

The church teaches that just like it is possible for us to love, human freedom also makes it possible for us to sin mortally. Mortal sin results in the loss of love and deprives the sinner of sanctifying grace. If a person does not repent and receive Christ's forgiveness and dies in a state of mortal sin, he or she will merit eternal separation from God: hell. A Christian should do everything possible with God's help to avoid mortal sin or to repent immediately and ask for God's forgiveness if he or she should commit deadly sin. For Catholics, the sacrament of reconciliation is the normal means by which mortal sins are forgiven (see Chapter 15).

What Is Venial Sin? *[CCC 1862-1866; 1875-1876]*

Venial sin partially rejects God; it is a stumbling block on the path of following Jesus. Venial sins typically involve slight matter. Or, with venial sins full consent of the will is lacking or ignorance is present in the sinner. These sins are *not* deadly. Unlike mortal sin, they do not destroy sanctifying grace, friendship with God, charity, or eternal happiness.

The theft of a small item, a sarcastic word, or not praying regularly are examples of venial sins.

Venial sin is something Christians should try to eradicate from their lives. The danger of all sin is that we can become attached to it. Repeating sinful acts can give a foothold to vices, bad habits that turn us from love. These vices, especially the so-called deadly or **capital sins**—*pride, envy, anger, sloth, greed, gluttony, and lust*—can lead us to sin mortally.

Venial sin also weakens love, attaches us to created goods rather than God, and merits temporal punishment.

All sin is personal. Sin also often involves cooperation in the sins of others and can produce social and institutional structures contrary to God's will. These so-called "structures of sin" result from our personal sin and both cause an evil society and lead people into committing sins.

Concluding Reflections

Traditionally, we speak of a person who has turned completely away from divine love and has killed a relationship with God as being in "the state of mortal sin." To correct this situation the sinner must repent, that is, turn back to God, admit his or her wrongdoing, and acknowledge the need for forgiveness. The Father always offers the grace, the invitation, to accept divine love again.

Catholics celebrate the sacrament of reconciliation in which God's healing love is presented to us as a sign which reassures us of divine love. The point of Jesus' parable of the prodigal son (Lk 15:11-32) is that God's love is steadfast and that God always extends mercy to us. However, we need to repent, to admit our wrongdoing, and to turn to our loving Lord to accept his love. In brief, a helpful way to image Christian morality is to see it as saying "yes" to God's love, letting it shine on us, and then living a life of light and love that shines out to others.

Prayer Reflection *[CCC 2447]*

> Though I command languages both human and angelic—if I speak without love, I am no more than a gong booming or a cymbal clashing (1 Cor 13:1).

After reflecting on this famous quotation from St. Paul, prayerfully examine your conscience. How are you currently responding to God's command to love?

To help in this examination, study the **spiritual** and **corporal works of mercy**, traditional ways Christians have used to express Christian love. If the Spirit prompts you to work more actively at living one of these works, make a positive resolution to do something specific this coming week. Check yourself next week to see if you followed through on your resolution.

Spiritual Works of Mercy
1. Counsel the doubtful.
2. Instruct the ignorant.
3. Admonish sinners.
4. Comfort the afflicted.
5. Forgive offenses.
6. Bear wrongs patiently.
7. Pray for the living and the dead.

Corporal Works of Mercy
1. Feed the hungry.
2. Give drink to the thirsty.
3. Clothe the naked.
4. Visit the imprisoned.
5. Shelter the homeless.
6. Visit the sick.
7. Bury the dead.

For Discussion

1. Early Christians were known by their deeds of love. Following the way of Jesus set the Christian apart from non-believers. How has your Christian faith in action distinguished you as a follower of Jesus Christ?
2. In your opinion, what are the three worst sins committed in today's world? Discuss how they disfigure people made in God's image and likeness.
3. Explain the validity of the moral principle, "A good end does not justify evil means to attain it." How is this sound norm often ignored?
4. How does faith help you to live a moral life? Discuss.

Further Reading

2 Samuel 7 (Yahweh's covenant with David)
Matthew 5–7 (the Sermon on the Mount)

Chapter Eighteen

Catholic Teaching on Social Justice

"Anyone who wants to become great among you must be your servant, and anyone who wants to be first among you must be your slave, just as the Son of man came not to be served but to serve, and to give his life as a ransom for many."
— Matthew 20:26-28

There is a story about a priest and a soap maker who were friends. One day while taking a walk in the city, the soap maker asked his friend, "What possible good can religion be? After thousands of years of preaching goodness, truth, and peace, look at all the misery and sin in the world. If religion is supposed to be so beneficial for people, why should this be?"

For awhile, the priest said nothing in reply. Shortly, they came to a school yard where some children were playing in the dirt. They were covered with grime. The priest then spoke up, "See those kids. You say that soap makes people clean, but still those children are filthy. I wonder how effective soap is after all."

The soap maker protested, "But, Father, soap is of no value unless people use it."

"Precisely," replied the priest. "And so it is with religion."[1]

Faith and religion are empty unless we put them into practice. Living a Christian, moral life makes our faith credible. St. James saw this connection when he wrote:

> How does it help, my brothers, when someone who has never done a single good act claims to have faith? Will that faith bring salvation? If one of the brothers or one of the sisters is in need of clothes and has not enough food to live on, and one of you says to them, "I wish you well; keep yourself warm and eat plenty,"

without giving them these bare necessities of life, then what good is that? In the same way faith: if good deeds do not go with it, it is quite dead (Jas 2:14-17).

This chapter will look at our participation as members of the human family. Highlighted will be some key themes and principles of Catholic social justice teaching.

What Is the Relationship Between the Individual and Society? *[CCC 1877-1882; 1890-1893]*

By nature, humans are social beings. We develop our potential as persons by dialogue and service of others. In fact, loving human relationships mirror Trinitarian life—a community of Persons bound in love. Our vocation as individuals and as a human community is to manifest God, to be transformed into the Lord's image, and to attain the happiness of union with God in eternity. We achieve this when we love God above all and love our neighbor as self. Thus, we must relate to others to achieve our eternal destiny. We must function socially.

By definition, a society consists of a group of persons bound together by a principle of unity that transcends the individual. Whether the institution is directly related to us, like the family or the state, or a voluntary organization to which we belong like a political party or neighborhood group, the *human person* must always be "the principle, the subject and the end of all social institutions" (*Church in the Modern World*, 25).

What Is the Principle of Subsidiarity? *[CCC 1883-1889; 1894-1896]*

Because social institutions exist for the benefit of individuals, they should be governed by the principle of **subsidiarity**. This principle holds that a larger social body should *not* take over the functions of the smaller group if the smaller body can effectively achieve for itself the common good. Rather, the community of the higher order should support the smaller community in its need and help coordinate its activities for the rest of the society, always taking into consideration the common good.

Practically, this principle has several important ramifications. First, just as God shares authority with creatures, leaders should share their power with those they serve. Second, this principle outlaws collectivism—forms of government that subordinate the individual to the state. Third, it limits state intervention and aims at harmonizing relations between individuals and societies and works toward international order.

Societies should promote the exercise of virtue among their members. They do so by recognizing that individuals are ends in themselves, not a means to some other purpose. Societies should appeal to the best in individuals and inspire them to inner conversion as the true way to obtain lasting and just social change.

With the help of God's grace, we can recognize that love is the true basis of any reform. It helps us respect the rights of others and empowers us to treat them justly and respond to them selflessly. "There is no solution to the social question apart from the Gospel" (CCC 1896).

Why Should We Obey and Respect Human Authority? *[CCC 1897-1904; 1918-1923]*

Authority is the quality invested in persons or institutions to make laws or give orders. All authority ultimately comes from God. Consequently, we should obey and respect those who hold positions of legitimate authority. The purpose of their offices is to maintain order in society and to promote the common good through just laws. In turn, citizens have the right to choose their political rulers. The church accepts a variety of political regimes that serve the common good as morally acceptable. Limited by the rule of law, legitimate authority promotes freedom and responsibility and serves the common good through just, moral, and equitable laws.

What Is the "Common Good"? *[CCC 1905-1917; 1924-1927]*

The Vatican II document *The Church in the Modern World* (26) defines the **common good** as "the sum of those conditions of social life which allows social groups and their individual members relatively thorough and ready access to their own fulfillment." It has three elements: (1) respect for the fundamental, inalienable rights of the human person; (2) the social development and spiritual and material well-being of the society (for example, food, clothing, health, work, culture, etc.); and (3) the creation of the conditions that enable a society to exist in peace with security and justice.

Within a nation, government officials must defend and promote the common good of civil society, the people, and intermediate bodies.

Internationally, interdependence among nations and peoples is increasing daily. Thus, nations should organize to promote a universal common good, always keeping in mind human progress, development, and the good of persons who must never be subordinated to the state. Such international cooperation must always proceed from truth, justice, and love.

The common good is promoted internationally and on every level when people participate according to their positions or roles in society. For example, employers must give a just wage to employees. Parents must provide food, shelter, and emotional support to their children.

Christians are also called to involvement in politics and public life. Such involvement helps to establish just social structures and also fights elements that dehumanize people or work against authentic human values.

What Is Social Justice? *[CCC 1928-1933; 1943-1944; 2419-2426]*

The church is interested in the achievement of social justice, that is, a just society which guarantees that individuals and associations obtain what is due them according to their nature and vocation. Since the end of the nineteenth century, the church has developed a rich tradition of social justice teaching which respects the rights and fundamental dignity of human persons. The church continues to take a leading role in the promotion of justice:

> Action on behalf of justice and participation in the transformation of the world fully appear to us as a constitutive dimension of the preaching of the Gospel, or in other words, of the Church's mission of the redemption of the human race and its liberation from every oppressive situation (Introduction to Justice in the World).

In short, the church's social teaching interprets historical events under the guidance of the Spirit with a view to applying the gospel of Jesus Christ to society. This social doctrine includes principles for reflection, provides criteria for judgment, and gives guidelines for action. It addresses how individuals and groups should apply the gospel to the systems, structures, and institutions of society. This is an important aspect of Catholic teaching because all human relationships take place within the framework of these systems, structures, and institutions.

Catholic social teaching rejects any theory or social system that makes profit the only norm and ultimate end of economic activity. Whether totalitarian, atheistic, communistic, unbridled capitalism, or individualistic, if these theories or systems make humans means to the end of profit, thus idolizing money and dehumanizing persons, they are morally unacceptable.

Ultimately, social justice rests on the profound respect for each person as another self. Following from the teaching of Jesus himself, we must respect everyone, especially those who are disadvantaged. And we must love those who think or act differently from us, even our enemies. Working for social justice means laboring to eradicate poverty, helping to build a more compassionate and peaceful society, and fighting injustice wherever we find it.

Efforts on behalf of social justice are a way to spread the gospel and put faith into action. Such work helps enflesh Jesus' message of love, justice, and peace to a suffering world.

What Are Some Central Themes of Catholic Social Justice Teaching? *[CCC 2419-2449]*

Besides the central themes of social justice discussed above, the following core issues appear frequently in Catholic social justice documents. A brief discussion of each follows.

• The profound dignity of the individual person
• The essential equality among humans
• The link between justice and love
• Political and economic rights
• Stewardship
• Economic justice
• Human solidarity among people
• Preferential option for the poor
• The promotion of peace among nations

What Is Meant by the Dignity of the Individual? *[CCC 27, 1700-1703]*

The social teaching of the Catholic church rests on the *inherent dignity of the human person*, each person made in the image of God with a capacity to know and love our Creator. Human dignity means we have freedom to shape our lives and our communities. It means that we have the capacity for love and friendship. God has appointed us master of all earthly creatures so that we might use them to God's glory (*Church in the Modern World*, 12). As the psalmist put it:

> Yet you have made him little less than a god, you have crowned him with glory and beauty, made him lord of the work of your hands, put all things under his feet (Ps 8:5-6).

Humans have dignity by the way God made us. But when God became human in the person of Jesus Christ, human nature was "raised in us also to a dignity beyond compare" (*Redeemer of Man*, 8). Our Lord became our way to the Father; he saved every human being. Jesus Christ, the full revelation of the Father and the perfect human being brings to light our vocation and identity as children of God.

How Are People Essentially Equal? *[CCC 1934-1938; 1945-1947]*

Because God created each of us with an identical human nature endowed with fundamental dignity and a common destiny, all people are essentially equal. Our human equality comes in our dignity as persons made in God's image and likeness with certain inalienable rights. Therefore, every form of discrimination, whether based on sex, race, color, socioeconomic condition, language, national origin, or religion is immoral and contrary to God's love for each of us.

Though we are equal in our humanity and dignity, we do have different talents and abilities. These differences are part of God's plan, something we can never fully understand, especially if we have been especially gifted. Our duty is to share our gifts generously with others and work in a special way to fight against sinful inequalities. Gross social and economic inequalities militate against social justice, human dignity, fairness, and peace.

How Are Love and Justice Linked? *[CCC 2011-2012]*

As stated in the bishop's letter *Justice in the World*, "love implies an absolute demand for justice, usually a recognition of the dignity and rights of one's neighbors." We cannot say we love if we do not respect and respond to the rights and basic needs of our neighbors. True love of God and neighbor are united. As St. John reminds us:

> Anyone who says "I love God"
> and hates his brother, is a liar,
> since whoever does not love the brother whom he can see
> cannot love God, whom he has not seen.
> Indeed this is the commandment that we have received from him,
> that whoever loves God, must also love his brother (1 Jn 4:20-21).

In applying this link to the uneven distribution of the world's goods, the Vatican II document *The Church in the Modern World* (69) reminds us that "God intended the earth and all it contains for the use of every human being and people. Thus, as all men follow justice and unite in charity, created goods should abound for them on a reasonable basis."

To love means to give oneself to another. It is impossible to love without sharing with others what is due them in justice. Love can go beyond justice, however. Justice is simply the *minimal* human and Christian response to others. The perfection of justice consists in loving others as we love ourselves.

What Are Some Basic Human Rights? *[CCC 1913-1917]*

Justice demands that a society be organized in a way that guarantees everyone the ability to participate in the political, cultural, and economic life of the society. Basic human rights are prerequisites to living a life of dignity in community. A right is a moral claim a person can make on other persons and on society in general. Here is a list of major human rights often discussed and defended in a number of church documents:

Basic human rights
• right to life and bodily integrity
• right to respect for one's person and a good reputation
• right to food, shelter, clothing

Economic rights
• right to work
• right to a just wage
• right to property
• right to rest
• right to medical care

Political rights
• right to participate in government
• right to judicial protection

Religious rights
• right to worship according to one's conscience

Social rights
• right to assembly
• right of free association

Cultural rights
• right to a basic education
• right to freedom of speech

Other rights
• right to choose one's state in life
• right to emigrate/immigrate
• right to development
• right to social security: in the event of sickness, unemployment, old age, loss of support (e.g., death of parents of minors)

Every right has a corresponding duty for others to respect, foster, and fulfill the right. Furthermore, the person has a duty corresponding to his or her right. For example, the right to a just wage corresponds to the duty to do an honest day's work. The right to participate in government carries the duty to cast an informed vote in elections. The right of free speech demands honesty and kindness in exercising it.

What Is the Meaning of "Stewardship"? *[CCC 2415-2418; 2451-2452; 2456-2457]*

Stewardship means respecting and sharing the earth's resources, since everyone is part of the community of creation. Stewardship also means we are co-creators with God in developing the earth, responsibly planning and conserving resources and unselfishly respecting the goods of this world. God's will for us is that we "should communicate with nature as an intelligent and noble 'master' and 'guardian,' and not as a heedless 'exploiter' and 'destroyer'" (*Redeemer of Man*, 15).

This is a tremendous responsibility that has reached critical stages today. Because we are only now becoming more aware that we have exploited nature in the past, we run the risk of destroying it. Pollution, refuse, scarcity of vital natural resources, and new illnesses result from an unchecked technology fueled by human selfishness and greed.

Specifically the seventh commandment charges us to respect the integrity of creation. Our dominion over mineral, vegetable, and animal beings is not absolute but must show concern for the quality of life of our neighbors, including future generations. This includes showing kindness to animals who are God's creatures. However, it is morally legitimate to use them for food and clothing and for rational medical and scientific experimentation. On the other hand, it is contrary to human dignity to cause the needless suffering and death of animals or to spend money on them to the detriment of poor people in our midst.

This teaching is based on our Jewish and Christian heritage that the riches of God's creation are for the common good of all people. Those who own these goods as personal property are their stewards, "ministers charged with working in the name of God, who remains the sole owner in the full sense, since it is God's will that created goods should serve everyone in a just way" (*Tertio Millennio Adveniente*, 13).

What Does the Church Teach About Economic Justice?
[CCC 2426-2436; 2458-2460]

The church teaches that the primary purpose of economic activity is to serve individuals and the human community. It is not meant only to increase goods, profit, or power. Humans must be the author, center, and goal of economic and social life. Everyone must have access in justice and love to the goods of God's creation.

The church also teaches that everyone has a basic right to participate in economic affairs according to his or her ability and talents, tempered by the common good. Work is a basic right because God created us to share in the tasks of co-creation and subduing the earth. Its value stems from humans themselves who are both the authors and beneficiaries of labor. Work is also a duty that helps us provide for our families and serve each other. Through it we honor God by developing and using our talents. By enduring the hardships of work, we can also share in Christ's work of redemption, grow in holiness, and sanctify the world by bringing Christ's Spirit to the marketplace.

The economic realm involves varying interests and often results in conflict. These should be settled peacefully, through negotiation if possible. As a last resort, workers have the right to strike when obtaining a proportionate benefit is necessary. However, violence is morally wrong. Using a labor strike as a weapon that damages the common good is also wrong.

The state must guarantee individual freedom, private property, a stable currency, efficient public services, and security so workers can enjoy the fruits of their efforts. In addition, people should have access to a job without discrimination and to a just wage that guarantees a dignified livelihood. In turn, workers must give an honest day's work for an honest day's pay and should contribute to their social security as required by legitimate authority.

Finally, employers are responsible for the economic and ecological impact of their operations. The good of persons must always be considered. Two key questions that must be asked of all those responsible for the economic welfare are: "What does the economy do *for* people? What does it do *to* people?" And these questions must be especially asked and answered regarding the economy's impact on the least among us, the poor and marginalized.

What Is the Call to Human Solidarity? *[CCC 1939-1942; 1947-1948]*

Solidarity—friendship or social charity—is a Christian virtue that sees to the just sharing of both spiritual and material goods, fair pay for services, and a peaceful effort to establish a just social order both nationally and internationally.

As social beings we live in a network of relationships. Society and the individual are engaged in reciprocal relationships. The individual is responsible for the well-being of society, and society has duties to the individual. Problems in the socioeconomic order demand all types of solidarity: among the poor themselves, between the wealthy and poor, among workers themselves, between employers and employees, and between nations and various population groups. In the words of Pope John Paul II:

> The exercise of solidarity within each society is valid when its members recognize one another as persons. Those who are more influential, because they have a greater share of goods and common services, should feel responsible for the weaker and be ready to share with them all they possess (On Social Concerns, 39).

Christians cannot escape the call of others, especially the weak. Love of God is united to love of neighbor. We are one human family, dependent on one another, and have the Christ-given call to be one. Jesus himself prayed for human solidarity:

> "May they all be one, just as, Father, you are in me and I am in you" (Jn 17:21).

Because we are one, Jesus commands us to love our neighbor as ourselves. The parable of the Good Samaritan illustrates well this double command to love self and neighbor. The Samaritan realized that when one person suffers everyone suffers because we are fundamentally brothers and sisters. Not to recognize and respect the dignity of a single person, especially one who is suffering, is to deny the Son of Man who came to teach us that we are one with him and with one another.

What Are the Demands of Global Solidarity? *[CCC 2437-2442]*

Belonging to one human family requires *global solidarity*. We have mutual obligations to promote the rights and development of all nations, whatever their boundaries. Rich nations have a special duty to ensure justice in the international order to facilitate the development of poor nations.

Providing direct help to those unfortunate nations suffering from natural catastrophes, famines, epidemics, and the like is an appropriate response of rich nations. However, it is also necessary for rich nations to support *reform* efforts in international economic and financial *institutions* to promote more equitable relationships with less advanced nations.

Concretely the papal encyclical *On Social Concerns* (43-45) outlines some steps necessary to help poor nations develop. These steps include:

- reforming the existing international trade system which unfairly discriminates against the products of new industries of the developing nations;
- reforming the world monetary and financial system which is marked by excessive fluctuation in exchange and interest rates to the detriment of the poorer countries;
- sharing technological resources with the developing nations and properly using them;
- reviewing and possibly correcting the operating methods, operating costs, and the effectiveness of existing International Organizations.

The encyclical encourages the formation of new regional organizations among the developing nations in a given geographical area based on equality, freedom, and participation in the community of nations.

Also, the papal encyclical *On the Development of People* and the pastoral letter of the United States bishops entitled *Economic Justice for All* outline other steps necessary to help poor nations develop. Among these are more direct development assistance, rectification of trade relationships, improved financing through a funding agency that will help provide low-interest loans, more foreign private investment, and recourse to a strong international organization like the United Nations to help bring about more harmonious international relations.

What Is the "Preferential Option for the Poor"? *[CCC 2443-2449; 2461-2463]*

Jesus had a special concern and love for the poor. We cannot call ourselves his disciples without seeking out and responding to the needs of the poverty-stricken in our midst. In fact, the Lord will judge us on how we meet their needs (see Mt 25:31-36).

The American bishops define poverty as "the lack of sufficient material resources required for a decent life" (*Economic*

Justice for All, 173). Economic disadvantage leads to oppression and powerlessness.

If we have an immediate love of wealth or use wealth selfishly, we cannot say we love the poor. Yet, if we share our wealth with the needy, we are only giving them their due. In the words of St. Basil:

> The bread you store up belongs to the hungry; the cloak that lies in your chest belongs to the naked; the gold that you have hidden in the ground belongs to the poor.[2]

A preferential love or option for the poor has been a major concern of the church since the time of Jesus, despite the sins and shortcomings of Christians. We demonstrate this love in the spiritual and corporal works of mercy: instructing, advising, consoling, comforting, forgiving, patiently enduring wrongs, feeding the hungry, clothing the naked, giving shelter to the homeless, visiting the sick and imprisoned, and burying the dead. The most important work of charity and justice for the poor, however, is almsgiving.

Concern for each other—poor and rich alike—includes the whole person, their physical, social, psychological, and spiritual development. True development works toward increasing each person's capacity to respond to God's call and live a fully human vocation.

To serve God faithfully in imitation of Jesus means paying attention and responding to the needs of the weakest in our midst. By doing so we exhibit the virtue of solidarity. Our benefit is that we will grow closer to God and each other.

What Does the Church Teach About Peace?
[CCC 2304-2305]

Peace is a blessing of Christ. The Prince of Peace and the church he founded as a sign of his peace teach that peace—the tranquillity of order—is the fruit of both justice and love. Peace results when persons are treated with dignity, communicate freely, and lovingly relate to each other as brothers and sisters. To be a disciple of Jesus Christ means to be passionately devoted to peace. Peace is not merely the absence of war. It is an enterprise of justice and must be built up ceaselessly.

> Peace cannot be obtained on earth unless personal values are safeguarded and men freely and trustingly share with one another the riches of their inner spirits and their talents. A firm determination to respect other men and peoples and their dignity, as well as the studied practice of brotherhood are absolutely necessary for the establishment of peace. Hence peace is likewise the fruit of love, which goes beyond what justice can provide (Church in the Modern World, 78).

What Does the Church Teach About War? *[CCC 2307-2309; 2312-2314; 2327-2328; 2330]*

The Beatitudes teach that peacemakers will be called children of God (Mt 5:9). The fifth commandment forbids killing. In light of these teachings, the church calls everyone to pray for peace and to work wholeheartedly to avoid war. However, the danger of war persists without an international authority with the power to prevent it. Thus, as a last resort, governments have the right and duty to pass laws to enlist citizens to help defend the nation.

Catholic teaching begins always with a presumption against war; it advocates the peaceful settlement of disputes. In extreme cases, though, some uses of force are permitted, for example, to defend against unjust aggression. The principles of the just-war tradition permit war if *all* the following conditions are met.

- There must be a real, lasting, grave and certain damage inflicted by an aggressor on a nation or a community of nations. If a situation threatens the life of innocent people, if basic human rights are violated, or if there is an imminent need for self-defense, then there would be just cause.

- The right to declare a war of defense belongs to those who have the legitimate responsibility to represent the people and are entrusted with the common good.

- The rights and values in the conflict must be so important that they justify killing.

- To be just, a war must be waged for the best of reasons and with a commitment to postwar reconciliation with the enemy. Needless destruction, cruelty to prisoners, and other harsh measures cannot be tolerated.

- War must be a last resort, justifiable only if all peaceful efforts have been tried and there are no alternatives.

- The odds of success should be weighed against the human cost of the war. The purpose of this criterion is to prevent irrational use of force or hopeless resistance when either will prove futile anyway.

- The damage to be inflicted and the cost incurred by the war must be proportionate to the good expected. Armed conflict must not produce evils and disorders graver than the evil to be eliminated. For example, if a large number of people would be destroyed over a dispute that only slightly affects the two countries, the decision to go to war would violate proportionality.

The moral law still holds in an armed conflict. For example, noncombatants, wounded soldiers, and prisoners deserve respect and humane treatment. Mass extermination of a people, nation, or ethnic minority is morally reprehensible and gravely sinful. Blind obedience to unjust orders, for example, participation in genocide, *cannot* excuse one's responsibility for participating in such a heinous crime.

What Is the Morality of Nuclear War and the Arms Race? [CCC 2314-2317; 2329]

Any act of war aimed indiscriminately at entire cities or extensive areas and their populations is a crime against God and humanity. Both actions merit total condemnation.

Because nuclear weapons have great potential for widespread and indiscriminate destruction, the American bishops have spoken out clearly against nuclear war (see *The Challenge of Peace*). There are major problems in trying to apply the just-war criteria to any kind of nuclear war. It is almost impossible to perceive any situation in which the first-use of nuclear weapons or limited nuclear war could be justified. One of the criteria of the just-war teaching is that there must be reasonable hope of success in bringing about peace and justice. It is doubtful whether there can be a reasonable hope once nuclear weapons have been used. Remember good ends (defending one's country, protecting freedom) cannot justify immoral means (the use of weapons which kill indiscriminately and threaten whole societies).

The arms race does not insure peace. It risks aggravating the causes of war—injustice, excessive economic and social inequalities, envy, distrust, and pride. The accumulation, production, and sale of arms are dangerous to international order and a grave injustice to the poor and needy. Over-armament intensifies the threat of conflict and squanders money that should be spent on the starving in our midst.

What Is the Role of Personal Conscience in a Person's Participation in a War? [CCC 2306; 2310]

The decision to fight in a just war or to be a nonviolent witness to peace, a pacifist, is a difficult one. The church respects the personal conscience of those who enter the military service out of loyalty to their country. They "should look upon themselves as the custodians of the security and freedom of their fellow countrymen." When they carry out their duties properly, "they are contributing to the maintenance of peace" (*Church in the Modern World*, 79).

By the same token, the church also respects those "who forego the use of violence to vindicate their rights and resort to other means of defense which are available to weaker parties, provided it can be done without harm to the rights and duties of others and of the community" (*Church in the Modern World*, 78).

Furthermore, the church supports laws which would make humane provision for conscientious objectors who refuse to bear arms, "provided they accept some other form of community service" (*Church in the Modern World*, 79).

Concluding Reflections

The justice of a society is measured by its treatment of the poor. To follow Jesus Christ means that we must have a "preferential option for the poor." Jesus strongly identified himself with those who had a marginal role in society. He bids his followers to respond in a special way to those whose dignity is threatened because of their position in society. The measure of our commitment to Jesus is how well we imitate the Lord who came to serve rather than be served.

Christian teaching recognizes that each person has basic human rights and that respect is due each person as a child of God, created in God's image to live in community. God loves everyone; Jesus died so that every person can be saved.

Jesus challenges us as individuals and as a Christian community to work for justice. It is not the role of the church's pastors to intervene directly into the political structures of society. This is part of the mission of the laity, to join with other citizens to promote the cause of justice. We do this when we speak out for the defenseless and become agents for peace and justice. We take up his challenge when we see and judge things from the vantage point of the poor. We respond to the Lord's mandate when we help people experience the good news of God's liberating salvation. Finally, and perhaps most important, we take Jesus' command to heart when we empty ourselves, both individually and as a church, so that we can experience God's power in the midst of poverty and vulnerability.

Prayer Reflection

You have already been told what is right
and what Yahweh wants of you.
Only this, to do what is right,
to love loyalty
and to walk humbly with your God (Mi 6:8).

But alas for you who are rich: you are having your consolation now.
Alas for you who have plenty to eat now: you shall go hungry.
Alas for you who are laughing now; you shall mourn and weep
(Lk 6:24-25).

For Discussion

1. What do you see as the most pressing social justice issue in to-
    day's society? How should Christians respond to it?
2. What can and should you be doing in the cause of world peace?
3. How do the needs of the poor have precedence in your life?

Further Reading

Amos 5–6 (a prophetic cry for repentance and justice)
Matthew 25:31-46

Chapter Nineteen

The Christian Call to Holiness

As the chosen of God, then, the holy people whom he loves, you are to be clothed in heartfelt compassion, in generosity and humility, gentleness and patience. Bear with one another; forgive each other if one of you has a complaint against another. The Lord has forgiven you; now you must do the same. Over all these clothes, put on love, the perfect bond. And may the peace of Christ reign in your hearts, because it is for this that you were called together in one body. Always be thankful.
— Colossians 3:12-15

The Christ of the Andes statue stands on the border of Chile and Argentina. It symbolizes a pledge between the nations that as long as the statue stands there will be peace and harmony between these two nations.

But the statue almost became the cause of open conflict. When the work was erected, someone indicated that our Lord's back was turned toward Chile. Chileans felt slighted. As tempers began to flare, a Chilean columnist cooled things down by writing, "The Argentineans need more watching over than the Chileans." This good-natured quip saved the day.

The conflict between these two Christian nations also highlights that we need help to live in peace as God's people. Called to eternal happiness, humans are flawed and in need of Christ's salvation. Thankfully, God has given us the Lord Jesus who guides us in right living through the law and showers us with the power of his grace to help us on the journey (CCC 1949). This chapter will focus on the moral law, grace, and the church's magisterium as sources of wisdom and strength in living out our Christian vocation.

What Is the Moral Law? *[CCC 1950-1953; 1975-1977]*

Moral law contains God's prescriptions for right human conduct. It teaches us what is good and how to act to attain eternal happiness. It points out the ways of evil that turn us from God and love.

There are four interrelated expressions of the moral law: the eternal law, which finds its source in God, the author of all law; natural law; revealed law; and civil and ecclesiastical laws. The fullest expression of the moral law and its unity is found in Christ, the one who teaches and bestows the justice of God.

St. Thomas Aquinas defines **law** as "an ordinance of reason for the common good." It is a rule of conduct enacted by competent authority that helps us serve our final end. All law is rooted in the moral law of God's providence—God's power, wisdom, and goodness.

What Is the Natural Law? *[CCC 1954-1960; 1978-1980]*

The natural law is written in the soul of each person. The natural law expresses the original moral sense and is a share in God's wisdom and goodness. It is the very basis of our fundamental rights and duties. Because we are made in God's image, this law makes it possible for our intellects to discover the truth. St. Thomas Aquinas pictured the natural law as the gift and light of understanding which God places in us, drawing us to do good and avoid evil. Because it is present in our hearts, the natural law is binding on all people in all places at all times. Although humans have applied natural law differently through the ages and adapted it to particular cultures, its general precepts are universal and permanent.

Natural law provides the foundation for moral rules and is the basis for living together in harmony with others. It also provides the grounding for various civil laws.

Because of human weakness and sinfulness, not everyone can grasp the dictates of the natural law. Thus, our loving God has given us grace and revealed to us the moral law through the course of salvation history. The first stage of God's revealed law is the Mosaic Law, summarized in the Ten Commandments. They contain the key precepts of the natural law.

How Is Moral Law Revealed? *[CCC 1961-1974; 1981-1986]*

God revealed the moral law to us in two stages: the law of the Old Testament and the new law of the gospel. Summarized in the Ten Commandments, the old law is imperfect, a preparation for the gospel. It shows what must be done and what must be avoided, but it does not provide the grace of the Holy Spirit to give us the strength to follow through. Its main function is to denounce and reveal sin.

The new law, the gospel of Jesus Christ, is the earthly perfection of the divine law, both natural and revealed. It is the work of Christ, most perfectly revealed in the Sermon on the Mount. It is also the work and grace of the Holy Spirit who guides us within through the law of love.

The law of the gospel surpasses the Old Testament law by bringing it to perfection. It does not add new precepts. Rather, the Spirit's life in us helps us reform our hearts so we might imitate the perfection of our heavenly Father. The new law requires purity of intention when we act, even challenging us to pray for and forgive our enemies. It calls us to be sincere in our religious practices of almsgiving, praying, and fasting. It finds its perfect summary in Jesus' Golden Rule—"So always treat others as you would like them to treat you" (Mt 7:12)—and in his new commandment—"Love one another, as I have loved you" (Jn 15:12).

In addition, the church recognizes the special value of the moral catechesis found in Romans 12–15:13, 1 Corinthians 12–13, Colossians 3–4, and Ephesians 4–6. The teachings contained in these passages and in the Sermon on the Mount reveal that the new law is really a *law of love* because it empowers us to put the Spirit's gift of love into action. It is also a *law of grace* because it gives us the strength to love obediently, through faith and the graces of the sacraments. Finally, the new law is a *law of freedom*, enabling us to act as children of God and friends of the Lord Jesus, sensitively responding to the inner call to love.

The new law also includes what we traditionally call the *evangelical counsels*, that is, poverty, chastity, and obedience. The purpose of these gospel virtues is to break down any barriers to the law of love and to perfect Christians who are striving to live totally for Christ.

What Is Justification? *[CCC 1987-1995; 2017-2020]*

Justification is the grace of the Holy Spirit that cleanses us from our sins and imparts to us God's righteousness, through faith in Jesus Christ and baptism. The Spirit's power unites us to the Lord's passion, teaching us to die to sin. In Christ's resurrection, we are born to a new life as members of his body, the church.

The grace of the Holy Spirit brings about conversion. It turns us to God and away from our sins and enables us to accept God's forgiveness and righteousness. The grace of justification empowers us to participate in divine life. It remits our sins, renews us inwardly, and—through the gifts of faith, hope, and charity—helps us live obediently to God's will.

Christ Jesus' passion, his gift of self-offering on the cross, merited for us justification. Granted through baptism, justification enables our freedom to cooperate with grace and the righteousness of God, the one who justifies us. We are helpless in the spiritual life without God's grace. But when we cooperate with it and follow the inner promptings of the Holy Spirit, we can be made holy.

The work of justification is God's greatest work of mercy. It not only glorifies our loving God and Christ our Savior, it also grants to us eternal life in heaven.

What Is Grace? *[CCC 1996-2005; 2021-2024]*

Grace is God's favor, the free and undeserved help that adopts us into the divine family, making us heirs to heaven and enabling us to live as children of the Father.

Grace is a supernatural gift, beyond human effort and totally dependent on God's gracious love for us. We call it *deifying* or *sanctifying grace* because it makes us holy. We also call it *habitual grace* because it is a permanent disposition to live godly lives. *Actual graces* are God's special helps for us to turn from sin and follow the Christian vocation once we have converted.

Grace requires our free response because God never forces grace on us. Yet God plants in our hearts a burning desire to know truth and to do good. Only God the Father can satisfy these desires. Thus, the Father initiates the work of grace by preparing for, preceding, and eliciting our free response. When we do respond in freedom, our freedom is perfected and our deepest longings are fulfilled.

In previous chapters we also discussed how each sacrament conveys *sacramental graces*, that is, gifts which are proper to a particular sacrament (see Chapters 12 and following) and *charisms* or special graces or gifts of the Holy Spirit given to help the church grow (see Chapter 5). There are also *graces of state* that accompany particular responsibilities or ministries within the church.

Since grace is a gift that conveys the life of God and helps us to live in tune with God's will, grace is in the supernatural order. Faith is required to know about the workings of grace in our lives. Neither our feelings nor our own works can tell us that we are justified and saved. However, through the eyes of faith and trust in God's mercy, we can see the effect of God's grace in our lives and in the lives of other Christians.

How Do We Gain Merit Before God? *[CCC 2006-2011; 2025-2027]*

Merit is defined as something owed for our good deeds. In truth, God does not owe us anything since everything we have and are is a pure gift from God. However, in God's wisdom and love, we have been brought into the work of divine grace. Any good we do is a result of God's prior grace, and from our free cooperation with that grace. Having adopted us into the divine family, the Father bestows true merit on us, granting us eternal life if we cooperate with the help and grace which he freely gives to us. We do not earn the initial grace that justifies us, but with the help of the Holy Spirit, we can "earn" (merit) for ourselves and for others the graces needed for holiness and eternal life. Our merit is gained primarily through love. In addition, if we act in accord with God's will and pray for the graces we need, we can merit temporal goods like health and friendship. However, we must always remember that it is the love of Christ Jesus that is the source of all merit before the Father. Allowing the Lord to live in us through grace is the true source of a godly life that wins us favor with God.

Is Everyone Called to Holiness? *[CCC 2012-2016; 2028-2029]*

The Vatican II document *Dogmatic Constitution on the Church* reminds us that God calls to holiness "all the faithful of Christ of whatever rank or status" (40). Holiness involves striving for the perfection of God the Father (Mt 5:48); it is the perfection of charity that has as its goal union with Jesus Christ.

The way to holiness, to the perfection of love, is the path of the cross—self-denial, penance, and mortification. "No pain, no gain" is an apt way to describe the spiritual life. Faithful Christians also exercise the virtue of hope that God will grant them the grace of persevering to the end of their life's journey and thus gain the eternal happiness of heaven.

How Does the Church Help Us to Live a Moral Life? *[CCC 2030-2040; 2047-2051]*

We live our Christian vocation as members of Christ's body, the church. As a nurturing mother, the church gives us the word of God with its instructions on how to live morally. The church also gives us the sacraments with their graces to help us live Christ-like lives. In the church we find examples of holiness like Mary and the saints; they show how to dedicate our lives in love to God. And the church reminds us to be in communion with the liturgy, especially the eucharist. Living morally is itself an act of spiritual worship to our loving God.

Furthermore, the magisterium (the pope and bishops), assisted by theologians and spiritual writers, helps ensure that the church remains the "pillar and bulwark of the truth." In their capacity as authentic teachers who instruct and guide with Christ's own authority, the pope and bishops hand down moral teaching and the basic principles of the moral and natural law. They normally do this through preaching and catechetical instruction. In addition, the gift of infallibility guarantees the truth of papal and magisterial teaching in matters pertaining to divine revelation. This charism of infallibility also ensures the truth of doctrinal and moral teachings that are necessary for the preservation, explanation, and practice of these truths of revelation.

As those Christ has entrusted with truth and life, we have the *right* to instruction in the truths of Christian moral living. We also have the *duty* to observe official church teachings on the moral life and to share our own experiences of living the gospel truths. Our example of living ethical lives in accord with gospel principles and church moral teaching can be a tremendous source of light not only to other Catholics, but to non-Catholics and non-Christians who are searching for truth and meaning in a world that often ignores objective standards of right and wrong.

Finally, the church calls individual Christians to consider the common good when they make moral decisions. Ultimately, personal conscience should not be opposed to either the dictates of the moral law or official church teaching.

What Are the Precepts of the Church? [CCC 2041-2043]

Belonging to the Catholic faith community involves certain basic commitments. Like all law, church law is reasonable, given by proper authority, published in a way that people know about it, and directed to the common good. The following precepts are meant to guarantee the minimum growth in love of God and neighbor for responsible Catholic living in today's church.

1. *To attend Mass on Sundays.* We keep the Lord's day holy by worshipping at the eucharist every Sunday, thus commemorating the Lord's resurrection. Sunday should be a day of relaxation, thanksgiving, and celebration. We respect this day by avoiding those activities that would hinder personal renewal, for example, by avoiding needless work and business activities and unnecessary shopping.

2. *To confess your sins at least once a year.* This precept ensures proper preparation for receiving the eucharist. The sacrament of reconciliation is a continuation of the conversion and forgiveness begun at baptism. Catholics celebrate the sacrament of reconciliation regularly as a means to experience the healing touch of the Lord, to help conquer sinful habits, and to grow in holiness.

3. *To receive the Lord in holy communion at least during the Easter season.* This obligation guarantees a minimum of reception of the Lord in connection with the Easter feast which is at the heart of the liturgical year. (Catholics in the state of grace, however, should receive holy communion frequently. We do so by approaching the sacrament reverently and by refraining from food or drink—other than medicine or water—for at least one hour before reception of holy communion.)

4. *Keep holy the holy days of obligation.* This precept is similar to the Sunday observance. It instructs us to participate in key liturgical feasts that honor the mysteries of the Lord, the Virgin Mary, and the saints (*CCC* 2043). In the United States, these feasts are:

Immaculate Conception of Mary—December 8
Christmas Day—December 25
Solemnity of Mary—January 1
Ascension Thursday—40 days after Easter
Assumption of Mary—August 15
All Saints' Day—November 1

5. *To observe the prescribed days of fasting and abstinence.* This practice helps us prepare for the liturgy by gaining mastery over our instincts and achieving the freedom to love. Catholics take seriously Jesus' command to pick up a cross and follow him. In the Sermon on the Mount (Mt 5—7), Jesus taught that prayer, fasting (and abstaining), and almsgiving (charity to the poor) are ways to holiness. These traditional means of self-discipline remain excellent ways to follow in the footsteps of Jesus.

In addition to these five precepts, the faithful have the duty *to provide for the material needs of the church.* As full members of Christ's body, we must support with monetary tithing the local church community—the parish and its staff, the charities run by the local diocese, and the like. We also belong to a worldwide community which has the Lord's own mandate to spread the good news. Thus, we should support the pope and the missionary efforts of the church.

A Catholic recognizes that service of others is not only a major mission of the church as an institution but an obligation of each member. Thus, Catholics will lend their talents and time to the local parish and will dedicate themselves to serving the human family in some way. Following Jesus means one must serve.

What Are the Ten Commandments? *[CCC Part Three, Life in Christ]*

The Ten Commandments, also called the Decalogue ("ten words") sum up and proclaim God's Law. The Ten Commandments are found in Exodus 20:2-17 and Deuteronomy 5:6-21. The summary below is from the *New American Bible*.

I	I, the Lord, am you God. You shall not have other gods besides me.
II	You shall not take the name of the Lord, your God, in vain.
III	Remember to keep holy the Sabbath day.
IV	Honor your father and your mother.
V	You shall not kill.
VI	You shall not commit adultery.
VII	You shall not steal.
VIII	You shall not bear false witness against your neighbor.
IX	You shall not covet your neighbor's wife.
X	You shall not covet anything that belongs to your neighbor.

Why Are the Ten Commandments Important for the Moral Life? *[CCC 2052-2082]*

The Commandments wonderfully express the natural law and can be discovered by reason. Yahweh gave the Law and the Commandments to the Chosen People as a seal to his covenant of love between them. The Ten Commandments are a revelation of God's holy will for a people called to be his own.

We should view the Ten Commandments as a response to God's loving initiative in calling and sustaining us as individuals and as a people. By observing them, we live a moral life. This itself is a response in love to a loving God who made us and calls us to himself.

Jesus acknowledged the importance of keeping the Commandments (for example, in Mt 19:16-19). However, his teaching delves into the inner spirit of the Law. He summarized the Law and the Commandments in his great injunction to love God with all our heart, soul, and mind and to love our neighbor as ourselves (see Mt 22:37-40).

The church has always taught the fundamental importance and significance of the Decalogue. In its catechetical efforts through the ages, the church has stressed how the first three commandments pertain to the love of God and the other seven to that of neighbor. Each commandment refers reciprocally to the others, thus linking the love of God and neighbor. (The next two chapters will follow this traditional categorization.)

The Council of Trent taught, and the Second Vatican Council reiterated, that Catholics have a serious obligation to observe the commandments, even though the matter of some actions and attitudes treated by a given commandment is slight. (For example, the fifth commandment forbids abusive language. Such language involves normally *slight* matter, but can be a grave offense depending on the circumstances or intention.) The content of the Ten Commandments states grave obligations because they teach the way to truth for humanity, underscoring our basic duties and highlighting, therefore, our fundamental human rights. Basically unchangeable, the Ten Commandments oblige in all times and in all places. God has written them on our hearts and gives us the graces necessary to make them the guiding rules of our lives.

Concluding Reflections

Our salvation, indeed our very existence, is a gift of God's enduring love for us. God justifies us, dispenses the graces we need to live holy lives, and makes it possible for our good works to benefit ourselves and others. A proper Christian response to this benevolence on God's part is thanksgiving. As St. Paul instructs: "In all circumstances give thanks, for this is the will of God for you in Christ Jesus" (1 Thes 5:18, NAB).

A most fitting way to express our gratitude for all of God's favors is to live an upright, moral life in response to God's love by observing the Commandments, following the teaching of Christ, and living virtuously. When we do so we build up the body of Christ, hasten the coming of God's reign, and make the gospel credible to others. A missionary is one who is sent. Our Lord Jesus sends us into the world to witness in both word and deed to the truth of the gospel. A moral life lived in a secular, materialistic world is a powerful magnet to restless hearts seeking truth and love. It is a prime way to continue Christ's own mission of proclaiming the good news.

Prayer Reflection

St. Paul teaches that the way to holiness is the imitation of Jesus Christ. Reflect on his profound words:

> I appeal to you, make my joy complete by being of a single mind, one in love, one in heart and one in mind. Nothing is to be done out of jealousy or vanity; instead, out of humility of mind everyone should give preference to others, everyone pursuing not

selfish interests but those of others. Make your own the mind of
Christ Jesus:
Who, being in the form of God,
did not count equality with God
something to be grasped.
But he emptied himself,
taking the form of a slave,
becoming as human beings are;
and being in every way like a human being,
he was humbler yet,
even accepting death, death on a cross.
And for this God raised him high,
and gave him the name
which is above all other names;
So that all beings
in the heavens, on earth and in the underworld,
should bend the knee at the name of Jesus
and that every tongue should acknowledge
Jesus Christ as Lord,
to the glory of God the Father.

— Philippians 2:2-11

For Discussion

1. Name occasions of grace in your life. Share some specific ways various events, people, or gifts have been "grace" to you.
2. How do you understand *holiness*? What does it mean for God to call *you* to holiness?
3. List and discuss several "laws" for human living that you think are clearly discoverable if people would honestly use their gift of reason.

Further Reading

Romans 12–15:13
Ephesians 4–6

Chapter Twenty

The First Three Commandments: Love of God

My dear friends, let us love each other, since love is from God and everyone who loves is a child of God and knows God. Whoever fails to love does not know God, because God is love. This is the revelation of God's love for us, that God sent his only Son into the world that we might have life through him. Love consists in this: it is not we who loved God, but God loved us and sent his Son to expiate our sins. My dear friends, if God loved us so much, we too should love each other.

— 1 John 4:7-11

A science experiment reports how some students put a live frog into a pot of water and slowly began to heat it. After awhile the water began to boil, but the frog never tried to jump out. Why not? Because the changes in the frog's surroundings were so gradual that it never noticed them until it was too late.

Christians can end up like the frog. Our moral environment, consisting of a humdrum world that often acts as though God does not exist, can subtly turn us away from what is really important. And we fail to notice that we are dying spiritually.

Jesus has an antidote to the moral coldness of our age. He teaches that we should have red-hot love for God, making God our first concern in life. He confirms the law of Deuteronomy 6:5: *"You must love the Lord your God with all your heart, with all your soul, with all your strength, and with all your mind"* (Lk 10:27). This injunction helps keep our minds and hearts focused. It highlights what is truly important in the moral life—a wholehearted, loving response to God who loved us into being and graciously sustains us, gives us Jesus, and destines us to eternal life.

This chapter will examine the requirements for loving God as expressed in the first three commandments.

What Does the First Commandment Require? *[CCC 2083-2087; 2090; 2093; 2133-2134]*

Exodus 20:2-5 gives the full text of the first commandment:

> "I am Yahweh your God who brought you out of Egypt, where you lived as slaves.
> "You shall have no other gods to rival me.
> "You shall not make yourself a carved image or any likeness of anything in heaven above or on earth beneath or in the waters under the earth.
> "You shall not bow down to them or serve them."

This commandment clearly calls us to accept and worship God and to manifest God's glory by acting as persons with dignity, created in the divine image and likeness.

The first commandment obliges us to exercise the virtues of faith, hope, and love. We demonstrate faith when we believe in God and his revelation, when we worship God, and when we witness to our own faith. We display hope when we trust God's word, mercy, and the promise of eternal salvation and take great care not to offend God so as to incur divine punishment. We exhibit love when we love God wholeheartedly and all of creation out of love for him. Jesus taught the meaning of love when he instructed, "If you love me you will keep my commandments" (Jn 14:15).

What Are Sins Against the First Commandment? *[CCC 2088-2089; 2091-2092; 2094]*

Sins against faith include voluntarily doubting all or part of any truth God has revealed through the Catholic church; this would include the sins of heresy, apostasy, and schism. *Heresy* is the denial of a truth of the faith. *Apostasy* is specially serious because it is a total denial of Christ and a repudiation of Christian faith. *Schism* is the refusal to recognize and accept the authority of the pope and a refusal to be in union with those Christians who do submit to papal jurisdiction.

The main sins against hope are presumption and despair. *Presumption* holds that a person can obtain salvation on one's own efforts or by God's granting salvation without any efforts at personal conversion or cooperating with divine grace. When people *despair*, they lack hope that God can forgive their sins or give them the help they need to attain salvation. Despair is an injustice to a merciful, good God who is always faithful to his promises.

Sins against God's love include religious indifference, by which one neglects or refuses God's love; ingratitude; lukewarmness; spiritual laziness that refuses the joy that comes from God's goodness; and outright hatred of God, a most serious offense. Hatred of God finds its roots in selfish pride; it contradicts God's love.

How Does Religion Help Us Develop a Relationship With God? [CCC 2096-2109; 2135-2137]

It is both natural and good for humans to bind themselves to a greater Power, to God, who is the source of life and all that is good. The theological virtues of faith, hope, and love lead to the moral virtues and to the virtue of religion by which we render God his due in justice. The virtue of religion enables us to revere and love our majestic, loving God. (The word *religion* derives from a Latin word that means "to bind together.") To fail to develop this virtue is to thwart an essential part of our spiritual nature, a nature that seeks out and responds in love to God the creator.

Religion requires us to worship God both individually and socially. Freedom of religion is a basic human right that civil law should protect. The act of religion and religious expression must be free because love is free. Catholics believe that the virtue of religion will lead people to seek the truth proclaimed by the Catholic church. "Christ is thus the fulfillment of the yearning of all the world's religions and, as such, he is their sole and definitive completion" (*Tertio Millennio Adveniente*, 6). Therefore, we as individuals and as a church community have the duty to proclaim in word and deed the gospel. We should do so lovingly, prudently, and patiently with those who respond to God in a different way than we do. We should also recall that people should not be forced to act against the dictates of their consciences in religious matters. Our human dignity guarantees people the right to pursue the divine as their inner lights lead them.

We can express the virtue of religion through adoration, prayer, sacrifice, and the keeping of our promises and vows.

* *Adoration* acknowledges that God is God and that we are not. When we adore God we recognize that we are nothing without God. In humility we then submit to and praise God and express our profound thanks for all God has done for us.

* *Prayer* lifts our minds and hearts to God in praise, thanksgiving, sorrow, petition, and intercession. The power of prayer helps us follow God's commandments.

- *Sacrifice*, a word that means "to make holy," must come from within, from a heart given over to God. When we unite our offerings to the only perfect sacrifice—Jesus's sacrifice on the cross—then we make our lives very pleasing to God.

- *Vows* are devotional, deliberate, and free promises of special dedication to God or promises to do some special good work for God. Religion enables us to keep the vows we make to God in the sacraments of baptism and confirmation, and matrimony or holy orders. The church especially recognizes the exemplary value of the evangelical counsels (vows) of poverty, chastity, and obedience.

What Practices Does the First Commandment Condemn? [CCC 2110-2122; 2138-2139]

The first commandment condemns the worship of false gods and sins like superstition, idolatry, divination, magic, irreligion, atheism, and agnosticism.

Superstition attributes special or magical powers to certain objects, acts, words, or external religious practices apart from proper interior dispositions, for example, of faith and humility. For example, it is superstitious to believe that a religious medal hanging from a car's rearview mirror alone has the power to prevent car accidents. What is also necessary are defensive driving techniques, a fine-tuned auto, a sober driver, and faith in God's divine providence and love. The medal can serve as a reminder to turn our lives over to God and to exercise the virtues of prudence and self-control when we begin a trip. To attribute divine powers to a medal is to engage in superstition.

Idolatry refers to the false worship of many gods (polytheism). An example of idolatry from the Hebrew scriptures is the worship pagans gave to gold and silver statues depicting their various gods. Today, people still make gods out of created beings, honoring and revering something in place of God. Satanic cults are idolatrous, but so is undue focus on "gods" like money, power, prestige, and sex. Jesus taught that we cannot serve both God and mammon. We will hate the one and love the other (Lk 16:13). Humans find meaning and fulfillment in worshipping God alone. Idolatry turns our hearts away from our true God by taking a created "good" and making it a "god."

Divination attempts to learn what is hidden (occult) or in the future by invoking Satan or the demons, conjuring up the dead, reading horoscopes or consulting the stars (astrology), consulting mediums, reading palms, dallying with Ouija boards, and similar practices. These activities do not respect a loving God who asks us to trust in his provident, parental care over our lives and our futures.

Magic, or *sorcery,* tries to control hidden powers either to one's own benefit or to another's harm. The church condemns these practices as contrary to the humble submission to God required of true religion.

Irreligion involves *tempting God* by challenging God in word or deed to manifest his goodness and divine wisdom. It does not respect God and displays a severe lack of trust in God's loving, providential care for us. Irreligion also reveals itself in *sacrilege,* that is, profaning the sacraments and other liturgical actions and treating disrespectfully things, places, or persons specially consecrated to God. Sacrilege is mortally sinful, especially when committed against Christ in the eucharist.

Finally, irreligion includes *simony,* the buying or selling of spiritual things. God's graces are free gifts that we can never purchase or sell. Persons with a true religious sense can only receive them with gratitude.

What Is Atheism? *[CCC 2123-2126; 2140]*

Atheism denies God's existence. It is a serious contemporary problem that takes many forms.

For example, *materialism* claims only those realities that can be perceived by the senses have any ultimate value. Materialists deny the existence of any spiritual reality, including God and the human soul. *Humanists* revere humanity as the supreme measure of all reality, as the absolute source of control in the universe. For them, humanity is the god. *Marxists* and *communists* look to socioeconomic laws and forces as the ultimate source of human freedom. Their brand of atheism wreaked tremendous brutality on human beings during the twentieth century, denying the inherent worth of the individual.

Atheism is a serious rejection or denial of God. However, particular circumstances or a person's intentions may diminish the blameworthiness for this offense. Atheism sometimes results because believers misrepresent God or fail to live lovingly, thus concealing God's true nature.

At other times atheism promotes a false idea of human freedom, stressing that depending on God assaults human freedom. Some atheists see religion as a drug that keeps people in check and content with their lot in life. Christians know, however, that true human dignity realizes itself when we acknowledge God and give ourselves over to a loving Creator who respects and supports our freedom.

What Is Agnosticism? *[CCC 2127-2128]*

An *agnostic* holds that no one can know with certainty that God exists. Not totally denying God's existence, the agnostic often slips into religious indifference, begging the important question of God's existence and the implications this would have for religious belief and practice. Though some agnostics may be on a genuine search for God, many are *practical atheists*, that is, they live their lives as though there were no God. Refusing to decide is, in fact, a kind of decision—in most cases a decision against the existence of a God whose acknowledged existence would require some type of religious response.

Does the First Commandment Permit the Veneration of Images? *[CCC 2129-2132; 2141]*

Because of the ancient Israelites' tendency to create and worship false idols, Yahweh forbade them to make any idolatrous image. However, God did instruct the Chosen People to make some images, for example, the bronze serpent, the ark of the covenant, and the cherubim.

Due to the Incarnation, the church finds it most fitting for Christians to venerate icons (pictures, mosaics, etc.) and statues of Jesus, his Blessed Mother, and the angels and saints. These sacred images remind us of and point us to the persons they represent. This traditional church teaching permitting veneration of sacred images was clearly stated at the Second Council of Nicaea in 787 against the *iconoclasts*, those who destroyed sacred images and considered their veneration idolatrous.

The church does caution, however, that we *worship* and *adore* God alone. We give special devotion and veneration to Mary because of her preeminent position in the church and her role as Christ's mother and our mother, too. Likewise, we venerate the saints as Christian heroes who inspire and intercede for us before the Lord. However, veneration and special devotion are not equal to the worship and adoration which is due God alone.

What Does the Second Commandment Require? *[CCC 2142-2145; 2160-2161]*

The second commandment—"You shall not take the name of the Lord your God in vain"—stresses the respect we must pay to God's holy name. Yahweh revealed the awesome, divine name to Moses and the Chosen People. In doing so, Yahweh commanded that we honor his mysterious, holy name in both speech and in sacred affairs in order to praise, reverence, adore, and glorify the Lord God. When we respect the divine name, we reverence the Mystery and the holy One behind the name. One way to exalt the Lord's name is to witness to our belief in the one, true, holy God and to venerate the name of *Jesus*, our savior, and his mother Mary, and all the saints.

What Does the Second Commandment Prohibit? *[CCC 2146-2152; 2162-2163]*

The second commandment prohibits any improper use of God's name or that of Jesus, Mary, or any saint. For example, if we *make a promise* or take a sacred *vow*, then we should be faithful to our word. Not to do so is to misuse God's name and make God out to be a liar.

Likewise, when we take an oath, that is, when we swear on God as a witness that we are telling the truth, we must keep it. Breaking an oath both disrespects God and is a misuse of human speech which should always act in conformity to the Truth, which is God.

To *perjure* oneself is to lie under oath. Perjury is a deliberate and deceptive taking of an oath with the intention not to keep it or, after taking it, failing to keep it. Oath-taking with the intent to commit evil seriously dishonors God's holy name, calling on God to witness a lie.

A most serious violation of the second commandment is **blasphemy**, a sin that is intrinsically gravely sinful. Blasphemy involves internal or external words of hate, defiance, or reproach against God and God's Son. Blasphemy can also extend to Christ's holy church, the saints, and sacred things. In addition, it is a form of blasphemy to invoke God's name to hide a crime or to enslave, torture, or kill people. It can never be justified.

Cursing calls evil down on another. If we fully intend grave harm to befall a person, our sin would be serious.

Is It Sinful to Take an Oath? *[CCC 2153-2155; 2164]*

Swearing to God under oath is a grave matter because God's name is so sacred that we should *never* take it in vain. In the Sermon on the Mount, Jesus calls his disciples to a higher norm of morality, instructing us not to swear, always to say "yes" when we mean yes and "no" when we mean no (Mt 5:33-34).

However, Catholic tradition, following St. Paul's lead (cf 2 Cor 1:23 and Gal 1:20), has not interpreted Jesus' teaching on oath-taking as an absolute prohibition of oaths. For serious and morally correct reasons (for example, in a legal trial) one may take an oath as long as it serves the cause of justice. Christians should not take immoral oaths required by illegitimate governments or legal entities that undermine human dignity or are contrary to Christian unity. A famous example of a saint who refused to take an oath was St. Thomas More. Had he taken an oath required by King Henry VIII of England, he would ultimately have been renouncing the pope's authority over the church, thus impugning his authority as Christ's vicar. Finally, Thomas More was convicted of treason and decapitated for his refusal to affirm Henry's Act of Supremacy. His martyrdom was a supreme witness to the truth, displaying a profound respect and love for Christ and his church.

How Are We and Our Individual Names Holy? *[CCC 2157-2159; 2165-2167]*

Through baptism the Lord makes us holy, sanctifying the name which we will take with us into eternity. Scripture tells us that God always knew us and calls each of us personally by name. As Christ's chosen ones, we and our individual Christian names are holy. Also, at baptism we receive the name of a patron saint, a model of holiness and an intercessor on our behalf. These truths should prompt us to begin our prayers, each day, and our undertakings with the Sign of the Cross. This powerful, but simple prayer reminds us of the loving God to whom we belong, assures us of God's love and our dignity, and strengthens us to live as those worthy of the name *Christian.*

What Does the Third Commandment Require? *[CCC 2168-2173; 2189]*

The third commandment teaches: "Remember the Sabbath day and keep it holy. For six days you shall labor and do all your work, but the seventh day is a Sabbath for Yahweh your God" (Ex 20:8-9). This commandment brings to mind the story of creation when God rested after six days. The Sabbath also memorializes God's freeing the Israelites from slavery in Egypt. God gave the Sabbath day to the Chosen People as a sign of the irrevocable covenant he made with them. This day was set aside for the people to praise God and God's works of creation and his saving acts for Israel.

God's dealings with Israel serve as a model for all humanity. The Sabbath is a day of rest and a respite from grinding work and the adoration of money. The Sabbath is a day for humans to turn to God in worship, thanksgiving, and renewal, a day to remember our dependence on God. Jesus respected the Sabbath law, but he also highlights its true meaning: "The Sabbath was made for man, not man for the Sabbath" (Mk 2:27).

How Do Catholics Observe the Sabbath Law? *[CCC 2174-2179; 2190-2191]*

For Christians no event in salvation history is more important than the Paschal Mystery of Christ's passion, death, resurrection, and glorification. Jesus' resurrection is the beginning of a new creation, the promise of our own eternal life. It took place on Sunday, the first day of the week. Sunday is properly call the "Lord's Day."

Christians assemble on Sunday to commemorate his Passover, to obey his command to break bread in his name, to worship, praise, and thank God for the gift of the Son and all the divine blessings on us. From the time of the apostles, Christians have observed the moral commandment of the old covenant by worshipping God publicly at the eucharist on the Lord's Day. Sunday is the preeminent holy day that commemorates God's decisive act for us through Jesus.

Today, Catholics continue to assemble on Sunday or the Sunday vigil (Saturday evening) in parish communities, led by pastors, to express, celebrate, and deepen our unity in Christ. We celebrate the eucharist in obedience to Christ and to derive the nourishment of the living Lord himself in order to live a Christian life both as individuals and in community.

How Is the Sunday Obligation Binding? *[CCC 2180-2183; 2192]*

Church law requires Catholics to participate in the Sunday Mass or its vigil and all other holy days of obligation. The eucharist is the foundation and heart of Christian life. To participate in the eucharistic celebration is to testify publicly that we belong to Jesus and are members of his body, the church. It is the preeminent opportunity to worship God as Jesus mandated, to derive strength and guidance from the Holy Spirit, and spiritual life from the resurrected Lord. Because of the central importance of the eucharist to Catholic and church life, we have a *serious* obligation to participate in the Mass on Sundays and holy days, unless excused for a proportionately serious reason like sickness or infant care or dispensation of one's own pastor. Deliberately failing to observe this duty is mortally sinful.

How Do We Make the Lord's Day Holy? *[CCC 2184-2188; 2193-2195]*

Positively, we sanctify the Lord's day by relaxing, spending quality time with our families, and doing charitable work for others like the elderly, poor, and needy. We also make Sunday holy by reading, reflecting, meditating, enjoying nature, and pursuing cultural activities that refresh the mind, heart, and spirit.

Because of the critical nature of their jobs and vocations, some people have to work on Sundays. However, they should also take care to set aside time for rest, prayer, and reflection. Christians especially should be careful not to make unnecessary demands on others on Sundays, demands that would prevent them from enjoying the Sabbath rest.

A commitment to refrain from unnecessary work and business activities that would keep us from worshipping God or relaxing the mind and body will help us observe the spirit of the third commandment.

Concluding Reflections

Someone once observed wisely, "Everyone has a reason for staying home from church—even those who are here." How true! But those who decide to come have even a greater reason for going—to worship a loving God who has given us life, friends, health, minds to enjoy beauty, and hearts to experience love. Without God, we would not exist. We are indebted beyond what we could ever repay.

Common sense dictates that we should adore a God who freely gives us life and so many other good things, especially the promise of eternal life in union with our beloved Jesus. The first three commandments remind us to keep things in perspective: to love God above all and to recognize that God deserves our respect, adoration, and love.

Prayer Reflection

The psalms are a rich resource for heartfelt prayers that worship and praise God. For example Psalm 146 expresses our promise to praise God all our lives.

> Alleluia!
> Praise Yahweh, my soul!
> I will praise Yahweh all my life,
> I will make music to my God as long as I live.
> He keeps faith forever,
> gives justice to the oppressed,
> gives food to the hungry;
> Yahweh sets prisoners free.
> Yahweh gives sight to the blind,
> lifts up those who are bowed down.
> Yahweh protects the stranger,
> he sustains the orphan and the widow.
> Yahweh loves the upright,
> but he frustrates the wicked.
> Yahweh reigns for ever,
> your God, Zion, from age to age.
>
> —Psalm 146:1-2; 7-10

For Discussion

1. How do you show love for God? Share at least two different ways.
2. What are some ways Christians can counteract the trend of vulgar, obscene, and blasphemous language in our day and age?
3. Besides Mass, what do you and your family do to make Sunday holy?
4. How would you respond to someone who does not go to Mass on Sunday because they say, "I can pray and worship God on my own?"

Further Reading

Psalms 145; 147–150 (other psalms of praise to almighty God)

Chapter Twenty-One

The Last Seven Commandments: Love of Neighbor

I give you a new commandment:
love another;
you must love one another
just as I have loved you.
— John 13:34

A story is told of a suburban man driving to work in the city. Each day he had to pass by a shelter for hungry and homeless people. On a particularly cold day he noticed a long line of needy people lined up around the block waiting for the center to open and dispense its morning fare of coffee and donuts. The scene depressed the man. So he cried out to the Lord, "Why don't you do something about this miserable scene? Why do you allow this suffering to go on?"

As the man drove into the parking lot at his place of employment, he distinctly heard an inner voice speak to him. It was the Lord. And the Lord said, "I did do something about it. I made you!"

This story reminds us that the Lord has chosen each of us to be his caring hands, his voice of truth, his compassionate eyes. He uses us to accomplish his work, to bring his love into the world. This chapter looks at the last seven commandments, which focus on love of neighbor and self and teach us virtues like fidelity, honesty, integrity, and self-control.

What Values Are Fostered by the Fourth Commandment?
[CCC 2196-2213; 2247-2250]

The fourth commandment instructs us: "Honor your father and your mother so that you may live long in the land that Yahweh your

God is giving you" (Ex 20:12). Interestingly, this commandment opens the second tablet of the Decalogue revealing that love of neighbor extends in a primary way to our parents. Charity does indeed begin at home. It requires honor, affection, respect, and gratitude shown not only to parents and other family members, but also to relatives and authorities who take the place of parents. Following this commandment results in peace and harmony in families and various other communities to which we belong.

The fourth commandment highlights the sacredness of the family which God created as the primary unit of society. A husband and wife join in marriage after giving free consent. They do so for their own good—their mutual enrichment and the sharing of love—and for the procreation and education of children. Moreover, the Christian family is a real community of persons equal in dignity. It is a living symbol of the unity among the three persons of the Blessed Trinity, and a "domestic church," a community of faith, hope, and love nourished by prayer, mutual respect, and the scriptures. There is a direct correlation between the well-being of married and family life and the happiness of individuals and the communities to which we belong—both civic and ecclesial. Civil authorities must recognize and protect the family for the sake of the raising of children in peace, dignity, and with free access to a religious education in God's ways.

Additionally, the family is the school for proper moral education. It teaches its members the virtues, respect, love, and acceptance of others. In a society that cares for and supports the family, we learn about other societal relationships, and come to recognize that everyone is a someone with profound dignity loved by God and thus deserving of just treatment and respect for their individual worth.

What Do Children Owe Their Parents? [CCC 2214-2220; 2251]

Children owe their parents gratitude for giving them the gift of life. They manifest this gratitude by showing parents respect and obedience as long as they live in their parents' home. Grown children must also respect their parents. They should meet their physical and spiritual needs in times of illness and loneliness and help them with problems associated with old age.

Children should also obey the reasonable and moral directions of teachers and others to whom their parents entrust them.

Brothers and sisters should also contribute to family unity by treating each other respectfully and lovingly.

In addition, Christians should thank all those who nurture their life in Christ, including parents, grandparents, catechists, pastors, and family friends.

What Are the Responsibilities of Parents? *[CCC 2221-2234; 2252-2253]*

Parents have a profound duty to respect their children not only as their own offspring but as unique persons endowed with dignity who are, above all else, God's children. Parents have the prime and inalienable right to educate their children, especially in the faith, proclaiming to them the gospel, teaching them to pray, and pointing out the way God is present in their lives. Parents must also create a welcoming home, a haven where their children can experience warmth, love, respect, forgiveness, and a spirit of unselfish service.

Parents educate their children in the Christian life of virtue through their own good example, teaching them to follow Christ Jesus and encouraging them to listen to the Lord who may be calling them to a vocation to the priesthood or religious life. Parents have a basic right to choose a school for their children that reflects their own values.

Parents of adult children must respect the right of their children to choose a vocation, profession, and spouse. Their role is that of advisor whose love and affection are unconditional, reflecting the love of almighty God for his children.

What Does the Fourth Commandment Require of the Civic Life? *[CCC 2235-2246; 2254-2257]*

The fourth commandment serves to remind those in authority that they must serve others. They should follow natural law, administer distributive justice wisely, and work for civic peace and harmony. They do this by respecting individual rights and encouraging people to work for the common good.

Citizens, on the other hand, should view public authorities as God's representatives. According to their abilities and talents, citizens must contribute to the common good, working in a spirit of truth, justice, peace, freedom, and solidarity. Furthermore, citizens have the duty to pay taxes, to vote, and to come to the defense of their country.

However, citizens also have the God-given responsibility *not* to obey laws issued by public authorities that contradict divine law. Armed resistance against unjust and oppressive governments is only permissible when very *strict* standards are met (see *CCC* 2243).

The church encourages contemporary societies to ground their vision of humans and their destiny in God's revealed truth. History has shown how societies have often become totalitarian when they are not grounded in a gospel view of human beings as persons of unique dignity who are children of a loving God. The church does not align itself with any given political philosophy or community. Rather, it encourages and respects the political freedom and individual responsibility of citizens. As Christ's presence in the world, the church must speak out at times on political issues, especially as they effect fundamental rights of human beings or the salvation of their souls.

What Does the Fifth Commandment Teach? *[CCC 2258-2262; 2268; 2302-2303; 2318-2320]*

The fifth commandment—"You shall not kill" (Ex 20:13)—teaches respect for the sanctity of human life. All human life is sacred. This is true from the first moment of conception until natural death brings a person to God. Only God is the Lord of life. Humans have utmost dignity because God wills us into being for our own sake, creating us in his image and likeness. Therefore, any direct and intentional killing by anyone is always gravely sinful.

The fifth commandment refers to the deliberate murder of innocent persons. The Old Testament teaches that murder arises out of anger and envy, as in Cain killing Abel, and is a result of original sin. Such killing violates human dignity, God's holiness, and Jesus' teaching to love neighbor as self. Jesus himself condemned anger that leads to revenge and to hatred that deliberately wishes another evil. These sinful attitudes of heart lead to grave sin, including murder.

When Is Killing Morally Justified? *[CCC 2263-2267; 2321]*

Killing in self-defense is morally permissible when, as a last resort, a person is protecting his or her own life or another person's life for whom he or she is responsible. In legitimate self-defense one only *intends* the effect of saving one's life against an unjust aggressor; the *killing* of the assailant is not willed, only permitted.

Analogously, public authorities have both the right and duty to defend citizens against unjust aggressors, especially in the case of a war defense. (For church teaching on war, see Chapter 18.) However, if bloodless means are enough to defend against aggressors, they *must* be used and killing avoided.

Also, many Christians today, including the American bishops, cannot reconcile capital punishment with a consistent "respect-for-life ethic." The purpose of punishing criminals is to redress the disorder caused by the offense, to preserve public order and personal safety, and to correct the offender. The poor and minorities, who cannot afford the costly appeals process of our legal system, have suffered capital punishment the most, a form of punishment that does not reform the criminal. Furthermore, there is little evidence to show that capital punishment deters crime, a key reason people have used to justify it. And though the church recognizes society's right to use the death penalty in grave cases, it is to the credit of Christian nations to follow Jesus' example of forgiving love and refrain from exercising it. *The Gospel of Life* teaches that because of the many means society has to deter crime today, capital punishment should very rarely be used. It should only take place

> in cases of absolute necessity: in other words, when it would not be possible otherwise to defend society. Today however, as a result of steady improvements in the organization of the penal system, such cases are very rare, if not practically non-existent (56, emphasis added).

What Are Some Evils Condemned by the Fifth Commandment? *[CCC 2268-2283; 2322-2325]*

Actions that directly and intentionally kill the innocent and actions or failures to act that cause the indirect killing of others are forbidden by the fifth commandment. Thus, murder is gravely wrong. Also:

- *Infanticide, fratricide, parricide,* and the murder of a spouse are especially serious because of the natural bonds involved in those relationships.

- Direct **abortion**, willed either as a means or an end, is a grave violation of the fifth commandment. Since the dawn of Christian history, the church has insisted that human life must be respected and protected from the very first moment of conception. Church teaching has not changed and cannot change: abortion is a grave evil. Because of this truth and to stress the evil of abortion, the church has attached the canonical penalty of automatic excommunication on anyone who procures an abortion.

The church teaches that society's laws must recognize the right to life of every human person. Everyone has a God-given right to life from the moment of conception. This right does not have to be earned.

It is morally permitted to medically care for a human embryo since it is truly a human person. However, any prenatal procedures engaged in for the purpose of abortion, medical experimentation that treats the embryo as disposable biological material, or genetic manipulation that is non-therapeutic are all seriously wrong.

- *Euthanasia*, means "easy death." *Direct* or *active* euthanasia ("mercy killing") is any "action or omission which of itself and by intention causes death, with the purpose of eliminating all suffering" (*The Gospel of Life*, 65). Regardless of one's intention (for example, to relieve pain), direct euthanasia is gravely wrong. Active euthanasia is to be distinguished from "aggressive medical treatment," that is, medical procedures that are disproportionate to any expected results or impose an excessive burden on the patient and his or her family. These extraordinary means can be refused. Of course, one must take ordinary means to care for oneself or to allow oneself to be cared for, but to forego extraordinary means is not equal to suicide or euthanasia. Additionally, a person can take painkillers to lessen suffering, even though one's life might be shortened. In this case, death is not willed as a means or an end, it is merely tolerated as inevitable.

- *Suicide* is a grave wrong because it ends the gift of life that comes from God. It is contrary to love of self and others and represents a rejection of God's absolute sovereignty over life and death. Additionally, it often gives scandal. Grave psychological problems, overwhelming fear in the face of anticipated suffering, torture, and the like, can reduce blameworthiness for a person who commits suicide. Although the action itself is gravely wrong, we can only commend the person who commits suicide to the unfathomable mercy of our loving God. It is our duty to pray for those who commit suicide.

The church also teaches the grave sin of assisted suicide:

> To concur with the intention of another person to commit suicide and to help in carrying it out through so-called "assisted suicide" means to cooperate in, and at times to be the actual perpetrator of, an injustice which can never be excused, even if it is requested (The Gospel of Life, 66).

What Is Scandal? *[CCC 2284-2287; 2326]*

Scandal is an attitude that leads others to do evil. Individuals, laws, institutions like the media, current fashions, or opinions can give scandal. Scandal is mortally sinful if it leads another person to commit a serious offense. It is especially grave when those in positions of authority, for example, teachers, perpetrate it.

How Does the Fifth Commandment Teach Us to Respect Life? *[CCC 2288-2300; 2326]*

We respect God's gift of life when we adopt healthy habits like getting proper exercise and rest, challenging the mind to grow, eating wholesome food, and avoiding harmful substances like drugs, alcohol, and tobacco. In our day, the trafficking in drugs and drug addiction (including alcoholism) are notorious cancers that destroy families, result in crime, and lead to the disintegration of persons. Living a wholesome life shows that we appreciate God's gift of life; it frees us to be persons for others.

Many moral issues today involve medical ethics. We show a profound respect for life when medical experimentation and initiatives (for example, organ transplants) conform to the natural law, respect human dignity, involve informed consent, and promote public health and the common good.

Other moral issues deal with the violation of fundamental human rights. Crimes like kidnapping, hostage taking, acts of terrorism, and torture are violent acts which are grave threats to human dignity. They are seriously immoral. So are bodily mutilations, amputations, and sterilizations unless they are performed for strictly beneficial medical reasons.

We also respect life when we allow dying persons to live their last moments in dignity and peace and treat human corpses with respect and love, demonstrating Christian hope in the resurrection.

Finally, we should always remember the Christian duty to promote, protect, and speak for others, especially the weak and helpless. Christians are, by definition, pro-life, that is, supportive of others' right to life including all that they need to live with dignity. Simply put, being pro-life means to fight the many assaults to human life that threaten our world today.

What Values Link the Sixth and Ninth Commandments? *[CCC 2331-2336; 2392-2393]*

The sixth commandment is "You shall not commit adultery" (Ex 20:14). The ninth commandment is "You shall not set your heart on your neighbor's spouse" (Ex 20:17). These two commandments embrace all aspects of human sexuality and teach us to use our sexuality in a way that respects God's plan for us.

God's gift of sexuality gives men and women an innate vocation and responsibility to love and to communion. Involving all aspects of the human person, sexuality affects especially our capacities to love and procreate. The sixth and ninth commandments teach us how to do so responsibly, that is, by accepting our sexual nature and acknowledging that males and females have equal personal dignity because we are created in God's image. The virtues of chastity, purity, and modesty empower us to live our sexuality according to God's plan.

What Is Chastity? *[CCC 2337-2350; 2394-2395]*

Chastity comes under the cardinal virtue of temperance that seeks to moderate according to reason our human appetites and passions. **Chastity** is that virtue which helps us integrate our sexuality with all aspects of our personhood. Its model is Christ Jesus himself who calls all persons to live chastely according to their state in life. Thus, married people are called to conjugal chastity. Single people and those in religious and vowed life must practice the virtue of chastity by living continently. Chastity also requires engaged couples to exercise self-control and reserve for marriage signs of affection that belong to marriage alone.

Chastity demands the difficult and lifelong task of self-mastery. It requires personal effort at all stages of life and a cultural effort that supports an individual's human dignity and a right to wholesome education. Chastity is a moral virtue but also a gift of the Holy Spirit who strengthens us in our spiritual efforts to integrate our sexuality. Means of self-mastery include a keen desire to resist temptations by avoiding "near occasions of sin" (like pornography). It also demands honest self-knowledge, works of self-discipline, obedience to God's commandments, practicing the moral virtues, a faithful prayer life, and frequent reception of the sacraments of reconciliation and eucharist.

What Are the Virtues of Purity and Modesty? *[CCC 2351; 2514-2533]*

The virtues of purity and modesty help us combat lust, a vice contrary to the virtue of chastity. *Lust* is the disordered craving for or enjoyment of sexual pleasure, that is, sexual pleasure sought for itself, isolated from its procreative and unitive functions.

Lust arises from carnal *concupiscence*, that is, the desires of our sense appetites contrary to human reason, our "flesh" warring against our "spirit." This tension in the human person results from original sin and inclines us to commit sin. Coveting others sexually is a form of concupiscence that allows strong, uncontrolled internal desires (lust) to turn others into objects of our pleasure. Jesus warned:

> "But I say this to you, if a man looks at a woman lustfully, he has already committed adultery with her in his heart" (Mt 5:28).

Sexual thoughts and desires are good. They become evil when we allow them to control us or when they cause us to look on others as objects for self-gratification.

Purity of the heart helps us in the struggle against carnal lust. It attunes our minds and hearts to God's holiness, not only in the areas of sex and chastity, but also in the virtues of charity and love of truth and right faith. To gain purity of heart, we must cooperate with God's grace by living chastely; by genuinely seeking God's will; by disciplining our feelings and imaginations, that is, by refusing impure thoughts when they arise; and by continual prayer for God's help.

Purity requires *modesty*, an integral part of the cardinal virtue of temperance. Modesty protects the mystery of persons and their love; it guards their intimate center by refusing to unveil what should remain discreet. Modesty requires patience and moderation in love relationships, decency in the clothes we wear, and a reserved and discreet attitude when talking about sex. Modesty governs unhealthy curiosity and demands respect of persons. In today's sex-saturated society, the virtue of modesty requires Christians to take an active role in purifying the social environment (especially various media) of an eroticism and sexual permissiveness that dehumanizes and inflames sexual appetites beyond God's moral law.

What Are Other Sins Contrary to the Virtue of Chastity? [CCC 2352-2359; 2396]

Masturbation, fornication, pornography, prostitution, rape, and homosexual acts all offend against the virtue of chastity.

- *Masturbation* is self-induced sexual pleasure. The church teaches that all voluntary sexual activity or pleasure—including thoughts, actions, and words—outside of marriage is objectively and seriously wrong. When we excite our sexual passions outside the commitment of marriage, we misuse the sexual powers that God has given us. Inexperience, habit, or circumstances, however, can diminish our blameworthiness in this area as we grow to maturity.

- *Fornication* refers to sexual intercourse engaged in by unmarried people and is also forbidden by Christian morality. Many acts of fornication are selfish and exploit the partner. But fornication is also wrong because God intends sexual sharing to express *total* love and commitment which is open to the sharing of life. Fornication seeks pleasure without responsibility. It lacks the unconditional love that the sacrament of marriage represents.

- *Pornography* removes the marital act from the intimacy of a loving marriage and depersonalizes it for deliberate display to others. It damages the dignity of those who create, sell, and use it to arouse their passions.

- *Prostitution* debases those who sell their bodies and seriously violates the virtue of chastity in those who pay for it.

- *Rape* is always a seriously, intrinsically evil act. Through force it violates another's sexuality and is an affront to their dignity as a child of God. Rape violates both justice and love. Similar acts that seriously offend against God's law are *incest* and the *sexual abuse of children*.

- *Homosexual activity* is objectively wrong because it frustrates the aims of God's gift of sexuality: unity between a husband and wife and the openness to the transmission of human life. However, persons with a *homosexual orientation* are not morally guilty for their condition. However, they must resist translating their sexual desires into actions.

Although homosexual acts themselves are seriously wrong, we must always be careful about judging a person's subjective blameworthiness. Prejudice against someone who has a homosexual orientation is wrong. We must accept such persons as our brothers and sisters. We must do so, however, without approving sexual activity that God's law forbids. (We must also disapprove in the same way of *heterosexual* premarital sex.)

In the area of sexual morality, Christ calls us to high standards, but as our brother and Savior, he knows what it means to be human. He extends his love and guidance to us through the church. He also gives us the Holy Spirit whose graces through the sacraments and prayer empower us to live a chaste, wholesome lives. As Christians blessed with the good news, we should also remember that failures in this area should not be occasions of self-hate but opportunities to grow and experience the love and forgiveness of the Lord.

What Does the Church Teach About Sexual Sharing Within Marriage? *[CCC 2360-2365; 2397]*

The church teaches that sexual intercourse (and all acts leading up to it) expresses a total, unreserved commitment of love. Sexual intercourse symbolizes that commitment of love and helps increase it. Such a commitment can take place only when a couple has declared publicly a lifelong devotion to each other. This can take place only in the sacrament of marriage. Marital sexual sharing is an authentic sign of the total gift of the husband to the wife and the wife to the husband. This beautiful symbol mirrors Christ's unconditional love for his body, the church.

The Bible reveals the holiness of sex when it tells us that the sexual love of marriage beautifully symbolizes God's love. For example, the Song of Songs compares God's love for the Chosen People to the passionate love that a husband has for his bride. And in Ephesians St. Paul refers to the church as the bride of Christ; Jesus is the bridegroom (Eph 5:25-33). The love of a Christian husband and wife should reflect Christ's love for his church.

> To sum up: you also, each of you, must love his wife as he loves himself; and let every wife respect her husband (Eph 5:33).

The sexual love between a husband and a wife is both a sign and pledge of their spiritual unity. Their sexual sharing, a source of both joy and pleasure within the marriage bond, has two purposes: *unitive*, that is, a loving bonding of a man and a woman as lifelong partners; and *procreative*, that is, a sharing in God's creative activity of bringing new life into the world. Each act of sexual intercourse should be open to these two ends of marriage: the sharing of life and mutual love.

What Does the Church Teach About Family Planning? *[CCC 2366-2369; 2398]*

The church teaches that a married couple must follow God's plan that each act of sexual intercourse be open to both the sharing of love *and* the transmission of life. For just and moral reasons, spouses may regulate the spacing of the birth of their children. The physical and psychological health of a spouse, family finances, or the current number of children could be legitimate factors to consider when a couple determines the size and spacing of their family. However, selfishness or greed—for example, not wanting a child because of a desire to attain a certain materialistic lifestyle—would be sinful motives for practicing birth control.

Moral methods of birth regulation include periodic abstinence from sexual relations and natural family planning methods. These are in harmony with objective criteria of morality because they respect normal, natural bodily functions. They respect the bodies of the husband and wife and encourage tenderness and authentic communication. Two popular and effective natural methods of birth control are the sympto-thermal method and the ovulation method, also known as the Billings method. The *Family Life Bureau* of most dioceses sponsors classes to help train couples in these methods.

What Does the Church Teach About Artificial Means of Contraception? [CCC 2370; 2399]

Church teaching holds that artificial means of contraception are contrary to God's will. Artificial birth control refers to pills or devices (like condoms or diaphragms) that interfere with the conception of a child. The church also teaches that sterilization—making the reproductive organs unfruitful—is also wrong except when the organs are diseased and threaten the health of the whole body.

This teaching rests on the Catholic view that marriage is directed to two aims simultaneously: the procreation (and rearing) of children and the mutual love and affection of the couple. Thus sexual relations which are selfishly engaged in by one partner without taking note of the feelings and desires of the other partner are wrong because one of the aims of marriage—mutual love—is destroyed. Likewise church teaching maintains that any artificial means used to frustrate the natural processes of procreation go against the very nature of marriage. Christian marriage is a sacrament, an effective sign of mutual love and openness to life. To rule out either of these purposes unnaturally or selfishly is to frustrate God's intent which is built into the very nature of marriage.

The classic statement of official church teaching in this regard is found in Pope Paul VI's encyclical entitled *Humanae Vitae* (*Of Human Life*):

> The church calling men back to the observance of the norms of the natural law, as interpreted by constant doctrine, teaches that each and every marriage act must remain open to the transmission of life (11).

In striving to live the ideal, sometimes people fall short. Thus, the pope and the bishops encourage married couples to frequent the sacraments of reconciliation and the eucharist to gain strength from the Lord.

Human life and its transmission should be judged from the point of view of our eternal destiny. The state may not usurp the fundamental rights of parents who have the primary duty to procreate and educate children.

What Does the Church Teach About Infertility? [CCC 2373-2379]

Sadly some couples are unable to have children because of infertility. Moral means of reducing infertility are allowed, but techniques that involve third parties through donated sperm or ova are seriously immoral because they intrude on the exclusive marriage union of the husband and wife. Medical techniques that involve only the married couple, but involve procedures that separate sexual lovemaking from the act of procreation, are also seriously disordered and not allowed.

A child is a gift from God. A child is not a thing, a piece of property. No one has an absolute right to a child. A couple suffering from infertility should join themselves to the cross of Christ. Many such couples have generous hearts which can show their love by adopting unwanted children or by committing themselves to other compassionate acts of service for others.

What Sins Violate the Sacredness of Marriage? *[CCC 2380-2391; 2400]*

The following violate the sacredness of marriage:

- *Adultery* is sexual intimacy engaged in by a married person with another who is not one's spouse. Adultery is a serious failure in the permanent commitment of a married couple who promised lifelong fidelity to each other. It is a serious injustice to one's spouse and one's children and brings about societal discord.

- **Divorce** is forbidden by the Lord who reinstituted God's original intent that marriage be indissoluble. The church will permit civil divorce when it is the only way legal rights can be protected or children cared for. Divorce is a serious offense against the sacramental bond of marriage. Sometimes it involves the desertion of a spouse and children, and so is an especially callous disregard of God's law. Sometimes a divorced spouse will remarry adding public adultery to the situation. At other times one partner who was unjustly abandoned is an innocent victim of a civil divorce; this spouse has not broken the divine law.

- Other sins against marriage include *polygamy* (having several spouses), *incest* (having sexual relations within a prohibited degree of relationship), the reprehensible crime of the *sexual abuse of children*, *free union* (living together without exchanging marriage vows), and so-called "trial marriages."

What Values Underlie the Seventh and Tenth Commandments? *[CCC 2401-2407; 2450-2452; 2534-2535]*

The seventh commandment is, "You shall not steal." The tenth commandment tells us, "You shall not covet your neighbor's goods." The seventh commandment requires just and loving stewardship of material possessions. It reminds us that God created the goods of creation for all humans. Although people have the right to private property and the fruits of their labors, personal ownership should be directed to the common good, as well as the welfare of the owner.

The seventh commandment mandates that we exercise the virtue of temperance in relation to material possessions so we do not become overly attached to them. It also requires the virtue of justice which recognizes our neighbors' property rights. Finally, it encourages us to practice solidarity by which we share our possessions with others, especially the most needy.

The tenth commandment recognizes that we desire to own things that give us pleasure. These desires are morally acceptable as long as they are kept within the bonds of reason and do not turn into coveting unjustly the belongings of others. The tenth commandment forbids the inordinate craving for another's goods that might lead us to immoral acts forbidden by the seventh commandment—acts like theft, robbery, and fraud.

What Else Does the Seventh Commandment Forbid? *[CCC 2408-2414; 2453-2455]*

The seventh commandment condemns *theft*, defined as taking another's property against his or her reasonable will.

Also forbidden is any unjust taking and keeping of another's property. This includes business fraud, paying unjust wages, price fixing, corruption, shoddy work, tax evasion, forgery, padding expense accounts, wasteful practices, and the destruction of public or private property (vandalism).

The seventh commandment requires that promises and contracts be kept. *Commutative justice* strictly requires equitable relations between individuals. Consequently, we must honor the property rights of others, pay our debts, fulfill any contractual obligations freely entered, and make reparation for any injustice caused another. Gambling is morally acceptable if we do so honestly and do not become addicted to it (a real danger), and thus deprive others of basic necessities. The seventh commandment also condemns the enslavement of people for profit or treating people as property to buy, sell, or exchange. No commercial or totalitarian motive can possibly justify this heinous assault on human dignity and freedom.

Incidentally, church tradition distinguishes commutative justice which regulates relations between individuals, *legal* justice which deals with the rights citizens owe their community, and *distributive* justice which governs what the larger society owes its citizens according to their needs and contributions.

Also, Catholic theology holds that one does not steal even when one is in need of life's essentials like food, clothing, or shelter.

Finally, the seventh commandment deals with many issues in the area of social justice, the economy, and the treatment of the poor. Chapter 18 discusses these topics in more detail.

What Else Does the Tenth Commandment Forbid? *[CCC 2536-2557]*

The tenth commandment forbids greed, avarice, and envy. *Greed* is the desire to amass unlimited wealth. *Avarice* is the passionate seeking of riches and the power that comes from them. *Envy*, a capital sin, is sadness at another's possessions and an inordinate desire to obtain them for oneself, even unjustly. Envy involves a lack of love and often arises from pride. When, due to envy, a person hopes for serious harm to another, it is an occasion of mortal sinfulness.

Greed, envy, and avarice lead to the commission of sins outlawed by the seventh commandment. Christians combat these sins of the heart, especially envy, through love, humility, and a willingness to be led by God. After all, we know that God alone can satisfy our restless hearts. The desire for wealth can quickly become idolatrous. Jesus teaches that we should choose him and his Father's kingdom first, and what we need will be provided for us. He instructs us to be poor in spirit, to be detached from earthly riches so we might enter God's kingdom in heaven.

Reflecting on and praying over what will truly make us happy—union with God—and allowing ourselves to be led by the Holy Spirit will help liberate excessive cravings over those transitory things that pass away all too quickly.

What Is the Teaching of the Eighth Commandment? *[CCC 2464-2474; 2504-2505]*

The eighth commandment—"You shall not bear false witness against your neighbor"—teaches us to witness to the God of truth. Negatively, the eighth commandment forbids misrepresenting the truth. Positively, it demands that we live the virtue of truthfulness in both words and deeds, guarding against duplicity, dissimulation, and hypocrisy.

When we follow this commandment, we are being just to others, we are witnessing to the truth, who is Jesus Christ, and we are making his truth known.

What Are Sins Against the Eighth Commandment? *[CCC 2475-2487; 2507-2509]*

Honoring the truth means respecting other people, their reputations, and their right to privacy. False witness in court and *perjury*—lying under oath—gravely obstruct justice. These sins condemn the innocent or unfairly exonerate or exacerbate the punishment of the guilty.

If we respect the truth and other people, we will not engage in *rash judgment*, that is, prejudicially assuming their moral culpability. Christians can combat rash judgment by always putting the most positive interpretation on another's thoughts, words, and deeds. *Detraction* (revealing another's faults without good reasons) and *calumny* (spreading lies about someone) violate the virtue of truthfulness. These sins assault the honor of a person's reputation and therefore offend both justice and charity.

Being truthful also prohibits *lying*. To lie means to speak a falsehood with the intent to deceive, that is, to lead into error someone who has a right to know the truth. Lying is contrary to the gift of speech whose purpose is to communicate truth. Lying is mortally sinful when it causes grave harm. Whenever we sin against justice and truth we must make a serious effort to repair the harm caused. This is especially true when we have damaged someone's reputation.

Do We Have an Absolute Right to Know the Truth? *[CCC 2488-2492; 2510-2511]*

Christian charity and prudent discretion indicate that not everyone who seeks information has a right to it. Thus, at times we should use discreet language or remain silent for the good and safety of others, to respect the common good, or to honor one's reasonable right to privacy. For example, priests may *never* reveal what they hear in confession (the "seal of confession"). And professionals like doctors and lawyers have the right to keep confidential secrets revealed to them unless grave harm would result from their silence. Everyone, including the media, must respect the privacy and freedom of public figures.

What Is the Relationship Between Truth and Society? *[CCC 2493-2503; 2512-2513]*

The communications media have a powerful impact in today's society. The media has a responsibility to provide the public with information based on truth, freedom, justice, and solidarity.

In addition, governments should refrain from manipulating the media for political, totalitarian, ideological, or economic motives. Society has a right to truthful information rooted in freedom, justice, and human solidarity.

Truth has its own beauty because it corresponds to reality. God's truth reveals itself in his magnificent creation and in the words of scripture. Through their creative works of art, humans express their relationship to God's truth and beauty. When human art (especially sacred art) reflects God's truth, beauty, and love, then it helps reveal the divine majesty and draws us to adore, pray, and love the Triune God.

Concluding Reflections

When it comes to living the moral life some people are like Christopher Columbus.

He didn't know where he was going.

He didn't know where he was when he got there.

He didn't know where he had been when he returned.

Christians, however, know clearly their destination: union with a loving God for all eternity. Moreover, they have a road map on how to get there: the Ten Commandments.

Note the word *commandments*. The list God gave to Moses on Mount Sinai was not called the "Ten Suggestions." These rules for the game of life teach us how to focus our love. They teach us how to make God the beginning, middle, and end of all our efforts. In short, they instruct us on how to love God above all, with all of our heart, with all our being, with all our strength, and with all our mind. And they teach us how to love our neighbor as we love ourselves.

The Lord himself taught us how to show our friendship to him: "If you keep my commandments you will remain in my love, just as I have kept my Father's commandments and remain in his love" (Jn 15:10).

Prayer Reflection

Use this "Morning Offering to the Sacred Heart" to help you dedicate your day to God.

> O Jesus, through the Immaculate Heart of Mary, I offer You my prayers, works, joys and sufferings of this day for all the intentions of Your Sacred Heart, in union with the Holy Sacrifice of the Mass throughout the world, in reparation for my sins, for the intentions of all our associates, and in particular for the intentions of our Holy Father for this month.

For Discussion

1. What are the most serious threats to human life today? What can you to promote the welfare of human life?
2. Do you believe the media are to blame for the degradation of sex in today's society or do they merely reflect current attitudes? What can a Christian do to promote a healthy attitude to sexual morality for various age groups?
3. Why do you think that some people routinely shade the truth?
4. For you, what does it mean to be a person of integrity?
5. How can the commandments help you to love God? your neighbor? yourself?

Further Reading

1 John 2:3–5:13

Part 4:

Christian Prayer

The Christian faith is to be believed, celebrated, and lived in a intense and personal relationship with the living and true God. The relationship is developed, nurtured, and maintained in prayer.

The *Catechism of the Catholic Church* describes prayer as God's gift. Only when we recognize that God is the giver, and we are the humble ones who receive his gifts are we open to prayer.

Prayer is also the place of covenant. Prayer comes from the heart. As the *Catechism* describes:

> The heart is our hidden center, beyond the grasp of our reason and of others; only the Spirit of God can fathom the human heart and know it fully (2563).

Thirdly, prayer is being in communion with God. Prayer is the habit of being in God's presence (*CCC* 2565).

This final chapter explores several questions having to do with the tradition of Judeo-Christian prayer, types of prayer, and how we, as Christians do pray.

Chapter Twenty-Two

Christian Prayer

"Ask, and it will be given to you; search, and you will find; knock, and the door will be opened to you. Everyone who asks receives; everyone who searches finds; everyone who knocks will have the door opened."
— Matthew 7:7-8

A famous actor attended a retirement party for an old pastor, known for his great holiness of life. The guests asked the actor to recite for them the pastor's favorite prayer, Psalm 23, "The Lord Is My Shepherd." He reluctantly agreed to do so on one condition—that the pastor would also pray it when he was finished.

The pastor was surprised because his speaking abilities were not the best. But he agreed to do so when the actor finished.

The actor in a deep and well-intoned voice delivered the prayer beautifully. The audience was spellbound and applauded him vigorously when he sat down. It was now the pastor's turn. His voice was not well-trained nor his diction faultless, but when he sat down there was not a dry eye in the room.

The actor rose and holding back the tears said, "My dear people, you heard some well-recited words that sounded nice to your ears. However, your holy pastor has touched your hearts. Here's the difference: I know how to read the Psalm. He knows the Shepherd."[1]

The goal of our Christian life is not simply to mouth pious words. Our goal is to know the Shepherd. And prayer is the way to attain this goal.

What Is Prayer? *[CCC 2558-2567; 2590]*

Prayer begins in humility, a gift from God that involves a divine dimension as well as human action. God seeks us first in prayer. The Holy Spirit moves us to respond in faith to the Father's calling. Prayer is our response to God's abiding, faithful love.

But what *is* prayer? There are many good definitions of prayer, for example, "the lifting of one's mind and heart to God." Prayer is also asking God for good things. Or prayer is our conscious turning to God, directing our thoughts and love to him. We can also define prayer as "the heart's response to our search for God."

In prayer, we enter into a dialogue with the Lord. We both *listen* to the Spirit and *speak* our own heartfelt prayers of adoration, contrition, thanksgiving, and supplication. (Note the acronym ACTS that spells out the various kinds of prayer conversations.) Conversational prayer involves an *active* dimension of taking our concerns, worries, petitions, and the like to God. It also involves a *passive* dimension where we pause and allow God to speak to us.

Thomas Merton defined prayer as "the consciousness of one's union with God, an awareness of one's inner self." This definition makes sense when we consider Jesus' revelation that we are his brothers and sisters, children of a loving Abba. When we pray, we become aware of ourselves as children of a most gracious God who loves us beyond compare. In Christian prayer we enter into communion with the loving Triune God.

Prayer awakens us to God's marvelous activity in our lives. St. Teresa of Avila imaged prayer as a conscious turning to the invisible friend who walks with us always. Prayer indeed deepens our friendship with the Lord and strengthens us for our journey to God. As food is to the body, prayer is to the spirit of Jesus' friends.

What Do the Hebrew Scriptures Teach About Prayer? *[CCC 2568-2597]*

The scriptures tell us how God unceasingly calls us to a mysterious meeting with him in prayer. Salvation history reveals prayer as a reciprocal relationship between God and human beings. For example, the book of Genesis uses the image of "walking with God" to describe humanity's intimate prayer relationship with God. Simply by creating us in his image, God has called us to pray. Genesis also describes how the patriarchs exhibited essential qualities of prayer. For example, Abraham modeled heartfelt faith in God's word.

The book of Exodus recounts many examples of Moses engaged in dialogue with God after God took the initiative. In this dialogue, Moses learned to communicate with God as one would with a friend. These conversations prompted Moses to pray for his people, an example of intercessory prayer. His face-to-face encounters with Yahweh helped Moses teach the Chosen People that the Lord is a just, loving, faithful God.

The Hebrew scriptures also show how religious leaders like Samuel, David, and Elijah taught prayer to the Israelites and how the Temple in Jerusalem became their center of worship. David, Yahweh's beloved king, became a model for submission, praise, and repentance in prayer. Ascribed to him are the Spirit-inspired Psalms, the songs of faith that exhibit a wide range of human emotions and longings, all fulfilled in Jesus Christ. The Psalms remain a timeless, essential part of the church's prayer life, a model for the prayerful expression of deeply felt personal and communal needs.

How Does Jesus Model Prayer? *[CCC 2588-2606; 2620]*

Jesus' very life was a model of prayer. He learned prayer in his family, from his mother, Mary, and his foster-father, Joseph. As a youngster, he also learned the prayer of his people, a practice he carried into his adulthood. For example, Luke reports how Jesus prayed every Saturday in the synagogue. Scripture also reveals that Jesus celebrated the various religious festivals so important to Jewish worship. Jews of Jesus' time prayed in the morning when rising, at noon, and in the evening before retiring. They also recited prayers before and after eating meals.

Jesus was well-versed in the scriptures, reciting the psalms often. He also prayed before making decisions. For example, after his baptism, Jesus made a forty-day retreat before launching his public ministry. He prayed the whole night before selecting his apostles. He prayed over his impending death on the cross, submitting himself in humility to the Father's will, though he feared death (see Lk 22:42).

Jesus often withdrew alone to hills and mountains to pray, for example, after the miraculous feedings of the thousands and at the time of the transfiguration.

Jesus prayed in different ways, thus exemplifying how we should approach the Father. For example, he *praised* the Father for revealing the divine will to the humble and lowly (see Lk 10:21). He *thanked* God when he raised Lazarus from the dead:

"Father, I thank you for hearing my prayer" (Jn 11:41).

He also *petitioned* God. For example, he prayed that Peter would not fall into temptation. And in his great priestly prayer of *intercession* (Jn 17), Jesus prayed that all of those the Father entrusted to his care may remain in the truth. We can take great comfort knowing that Jesus prays for us.

A final example of Jesus at prayer is his final moments while he hung from the cross dying. He prayed for us sinners, and forgave those who put him to death. His final words were an act of self-abandonment to the Father:

"Father, *into your hands I commit my spirit*" (Lk 23:46).

Jesus' life and death reveal that prayer was vital for him, God's own Son. Praying kept Jesus' close to the Father and helped him live for us, his brothers and sisters. His example teaches us that we must cultivate a prayer-life so we can be close to God and learn to live for others.

How Does Jesus Teach Us to Pray? *[CCC 2607-2616; 2621]*

Jesus offers much wise advice on how to pray. First, he *calls us to conversion and reconciliation* with our sisters and brothers before we pray. A pure heart enables us to love our enemies, pray for our persecutors, and approach God with a loving spirit. Thus, we should *pray with forgiving hearts:*

"And when you stand in prayer, forgive whatever you have against anybody, so that your Father in heaven may forgive your failings too" (Mk 11:25).

Jesus also tells us to *pray to the Father in secret* and not heap up empty words the way hypocrites do. When we *keep our prayers short*, we display confidence in God's goodness and generosity.

We should also *pray with childlike simplicity* and *with faith* in God (cf. Mt 21:22). The Lord always hears our petitions, and will give us what is good for us.

"If you then, evil as you are, know how to give your children what is good, how much more will the heavenly Father give the Holy Spirit to those who ask him!" (Lk 11:13).

Jesus also teaches that we should *persist in prayer*, not giving up easily. Persistence is a sign of faith in Jesus' word (cf. Lk 11:5-8).

Another point Jesus makes is to *pray with others*, assuring us that when we gather in his name he is with us (Mt 18:19-20). At the Last Supper, he instructed us to "break bread" in his name, something we do in our celebration of the eucharist.

Jesus also teaches us to pray with humility (Lk 18:9-14), with attention to his presence and future coming (Lk 21:34-36), and with a sincere heart that is ready to do God's will in all (Mt 7:21). Further, Jesus tells us to pray in his name (Jn 14:13) with the Spirit of truth he and the Father give to us to guide and lead us. Christian prayer in the Lord's name is a communion of love with the Father both through and in Christ the Lord. Finally, when we pray to Jesus, he, the merciful one, hears our prayer and answers it. The famous *Jesus Prayer* is an excellent way to petition the Lord: "Lord Jesus Christ, Son of God, have mercy on me a sinner."

Finally, as covered on pages 326-331, Jesus teaches us the perfect prayer—the Lord's Prayer—in which he invites us to address God as our loving Father.

What Can We Learn About Prayer From Mary? *[CCC 2617-2619; 2622]*

Mary exhibited two qualities necessary for a good Christian prayer life: faith and humility. Faith, the virtue of trusting on the word of another, was at the heart of Mary's life. Not fully understanding why or how, Mary accepted in faith the invitation to become God's Mother:

> "You see before you the Lord's servant, let it happen to me as you have said" (Lk 1:38).

Her humble and trusting response to God's desire to work through her illustrates what we all owe our loving Creator. Her *Fiat* ("Let it happen") is Christian prayer at its best.

Mary's faith helped bring forth Jesus, the Word made flesh. But Mary was also humble. She knew that all that was happening in and through her took place through God's power.

> "For the almighty has done great things for me" (Lk 1:49).

Her Magnificat (see Lk 1:46-55) is the song of the Mother of God and of the church, expressing praise and humble gratitude to God who is the source of all blessings.

Mary's faith and humility teach us the proper dispositions for prayer. She also prayed often, an example for our own prayer life. She rushed off to visit her cousin Elizabeth and sang joyfully with her of God's great goodness. She went to the Temple for the key Jewish feasts. After Jesus' ascension into heaven, Mary helped the early Christian community in prayer. She remains the Mother of the church today.

> With one heart all these joined constantly in prayer, together with some women, including Mary the mother of Jesus, and with his brothers (Acts 1:14).

What Are the Basic Prayer Forms? *[CCC 2623-2649]*

The Catholic tradition has a rich variety of prayer. Prayers can be private. Or, prayers can be public like the liturgy. Prayers can use the words of others, like the traditional blessing before meals, or can be spontaneous words thanking God for his blessings. In addition, prayers can be vocal—said aloud—or silent, those whispered in the heart.

The Holy Spirit has instructed the church in various forms of prayer, inspiring different expressions through the ages. The basic types, also revealed in scripture, are as follows:

- *Blessing and adoration.* When we bless God we respond to God's gifts. We can bless God because God first blesses us. Adoration of God recognizes that God is the creator and we are the creatures. Adoration pays God homage as our sovereign Lord. Prayer of adoration is loving God for his own sake, simply because God is goodness itself and worthy of our love.

- *Petition.* Prayers of petition are prayers of supplication, prayers of asking. A prime prayer of petition is asking God for forgiveness. Prayer for forgiveness begins in humility and acknowledges God as a loving Abba who extends divine mercy to us through Jesus Christ.

Believing in the good news of God's love, we can indeed ask God to fulfill our needs. Jesus instructs us to approach God with the confidence of trusting children and to ask for what we need. The Lord also tells us to pray for the coming of God's reign and the gift of the Holy Spirit who gives us the strength to lead a Christian life.

- *Intercession.* Intercessory prayers are petitions for others. When we pray for others, we imitate the Lord Jesus who prayed for everyone at the Last Supper (Jn 17) and who continues to intercede for us until the end of time. Following Jesus' example, we should pray in a special way for the needy and even our enemies.

- *Thanksgiving.* We express gratitude to God for his many gifts: our beautiful world, our family and friends, our health and talents, the Lord Jesus and the gift of salvation he has won for us. A spirit of gratitude shows we do not take anything for granted. God deserves our thanks; without our loving God, we would not even exist.

  Give thanks to Yahweh for he is good, his faithful love lasts forever (Ps 107:1).

- *Praise.* Prayers of praise sing to and glorify God simply because God is God—gracious, loving, saving. When we praise God, the Holy Spirit joins our hearts and enables us to recognize our Lord and brother Jesus and to call God "Abba." True prayers of praise show no self-interest. They take joy in God alone: "Praise the Lord! Alleluia!"

Catholics recognize the uniqueness of the eucharist which exemplifies all forms of prayer. Through the eucharist, we bless, adore, and praise God. We thank the Lord for all the blessings we have. (Recall that *eucharist* means "thanksgiving.") We ask for forgiveness, the fulfillment of all our needs, and look to the needs of everyone—praying for and with them. And in holy communion, by the power of the Holy Spirit, the Lord comes to us in a special way, uniting us to God and our Christian brothers and sisters.

How Does the Holy Spirit Teach Us to Pray? *[CCC 2650-2662; 2744-2745]*

Through the centuries, the Holy Spirit has been the true teacher of prayer to the Christian community. The Spirit teaches through the living Tradition of the church, guiding us to various sources for nourishment in the spiritual life. These sources include the holy scriptures and the sacred liturgy.

Other sources of Christian prayer include the theological virtues of faith, hope, and love. Faith enables us to enter into prayer. The Holy Spirit teaches us to pray in hope, and by doing so our hope is nourished. Prayer attracts us to Christ's love and enables us to love him as he has loved us. Love, which is of God, is a prime source of prayer. These virtues help us realize that every moment and every event of every day is a prayer opportunity because the Holy Spirit is always present to us. Thus, we can and ought to meet God in the present, in the now of life. The Spirit who lives within teaches us that all of life is a prayer.

How Should We Pray? *[CCC 2663-2698; 2720; 2757]*

The church's rich tradition has given us many teachings on how to pray. A key teaching is that we should address our prayers primarily to the Father. However, we should also direct prayers to Jesus and frequently invoke his sacred name. Jesus, the Son of God, is the way to the Father. The church also tells us to invoke the Holy Spirit. And throughout the ages the church loves to pray in communion with the Blessed Mother because of her exemplary and singular cooperation with the Holy Spirit. The "Hail Mary" is a privileged prayer that praises God for his goodness manifested in Mary. It also commits to Mary, our Mother, our petitions and praises, trusting that she will also pray for us to her Son.

The church also reminds us that the Christian family is the key source for learning prayer. Parents and catechists help teach children how to pray. Other helpers in developing a mature prayer life include ordained ministers, those in consecrated life, prayer groups, and spiritual directors.

Through the ages, many saints and other Christian seekers have developed different spiritualities, different ways to pray. Behind them all, however, is the Holy Spirit who guides us in prayer to the Triune God. These spiritual traditions have many common features on how to get started in prayer, including the following:

- *Place.* We can pray anywhere, but it is good to find a special place where we can slow down, relax, and focus our attention. The outdoors or a special place in the house with a Bible and sacred images (family oratories) are appropriate places for prayer. The parish church in front of the Blessed Sacrament, a monastery, or a place of pilgrimage are other excellent places to pray.

- *Time.* Scripture tells us to pray always simply because prayer is a vital necessity for following Jesus. Prayer and the Christian life are inseparably linked. Thus the church commends that we pray daily, for example, morning and evening prayers, grace before and after meals, and the liturgy of the hours. It also tells us of our duty to worship on Sundays and holy days and commends that we incorporate the liturgical year into our prayer life.

Concerning daily prayer, it is a good idea to commit ourselves to a regular prayer time each day. The biggest excuse most Christians have for not praying is that they cannot find the time. However, we could all really spare ten or fifteen minutes each day to spend with the Lord, if we discipline ourselves to find a special time and stay with it. Prayer is a habit. We learn to pray by praying.

- *Relaxation.* Prayer demands our attention. If we are tired, distracted, or edgy, we cannot pray well. Masters of the spiritual life suggest that we assume a body position that keeps us alert but also helps us relax. Sitting in a chair with our backs in a straight line, lying on the floor, kneeling, sitting in the lotus position are all acceptable prayer positions.

We should also spend some time calming our bodies so our minds and spirits are free to commune with the Lord. Becoming aware of our various senses, rhythmic breathing, listening intently for the sounds around us, noticing the tensions in our body and consciously allowing them to fade away—all of these can help us get ready for prayer.

- *Proper attitude.* Prayer helps us grow in friendship with the Lord. God gives us the gift of wanting to pray, but we have to do our part and accept the gift. This requires discipline, humility, trust in God's presence, and perseverance. Prayer requires openness and devotion to God. It is always good to begin our prayer by recalling God's presence and friendship, and the many gifts God has bestowed on us.

What Are the Expressions of Prayer? *[CCC 2700-2719; 2721-2724]*

The three main expressions of prayer are vocal prayer, meditation, and mental prayer.

When we express our interior feelings in *vocal prayer* we are imitating the Lord himself who often prayed aloud and taught his disciples to do the same (for example, in the Our Father). In vocal prayer we often join our prayer with others, thus strengthening our spiritual relationship with our Christian brothers and sisters.

Meditation is a "tuning into God," thinking about his presence in the world or our life. It is an active form of prayer that involves our thoughts, imaginations, emotions, and desires. It seeks to know how the Lord reveals himself to us in our daily life. Its goal is to know and to love the Lord so we may serve him better.

The Catholic tradition has many spiritual traditions and masters that teach meditation (for example, St. Teresa of Avila and St. Ignatius of Loyola). They often recommend that we meditate on a scripture passage, especially from the gospels, the liturgical texts of the day or season, the spiritual writings of the saints and spiritual guides, an icon, or events in our own lives.

Mental prayer centers on the Lord, for example, on the mysteries of Christ's life. Mental prayer often leads to *contemplation*, the silent, wordless prayer of simply being in the presence of our all-loving God. In a story he told to explain contemplative prayer, St. John Vianney gave a peasant's description of how he spent his time sitting daily with Jesus before the tabernacle, "I look at him and he looks at me."

In contemplative prayer, we empty our minds of thoughts and images and simply allow the divine presence to penetrate our being. We do not have to do anything at all. We simply enjoy the Lord's company the way two lovers sit on a seashore speechless, enjoying a beautiful sunset. To be able to pray this way is a great gift from and to God.

How Should We Combat the Obstacles to Prayer? *[CCC 2725-2743; 2746-2756; 2758]*

Prayer can be difficult at times, a real battle involving human weaknesses and temptations. One of these temptations is the idea that prayer is simply a psychological exercise, rather than a gift of God's grace. Another is the secular attitude that glorifies human reason or sensuality, both of which see no purpose to the spiritual life. Yet another is the pragmatist's view that prayer has no practical value.

If we resist these attitudes and temptations and pray regularly, we still face the two main difficulties of distractions and dryness. Faith, conversion, and watchfulness help combat these difficulties. Vigilance is especially necessary so we do not weaken in our faith or fall into a type of spiritual depression because of a lax attitude toward prayer. We must also look to Jesus' example of praying to do God's will—summed up beautifully in Jesus' priestly prayer of unity in John 17. We must especially recommit ourselves to prayer when we feel that we are in a spiritual desert and God does not hear or answer us.

A further word about distractions, which is a typical problem faced by everyone who prays regularly. A wandering mind, reliving the day just past, an overactive imagination, attending to external noises—these can distract us when we pray. It is usually not a good idea to fight distractions head on.

Rather, gazing at an icon, crucifix, or lit candle can help us refocus. Or turning inwardly to the Holy Spirit and asking for his help during our time of prayer, or repeatedly reciting a particular prayer-word or phrase like "Jesus help me" or "Loving Abba"—these practices can help "distract us from the distractions" and bring us back to our special time with the Lord. We should always remember that the Lord values our attempts at prayer even if distractions bombard us or our prayer seems dry and empty. Wanting to pray is itself a prayer.

What Is the Special Value of the Lord's Prayer? *[CCC 2759-2776; 2799]*

Tertullian, a church father, called the Lord's Prayer "the summary of the whole gospel." The Our Father is the preeminent Christian prayer. It is prayed in liturgical celebrations, for example, the liturgy of the hours, the sacraments of initiation, and especially the eucharist. The Lord's Prayer is recited on special occasions, and whenever we gather to pray. It is central to a Christian's daily prayer.

The Lord's Prayer appears in the gospels of both Luke and Matthew. Luke's version of the Lord's Prayer has five petitions. In Luke's gospel, the apostles approach Jesus who is praying quietly. They ask him to teach them how to pray. Jesus then gives them the Lord's Prayer, a prayer that marks them as his special disciples, ones who can dare to address God as *Abba*, "daddy" or "Dear Father." This is the prayer that identifies Jesus' disciples as *Christians*.

Matthew's version, with seven petitions, is the one the church has adopted in its liturgical tradition. The conclusion we pray at Mass—"For the kingdom, the power and the glory are yours now and forever"—comes from the *Didache*, a first-century catechetical manual, and the *Apostolic Constitutions*. This doxology (a word that means "short hymn of praise") reiterates the first three petitions to our heavenly Father: the glorification of God's name, the coming of the kingdom, and the power of God's saving will.

Matthew's gospel sets Jesus' teaching of the Lord's Prayer in the Sermon on the Mount (Mt 5–7). There Jesus offers instruction on the Christian way of life, including how we should pray. Jesus tells us to pray humbly and not babble on. He teaches the Our Father as a short, but profound example of prayer which relies totally on God. We address this prayer to the Father as taught by Jesus and inspired by the Holy Spirit. Thus, it brings us into communion with the Father and the Son in the Holy Spirit.

What Is the Meaning of the Lord's Prayer? *[CCC 2777-2785; 2803-2806; 2857]*

The Lord's Prayer is the "Our Father." We know we can relate to God as Father because the Holy Spirit allows us to participate in the very personal relationship that the Son has with the Father. As prayed by the church, the Lord's Prayer consists of seven petitions. The first three glorify the Father—the sanctification of his name, the advent of the kingdom, and the fulfillment of his will. The last four take our needs to this loving Father: requesting the nourishment we need to live, the healing of our sins, and the victory in the battle of good over evil. Let us examine each element of this prayer.

Our Father [CCC 2786-2793; 2797-2798; 2800-2801]

Jesus invites us to call God *Abba*, to address the almighty God intimately, securely, and with childlike trust. Jesus teaches us that God is good, gracious, and absolutely loving.

Jesus' invitation to call God *Abba* infers two very important truths. First, God is a loving parent. Like little children, we should humbly trust our Abba to care for our needs.

Second, God is *our* Father. We are God's people, belonging to him. We are invoking the new covenant in Jesus Christ and our communion with the Blessed Trinity. "Our" affirms that we are brothers and sisters to one another; every person is intimately related to us. If we believe what Jesus teaches us by this prayer, we will commit ourselves to understand, love, and respond to *everyone* who comes into our lives.

Who art in heaven [CCC 2794-2796; 2802]

The biblical expression "in heaven" does not refer to a place but to God's way of being, his majesty. Christians affirm that through Jesus, God lives in the hearts of the just. When we invoke the Father, we profess that we are his people who are in union with Christ in heaven. At the same time, we await the day when our heavenly reward will be fully ours.

Hallowed be thy name. [CCC 2807-2815; 2858]

When we pray in Jesus' name for the "hallowing" of God's name, we enter into the Father's plan by praying that everyone on earth will regard him as holy (as he is in heaven). The Father is the source of all holiness, of all that is good, of all love. We make the Father's name holy when we believe in God's love and act on it by taking on the identity of our Savior, Jesus Christ. When we live up to the name *Christian*, others will come to know and praise the Father because they can see his image in us.

Thy kingdom come; thy will be done on earth as it is in heaven. [CCC 2816-2827; 2859- 2860]

With the coming of Jesus Christ, the Father's kingship (also, kingdom or reign)—firmly established in heaven—has broken into our world. Jesus has inaugurated this reign through his own ministry. He preached the gospel to the poor, brought liberty to captives, wholeness to the broken, and healing and salvation to everyone. Thus, God's kingdom is righteousness, peace, and joy in the Holy Spirit.

When we pray "thy kingdom come," we petition primarily for Christ's return, the final coming of God's kingdom. However, we are to live, experience, and work for God's kingdom right now, though it will not be fully established until the end of time. Then there will be full righteousness, peace, and joy.

The Father wills that his reign of peace, justice, truth, and service advance in our world. To pray for the coming of this kingdom means to join Jesus in his work: to feed the hungry and give drink to the thirsty, to welcome the stranger, to clothe the naked, to visit the sick and the imprisoned, to respond to the needs of all those who come into our lives, especially those Jesus called "the least of these."

Give us this day our daily bread. *[CCC 2828-2837; 2861]*

When we pray "give us," we show our trust in Abba. When we ask for bread, we are requesting what bread represents—our very life. Bread also suggests a meal and the companionship which comes with a meal. When we pray for bread we are praying for life's requirements: what we need for physical life (food, shelter, clothing), psychological life (friendship, love, companionship), and spiritual life (scripture, the teachings of the church, and the body of Christ received in holy communion).

When we pray for *our* bread, we ask for our needs plus the needs of all people. The Lord's Prayer challenges us to share with others, especially the less fortunate. It prods us to be both just and loving. The parable of the last judgment (Mt 25:31-46) and the parable of Lazarus and the rich man (Lk 16:19-31) teach us that God's children *must* share their material goods with the poor.

The word "daily," in the original Aramaic which Jesus spoke, may also have meant something similar to "for tomorrow, today." When we pray for our *daily* bread, we also pray for the fullness of God's material and spiritual blessings which will be ours in heaven. We dare to ask our Father to give us a taste of the heavenly feast of the coming kingdom in "God's today," an eternal reign that is anticipated in the eucharist.

And forgive us our trespasses as we forgive those who trespass against us. *[CCC 2838-2845; 2862]*

It is difficult both to forgive and to ask for forgiveness. When we ask God for forgiveness, we honestly admit that we are sinners who need God's saving love. We acknowledge that we need the Spirit who will enable us to repent of our selfishness and turn to a more loving life of service. We confess in humility that we need Jesus' help on our journey to the Father.

But we must also forgive others. Jesus connects God's forgiveness of us to our forgiveness of others. As the gospel of John teaches, it is impossible to love the God we cannot see if we cannot love the brother or sister we do see (1 Jn 4:20). Forgiveness turns us into other Christs. The Lord's Prayer calls us to forgive as we have been forgiven. When we forgive those who have hurt us, we are sharing love and understanding, thus encouraging others to respond to us in the same way. Forgiveness is the basic condition that reconciles God's children with the Father and each other.

And lead us not into temptation. *[CCC 2846-2849; 2863]*

This petition is asking God *not* to allow us to take the path that leads to sin. It also asks God to let us persevere to the end of our days, when we struggle with our final test: death.

To follow Jesus means to pick up his cross and to willingly endure suffering in his name. In this petition we pray that God will strengthen us to overcome any difficulties that might steer us away from Christ. This petition also calls us to fight the temptations of a godless society: consumerism, pornography, permissive abortion laws, materialism, and the like. Thus, through this petition we are praying for fortitude, watchfulness, perseverance, and a discerning heart that can distinguish between trials that strengthen us spiritually and temptations that lead to sin and death.

But deliver us from evil. Amen. *[CCC 2850-2856; 2864-2865]*

Finally, in solidarity with the communion of saints, we pray to God to manifest the victory Christ has already won over Satan, the evil one. As individuals and as a community, we ask the Father to deliver us from the snares of Satan and a sensuous, materialistic, and violent society that ignores God and tempts us to rely solely on ourselves. We pray that God may spare us from the evil of accidents, illness, and natural disasters. We pray that God will strengthen us to confront the evil for which we too share some blame—using others, injustice, prejudice. And we pray that no situation arises that might tempt us to deny our loving Creator. This would be the worst evil of all.

One final note: In praying this petition, we are praying with the Holy Spirit and the entire church for the coming of the Lord. His second coming will deliver all humanity forever from the snares of Satan.

When we end our prayer with "Amen," we are saying, "So be it." We are assenting to our "Lord's Prayer," thus making it our prayer, too.

Concluding Reflections

Think of your closest relationship. You know how vitally important this person is to you—and you to him or her. You cherish what the person says and who the person is. You like spending time together, laughing, talking, knowing each other more and more deeply. You give meaning to each other's lives.

Friends of the Lord Jesus cherish their friendship with him, too. They know that to deepen their friendship with him, they must make some time for him. Thus, prayer is vitally important in their lives. Prayer—like friendship—demands commitment and fidelity. It means that we take time out of our schedules to spend with the Lord. The question is: Do we want to grow in our relationship with the Lord?

Someone once said that if you are too busy for prayer, you are too busy. Are you too busy?

Prayer Reflection

The *Angelus* commemorates the Incarnation. Catholics traditionally recite it in the morning, at noon, and in the evening. It recalls the angel Gabriel's announcing to Mary that God chose her to be the mother of the Lord. It also gives Mary's humble acceptance. The *Angelus* also includes three Hail Marys and a closing prayer.

Angelus
The angel of the Lord declared unto Mary.
R: And she conceived by the Holy Spirit.
Hail Mary. . . .
Behold the handmaid of the Lord.
R: May it be done unto me according to your word.
Hail Mary. . . .
And the Word was made flesh.
R: And dwelled among us.
Hail Mary. . . .
Pray for us, O holy mother of God.
R: That we may be made worthy of the promises of Christ.
Let us pray: We beseech you, O Lord, to pour out your grace into our hearts. By the message of an angel we have learned of the incarnation of Christ, your Son; lead us, by his passion and cross, to the glory of the resurrection. Through the same Christ our Lord. Amen.

For Discussion

1. What is the most meaningful way for you to pray?
2. Based on your own personal experience of prayer, what advice would you give to an adolescent on how and why to pray?
3. "Prayer can change the world." Discuss.

Further Reading

Using the steps for praying with scripture from Chapter 3 (pp. 57-58), meditate on the death of Jesus by reading Luke 23. Put yourself in the scene beneath the cross and look at Jesus looking at you.

Appendix

Additional Information

Being Catholic: A Summary

Listed below are some of the identifying marks of Catholicism:

A Catholic is a Christian who belongs to a certain faith community (the church) that shares Jesus' vision and responds to his presence in our midst. A Catholic loves each member of this community and uses his or her unique talents to contribute to it in a positive way.

A Catholic believes in God the Father. This loving Father has made us brothers and sisters to everyone who has ever lived. Moreover, he has sent us his Son Jesus Christ who won for us our salvation and gave us eternal life.

A Catholic believes in the presence of the Holy Spirit, accepting and using the many gifts he showers on us. By the power of this Holy Spirit, a Catholic accepts Jesus into his or her life.

A Catholic attempts to live in harmony with Jesus' teaching: loving God above all things; loving neighbor as oneself; forgiving enemies; extending special care to the poor, the lonely, and the outcast.

A Catholic prays and lives a sacramental life, for example, by recognizing a need for forgiveness through the celebration of the sacrament of reconciliation. Moreover, a Catholic cherishes the eucharist as a special sign of God's nourishing love, a way to encounter the living Lord Jesus. A Catholic participates fully in the eucharistic celebration every week.

A Catholic reveres and reads the Bible, the word of God.

A Catholic acknowledges the role of proper authority in the church, for example, by seeking direction for moral decisions from the church's official teachers, the pope and the bishops in communion with him.

A Catholic serves others and shares his or her faith in publicly acknowledging Jesus Christ and his church. He or she is willing to stand up to ridicule and suffering in the name of the gospel truth.

A Catholic is open to all people and to truth wherever it is found.

A Catholic is passionately committed to life.

A Catholic is all of the items on this list and more. You might try to summarize in your own words what it means to be a Catholic. More than likely you will add some traits that are a special part of your own faith practices.

Organization in the Church

The church is organized to carry on a worldwide mission of preaching Jesus' message and serving the needs of individual people. Its structure can be viewed from the vantage point of the local, national, and international levels.

Local: The Parish and the Diocese

In truth the smallest church unit is the Christian family. But the family needs the support of a community to live out its Christian vocation. So most Catholics experience Christian community in the local *parish* which usually embraces all Catholics living in a given geographical area. The bishop appoints a *pastor* to serve the pastoral needs of the people and to supervise the temporal affairs of the parish plant in cooperation with God's people. The pastor, the symbol of unity in the parish, often serves with a pastoral team which coordinates the efforts of the many organizations within a parish.

In between the parish and the diocese is a *deanery* which consists of a group of parishes located in a certain geographical region. These pastors of these parishes work with the bishop on a regional basis.

The *bishop* is the chief shepherd of a *diocese*, which is typically associated with a geographical area. He presides from the *cathedral*, the bishop's church. He is aided in his work by priests, and his chief consulting body is a *priests' council*. The bishops' staff works out of the *chancery* which includes organizations like Catholic Charities, the Office of Education, Liturgy Commission, Family Life Bureau and the like.

National: NCCB and USCC

The *National Conference of Catholic Bishops (NCCB)* is made up of all the bishops in the United States. This conference meets at least once a year to discuss and set policy on issues related to the liturgy and church ministry as well as issues of social concern. In recent years the American bishops have issued important pastoral letters on peace and the economy.

The *United States Catholic Conference (USCC)* handles the public, educational and social concerns of the church. With its offices in Washington, this organization of the bishops carries on many of the administrative functions of church programs on both the national and international levels.

International: The Pope, Curia, Synods, Ecumenical Councils

The *pope* is the chief shepherd, teacher and law-maker of Roman Catholicism. His headquarters and administrative offices are in the Vatican, an independent city within Rome's city limits.

The pope is assisted in the day-to-day operation of the church by the *curia*, the bureaucracy which runs the church. Cardinals (an honorific title given to some bishops with the right to elect the pope) and bishops head various congregations and other agencies. Some examples are the Congregations for the Clergy and Laity, the Secretariat for Christian Unity, and the Commission on Justice and Peace.

The *synod of bishops* is a representative body of bishops assembled periodically by the pope to advise him on important church concerns. It is not a legislative body.

The most important teaching body and law-making assembly in the church is the ecumenical council. There have been 21 such councils in the history of the church. An ecumenical council is made up of the pope and all the bishops of the world. Vatican II was the last ecumenical council to meet (1962-1965); it took up major issues in the area of doctrine, church life, and the church's relationship to the world.

Religious Vocations

In general, *vocation* means "calling," an invitation by the Lord to a special kind of service. One can be called to serve God as a married person, in the single life, as a priest, or in religious life.

Down through the centuries certain Christian men and women have consecrated themselves to God and the work of his kingdom by taking vows of poverty, chastity and obedience. These Christians ordinarily live a common life in a religious community which typically was founded to engage in a specific work (ministry) to help build up God's kingdom.

By taking the vow of poverty, those living the religious life are attempting to free themselves of the things of this world so that they can be attached to the One who is really important, Jesus Christ. By vowing chastity for the sake of the gospel, religious become a sign to the world that they belong simultaneously to Christ and to all people. Through the vow of obedience, religious commit themselves to serve their community, which in turn is dedicated to serving the Christian community. All three vows are positive ways to liberate those living them to a more active life of prayer and service in God's church.

Sisters (or nuns) are women who take the three vows and belong to a community dedicated to some specific ministry like social work, care of the sick, religious education, or parish ministry. Religious orders of brothers also live a communal, vowed life in working for the kingdom. There are also priests who belong to a particular religious community. These ordained religious typically undertake the specific work of their community, for example, teaching, missionary work, or preaching.

Some Traditional Prayers

Sign of the Cross

In the name of the Father,
and of the Son,
and of the Holy Spirit. Amen.

Our Father

Our Father
who art in heaven,
hallowed be thy name.
Thy kingdom come;
thy will be done be done on earth as it is in heaven.
Give us this day our daily bread
and forgive us our trespasses
as we forgive those who trespass against us.
And lead us not into temptation,
but deliver us from evil.
For the kingdom, the power and the glory are yours
now and forever. Amen.

Glory Be

Glory be to the Father
and to the Son
and to the Holy Spirit,
as it was in the beginning,
is now,
and ever shall be,
world without end. Amen.

Hail Mary

Hail Mary, full of grace,
the Lord is with thee.
Blessed art thou among women
and blessed is the fruit of thy womb, Jesus.
Holy Mary, mother of God,
pray for us sinners now
and at the hour of our death. Amen.

Memorare

Remember, O most gracious Virgin Mary,
that never was it known
that anyone who fled to your protection,
implored your help,
or sought your intercession was left unaided.
Inspired by this confidence,
I fly unto you,
O Virgin of virgins, my mother,
To you I come, before you I stand,
sinful and sorrowful.
O Mother of the Word incarnate,
despise not my petitions,
but in your mercy hear and answer me. Amen.

Hail, Holy Queen

Hail, holy Queen, Mother of Mercy,
our life, our sweetness and our hope!
To you do we cry,
poor banished children of Eve;
to you do we send up our sighs,
mourning and weeping in this valley of tears.
Turn then, O most gracious advocate,
your eyes of mercy toward us,
and after this exile,
show us the blessed fruit of your womb, Jesus.
O clement, O loving, O sweet Virgin Mary.
V. Pray for us, O holy mother of God,
R. that we may be made worthy of the promises of Christ.
Amen.

Morning Offering

O Jesus, through the immaculate heart of Mary, I offer you my prayers, works, joys and sufferings of this day in union with the holy sacrifice of the Mass throughout the world. I offer them for all the intentions of your Sacred Heart: the salvation of souls, reparation for sin, the reunion of all Christians. I offer them for the intentions of our bishops and all members of the apostleship of prayer and in particular for those recommended by our Holy Father this month. Amen.

Apostles' Creed

I believe in God, the Father almighty,
Creator of heaven and earth.

I believe in Jesus Christ, his only Son, our Lord.
He was conceived by the power of the Holy Spirit,
and born of the Virgin Mary.
He suffered under Pontius Pilate,
was crucified, died, and was buried.
He descended to the dead.
On the third day he rose again.
He ascended into heaven,
and is seated at the right hand of the Father.
He will come again to judge the living and the dead.

I believe in the Holy Spirit,
the holy catholic Church,
the communion of saints,
the forgiveness of sins,
the resurrection of the body,·
and life everlasting. Amen.

Act of Faith

O my God, I firmly believe that you are one God in three divine Persons, Father, Son and Holy Spirit. I believe that your divine Son became man and died for our sins, and that he will come to judge the living and the dead. I believe these and all the truths which the holy Catholic church teaches, because you have revealed them, who can neither deceive nor be deceived. Amen.

Act of Hope

O my God, relying on your infinite goodness and promises, I hope to obtain pardon of my sins, the help of your grace, and life everlasting, through the merits of Jesus Christ, my Lord and Redeemer. Amen.

Act of Love

O my God, I love you above all things, with my whole heart and soul, because you are all good and worthy of all my love. I love my neighbor as myself for the love of you. I forgive all who have injured me, and I ask pardon of all whom I have injured. Amen.

Act of Contrition

O my God, I am sorry for my sins with all my heart. In choosing to do wrong and failing to do good, I have sinned against you whom I should love above all things. I firmly intend, with your help, to do penance, to sin no more, and to avoid whatever leads me to sin. Our Savior Jesus Christ suffered and died for us. In his name, my God, have mercy. Amen.

Angelus

The angel of the Lord declared unto Mary.
R: And she conceived by the Holy Spirit.
Hail Mary . . .
Behold the handmaid of the Lord.
R: May it be done unto me according to your word.
Hail Mary . . .
And the Word was made flesh.
R: And dwelled among us.
Hail Mary . . .
Pray for us, O holy mother of God.
R: That we may be made worthy of the promises of Christ.
Let us pray: We beseec you, O Lord, to pour out your grace into our hearts. By the message of an angel we have learned of the incarnation of Christ, your Son; lead us, by his passion and cross, to the glory of the resurrection. Through the same Christ our Lord. Amen.

Grace at Meals

Before Meals
Bless us, O Lord,
and these your gifts,
which we are about to receive from your bounty,
through Christ our Lord. Amen.

After Meals
We give you thanks, almighty God,
for these and all the gifts
which we have received
from your goodness
through Christ our Lord. Amen.

Prayer to Our Guardian Angel

Angel of God, my guardian dear, to whom God's love entrusts me here, ever this day (night) be at my side, to light and guard, to rule and guide. Amen.

Prayer for the Faithful Departed

Eternal rest grant unto them, O Lord.
R: And let perpetual light shine upon them.
May their souls and the souls of all the faithful departed,
through the mercy of God, rest in peace.
R: Amen.

The Jesus Prayer

Lord Jesus Christ, Son of God, have mercy on me, a sinner.

The Divine Praises

(These praises are traditionally recited after the benediction of
the Blessed Sacrament.)
Blessed be God.
Blessed be his holy name.
Blessed be Jesus Christ, true God and true man.
Blessed be the name of Jesus.
Blessed be his most Sacred Heart.
Blessed be his most Precious Blood.
Blessed be Jesus in the most holy sacrament of the altar.
Blessed be the Holy Spirit, the Paraclete.
Blessed be the great mother of God, Mary most holy.
Blessed be her holy and Immaculate Conception.
Blessed be her glorious Assumption.
Blessed be the name of Mary, Virgin and Mother.
Blessed be St. Joseph, her most chaste spouse.
Blessed be God in his angels and in his saints.

Prayer for Peace (attributed to St. Francis of Assisi)

Lord, make me an instrument of your peace.
Where there is hatred, let me sow love;
where there is injury, pardon;
where there is doubt, faith;
where there is despair, hope;
where there is darkness, light;
where there is sadness, joy.
O Divine Master,
grant that I may not seek so much to be consoled as to console;
to be understood, as to understand,
to be loved, as to love.
For it is in giving that we receive,
it is in pardoning that we are pardoned,
and it is in dying that we are born to eternal life.

Stations of the Cross

The stations of the cross are a type of meditative prayer based on the passion of Jesus. This devotion grew out of the custom of Holy Land pilgrims who retraced the last steps of Jesus on his way to Calvary. Most Catholic churches have the stations depicted on the side walls to help us imagine the sufferings of Jesus and focus on the meaning of the Paschal Mystery.

Traditionally there have been fourteen stations, ending with the laying of Jesus in the sepulcher. In recent years a fifteenth—depicting the resurrection—is added to show the glorious conclusion to Jesus' sacrifice for us.

We pray the stations either as a group or individually by meditating on the following scenes:
1. Jesus is condemned to death
2. Jesus takes up his cross
3. Jesus falls for the first time
4. Jesus meets his mother
5. Simon of Cyrene helps Jesus carry his cross
6. Veronica wipes the face of Jesus
7. Jesus falls for the second time
8. Jesus consoles the women of Jerusalem
9. Jesus falls the third time
10. Jesus is stripped of his garments
11. Jesus is nailed to the cross
12. Jesus dies on the cross
13. Jesus is taken down from the cross
14. Jesus is laid in the tomb
15. The resurrection of the Lord

Selective Glossary of Terms

Abba —A term of endearment from the Aramaic language meaning "daddy." Jesus used this word to teach that God is a loving Father.

Abortion—The deliberate killing of unborn human life by means of medical or surgical procedures. Direct abortion is seriously wrong because it is an unjustified attack on innocent human life.

Absolution—The statement by which a priest, speaking as the official minister of Christ's church, declares forgiveness of sins to a repentant sinner in the sacrament of reconciliation. The formula of absolution reads: "I absolve you from your sins; in the name of the Father, and of the Son, and of the Holy Spirit. Amen."

Agnostic—Someone who claims that we cannot be certain if there is a God or not.

Angels—Spiritual beings, created by God, that are superior in knowledge to humans. The word *angel* means "messenger."

Annulment—An official church declaration that what appeared to be a Christian marriage never existed in the first place.

Anointing of the sick—A sacrament of healing in which the Lord extends his loving, healing touch through the Christian community to those who are seriously ill or dying.

Apostasy—A total denial of Christ and a repudiation of the Christian faith.

Apostle—One who is sent by Jesus to continue his work.

Assumption—The official church dogma that the body of the Blessed Mother was taken directly to heaven when her life on earth ended.

Atheist—Someone who, for various reasons, denies the existence of God.

Baptism—The first sacrament of initiation that makes a person a child of God and an heir to God's promises of eternal salvation.

Beatific vision—Seeing God "face-to-face" in heaven; the final union with God in eternity.

Bible—The inspired word of God; the written record of revelation.

Bishop—A successor to the apostles who pastors and governs the local church in a given territory and pastors and governs the worldwide church in union with the pope.

Blasphemy—An insult or contempt of God or of holy persons and things.

Canon (of the Bible)—The official list of the inspired books of the Bible. Catholics list forty-six Old Testament books and twenty-seven New Testament books in the canon.

Canon Law—The code of church laws that governs the life of the Catholic community.

Canon of the Mass—The eucharistic prayer which includes the words of consecration. It is the central prayer of the liturgy of the eucharist. There are several canons in today's eucharistic rite.

Canonization—The process whereby the pope ultimately declares that a martyr and/or a person who lived a heroic Christian life of virtue is now in heaven and worthy of honor and imitation by Christians and Catholics.

Capital sins—Moral vices that give rise to many other failures to love. They are: pride, avarice, lust, anger, gluttony, envy, and sloth.

Cardinal virtues—The four hinge virtues from which moral living springs. They are: *prudence*, or moral common sense concerning the best way to live morally; *justice*, or giving each person his/her due by right; *fortitude*, or courage to persist in living a Christian life; and *temperance*, or moderation in controlling our desires for physical pleasures.

Catechesis—The process of religious instruction and formation in the major elements of the Christian faith.

Catechumen—A person who is studying the main elements of the Christian faith in preparation for the sacraments of initiation.

Catholic—A Greek word that means "universal." The term *Catholic church* refers to the Christian community that is open to all people everywhere and in all ages and which preaches the fullness of God's revelation in Jesus Christ.

Celibacy—The state of being unmarried and abstaining from sexual relations that priests and other religious choose in order to dedicate their lives totally to the Lord and the people of God.

Charism—A gift of the Holy Spirit that enables the recipient to do good works in the building up of Christ's body. Examples include wisdom, prophecy, zeal in witnessing to Christ, discernment of spirits, and exemplary loving service of others.

Charity—Love of God above all things and love of neighbor as oneself; the greatest of the three theological virtues.

Chastity—The virtue that enables us to act morally in sexual matters according to our station in life.

Christ—Greek translation of the Hebrew word *messiah*; a significant title of Jesus meaning "the anointed one."

Church—For Christians, the community of God's people who profess faith in the risen Lord Jesus and live lives of loving service under the guidance of the Holy Spirit.

Common good—Those spiritual, material, and social conditions needed for a person to achieve full human dignity.

Communion of saints—The entire community of Christians—those on earth, in purgatory, and in heaven.

Confirmation—A sacrament of initiation that seals the recipient with the Holy Spirit and bestows gifts that enable the confirmed Christian to live courageously for Jesus Christ.

Conscience—The practical judgment that helps a person decide the goodness or sinfulness of an action or attitude. It is the subjective norm of morality which we must form properly and then follow.

Contrition—Heartfelt sorrow and aversion for sins committed, along with the intention of sinning no more.

Corporal works of mercy—Charitable works Jesus taught (see Mt 25:35-40) as ways to respond to him through others. They include: feeding the hungry, giving drink to the thirsty, clothing the naked, visiting the imprisoned, sheltering the homeless, visiting the sick, and burying the dead.

Covenant—The open-ended contract of love God made with the Israelites and with all people everywhere in the person of Jesus Christ.

Creed—A formal statement of faith. Catholics recite the Nicene Creed at Mass each Sunday. The Apostles' Creed is another summary of Christian faith.

Deacon—An ordained minister who assists a bishop or priest.

Disciple—A follower of Jesus. Christians are disciples who try to model their lives on Jesus Christ.

Divine providence—See *Providence*

Divine revelation—See *Revelation*

Divorce—The legal dissolution of a marriage. Based on the teaching of Jesus, the church cannot dissolve valid Christian marriages which are lifelong covenants of love. Nor can the church remarry a divorced person who has previously entered a valid Christian marriage while the first spouse is still living.

Dogma—A church doctrine (teaching) issued with the highest authority and solemnity; a core teaching of the church.

Ecumenical council—A worldwide, official assembly of the bishops under the direction of the pope. There have been twenty-one ecumenical councils, the last being the Second Vatican Council (1962-1965).

Ecumenism—The movement that seeks Christian unity and eventually the unity of all peoples throughout the world.

Encyclical—A papal letter written on some important issue and circulated throughout the worldwide church. Encyclicals are often addressed not only to Catholics but also to all Christians and people of good will throughout the world.

Eschatology— Teaching about the last things—death, judgment, heaven, hell, purgatory, the Parousia, and the resurrection of the body.

Eucharist—A sacrament of initiation that makes one a full member of Christ's body. The word is derived from the Greek word for "thanksgiving." Other names for this sacrament are the Mass and the Lord's Supper. The eucharist is the summit of Christian worship which celebrates and creates Christian unity.

Evangelist—A person who proclaims the good news of Jesus Christ. "The four evangelists" refers to the authors of the four gospels: Matthew, Mark, Luke, and John.

Extreme unction—Latin for the "last anointing," this was the common name for the sacrament of the anointing of the sick until relatively recent times.

Faith—One of the three theological virtues. Faith refers to (1) personal knowledge of God; (2) assent of the mind to truths God has revealed, made with the help of his grace and on the authority and trustworthiness of his revealing them; (3) the truths themselves (the content of faith); and (4) the lived witness of a Christian life (living faith).

Fathers of the Church—An honorary title given to outstanding early Christian theologians whose teaching has had lasting significance for the church.

Fruits of the Holy Spirit—Spiritual fruits given by the Holy Spirit. They are: love, joy, peace, patience, kindness, goodness, generosity, gentleness, faithfulness, modesty, self-control, and chastity (see Gal 5:22-23).

General judgment—The event that will take place at the end of time when Jesus comes to fully establish the kingdom of God, bring final victory over evil, and judge the living and the dead.

Gifts of the Holy Spirit—God-given abilities that help us live a Christian life with God's help. Jesus promised these gifts and bestows them through the Holy Spirit, especially in the sacrament of confirmation. The seven gifts are wisdom, understanding, knowledge, counsel (right judgment), fortitude (courage), piety (reverence), and fear of the Lord (wonder and awe).

Gospel—Literally, "good news." Gospel refers to (1) the good news preached by Jesus; (2) the good news of salvation won for us in the person of Jesus Christ (he is the good news proclaimed by the church); (3) the four written records of the good news—the gospels of Matthew, Mark, Luke, and John.

Grace—The free gift of God's life and friendship.

Heaven—Perfect life with the Blessed Trinity and the communion of saints for all eternity; the state of supreme, definitive happiness that will fill all human desires.

Hell—Eternal separation from God brought on by a person who dies with unrepented mortal sin on his or her soul. Hell results from a free choice to turn away from God.

Heresy—A false teaching that denies an essential (dogmatic) teaching of the church.

Hierarchy— The sacred leadership in the church. The hierarchy is made up of the body of ordained ministers in the church: pope, bishops, priests, and deacons. The pope is the symbol of unity in the church and the successor to St. Peter.

Holy orders—A sacrament of vocation whereby Christ, through the church, ordains men to serve as deacons, priests, or bishops.

Hope—One of the three theological virtues. Hope enables us to firmly trust in God's salvation and to be sure that God will bless us with the necessary gifts to attain it.

Idolatry—Worship of anyone or anything other than the true, living God. To put anything before God is a violation of the first commandment.

Immaculate Conception—The church dogma that teaches that the Blessed Mother was free from sin from the very first moment of her human existence. (This dogma is sometimes confused with the doctrine of the *virginal conception* which holds that Jesus was conceived of the Virgin Mary by the power of the Holy Spirit without the cooperation of a human father.)

Immanent Trinity—see *Trinity*

Incarnation—A key theological term for the dogma of the Son of God becoming man in Jesus Christ, born of the Virgin Mary. (The term literally means "taking on human flesh.")

Infallibility—The gift (or charism) given to the church by Christ whereby it is protected from error in matters of faith and morals. This gift is most exclusively exercised by a pope or by an ecumenical council of bishops teaching in union with him.

Inspiration—The guidance of the Holy Spirit given to human authors in the writing of the sacred scriptures.

Kerygma—The core or essential message of the gospel—Jesus Christ is Lord! An excellent example of the kerygma is found in Acts 2:14-36.

Kingdom of God—see *Reign of God*

Law—A reasonable norm of conduct given by proper authority for the common good. In the Hebrew scriptures the Law is summarized in the Ten Commandments. Jesus taught the law of love of God and neighbor.

Liturgy—The official public worship of the church. The seven sacraments, especially the eucharist, are the primary forms of liturgical celebrations.

Liturgy of the hours—The official daily prayer of the church; it is a set of prayers for certain times of the day. It is also called the divine office.

Magisterium—The official teaching authority of the church. The Lord bestowed the right and power to teach in his name on Peter and the apostles and their successors, that is, the bishops and the pope as their leader.

Matrimony—A sacrament of vocation in which Christ binds a man and woman into a permanent covenant of love and life and bestows his graces on them to help them live as a community.

Meditation—A prayer form that uses the mind and heart to help us hear the word of the Lord.

Miracles—Mighty works, wonders, and signs that revealed the presence of God's kingdom in the person of Jesus, thus proving that he was indeed the Messiah, Son of God.

Mortal Sin—Personal sin that involves serious matter, sufficient reflection, and full consent of the will. It results in total rejection of God and alienation from him.

Mystery—A reality filled with God's invisible presence. The term is often applied to the church and to the sacraments.

Natural law—God's plan written into the way he made things. Human intelligence and reflection can aid us in discovering the natural law and living a life in harmony with it.

Original sin—The state or condition of sin into which all generations of people are born since the time of Adam's turning away from God.

Parousia—The second coming of Christ, which will usher in the full establishment of God's reign on earth as it is in heaven.

Particular judgment—God's judgment on us immediately after death on whether we go to purgatory, heaven, or hell.

Paschal Mystery—God's love and salvation revealed to us through the life, passion, death, and resurrection and glorification of his Son Jesus Christ. The sacraments celebrate the Paschal Mystery and enable us to live it in our own lives.

Passions—Feelings that incite us to act in a good or bad way.

Personal sin—A personal failure to love God above everything and our neighbor as ourselves.

Prayer—Conversation with God. Joining one's thoughts and love to God in adoration and blessing, petition, intercession, thanksgiving, and praise.

Priest—A mediator between God and people. Though all baptized Christians share in Jesus' priestly ministry, the Catholic church celebrates the sacrament of Holy Orders which ordains certain men to the office of priesthood.

Providence—God's actual interest in guiding creation to perfection.

Purgatory—Purification after death for those who die in God's friendship, yet still need to be purified to attain holiness before entering heaven.

Reconciliation—A sacrament of healing, also known as penance or confession, through which Christ extends his forgiveness to sinners.

Reign of God—The reign of God (also called kingdom of God) proclaimed by Jesus and inaugurated in his life, death, and resurrection. It refers to the process of God reconciling and renewing all things through his Son, to the fact of his will being done on earth as it is in heaven. The process has begun with Jesus and will be perfectly completed at the end of time.

Repentance—From the Greek word *metanoia*, it means change of mind or change of heart. A key aspect of following Jesus is to turn from our sins and embrace the way of the cross.

Resurrection—God's gift of eternal life given to humans who will receive a glorified body in union with Jesus Christ at the end of time. Through Jesus' death and resurrection all people have been saved.

Revelation—God's free self-communication to us through creation, historical events, prophets, and most fully in the Son Jesus Christ.

Sacrament—A visible sign of an invisible grace. An efficacious symbol. Traditionally sacrament is defined as an outward sign instituted by Christ to confer grace. The seven sacraments are baptism, confirmation, eucharist, reconciliation, anointing of the sick, matrimony, and holy orders.

Sacramental character—A lasting effect which the sacraments of baptism, confirmation, and holy orders bestow on their recipients. Baptism marks us as a child of God; confirmation seals us as a witness for Jesus Christ; holy orders permanently designates a man as a deacon, priest, or bishop—a special minister for God's people. As a result, these sacraments may be conferred only once.

Sacramentals—Sacred signs that resemble the sacraments and prepare a person to receive them.

Salvation—The process of healing whereby God's forgiveness, grace, and loving attention are extended to us through Jesus Christ in the Holy Spirit. Salvation brings about union with God and with our fellow humans through the work of our brother, Lord, and savior, Jesus Christ.

Salvation history—The story of God's saving action in human history.

Salvific Trinity—see *Trinity.*

Schism—A break in Christian unity that takes place when a group of Christians separates itself from the body of Christ. This happens historically when the group breaks its union with the pope, for example, when the Eastern Orthodox church broke with the Roman Catholic church in 1054.

Social justice —The church teaching that deals with the obligations of individuals and groups to apply the gospel to the systems, structures, and institutions of society.

Spiritual works of mercy—Good actions that apply gospel love to those in need. They include: counseling the doubtful, instructing the ignorant, admonishing sinners, comforting the afflicted, forgiving injuries, bearing wrongs patiently, and praying for the living and the dead.

Subsidiarity—The principle of Catholic social teaching that holds that a higher unit of society should not do what a lower unit can do as well (or better).

Tabernacle—The holy receptacle in which the Blessed Sacrament is reserved.

Theological virtues—Three key virtues bestowed on us at baptism which relate us to God. They are: *faith*, or belief in and personal knowledge of God; *hope*, or trust in God's salvation and God's bestowal of the graces needed to attain it; and *charity*, or love of God, love of neighbor, and love of self.

Tradition—The process of handing on the faith as well as that which has been handed on. Tradition can be found in the scriptures, church doctrine, writings of the church fathers, the liturgy of the church, and the living and lived faith of the church through the centuries.

Transubstantiation—The official Catholic church teaching that the substance of the bread and wine is changed into the substance of the body and blood of Jesus Christ at the consecration of the Mass.

Trinity—The Christian dogma that holds that there are three persons in one God: Father, Son, and Holy Spirit. *Immanent Trinity* refers to the inner life of the Trinity, the relations of the three divine persons to another. *Salvific Trinity* refers to the active work of the Triune God in salvation history: the Father as Creator, the Son as Redeemer, the Holy Spirit as Sanctifier.

Venial sin—Personal sin that weakens but does not kill our relationship with God.

Vice—A bad habit or disposition (like lust) that turns us from good to embrace evil.

Virgin birth—The doctrine that holds that Jesus was conceived through the Virgin Mary by the power of the Holy Spirit without the cooperation of a human father.

Virtue—A good habit that enables us to live moral lives; a virtue (e.g., faith hope, and charity) is the Spirit-given ability to live the Christian life joyfully and courageously.

Yahweh—The sacred Hebrew name for God. It means "I am who am" or "I cause to happen." Because the name was too holy to say aloud, the word *Lord* (*Adonai* in the Hebrew) was substituted whenever the sacred Hebrew texts were read aloud.

Index

Notes

Introduction

1. *The Way of a Pilgrim*, trans. Helen Bacovin (Garden City, New York: Doubleday, 1978), p. 13.

Chapter 2

1. Rudolph Otto, *The Idea of the Holy* (New York: Oxford University Press, 1928), p. 71.
2. St. Francis de Sales, *Introduction to the Devout Life*, trans. and ed. John K. Ryan (Garden City, NY: Image Books, 1972), pp. 106-107.

Chapter 9

1. Adapted from Brian Cavanaugh, T.O.R., *Fresh Packet of Sower's Seeds: Third Planting* (New York: Paulist Press, 1994), pp. 78-79.

Chapter 13

1. F.H. Drinkwater in Tony Castle, *"Quotations for All Occasions"* (London: Marshall Pickering, 1989), p. 12.

Chapter 14

1. Quoted in Ronda DeSola Chervin, *Quotable Saints* (Ann Arbor, MI: Servant Publications, 1992), p. 79.
2. Ibid, p. 80.
3. Quoted in Jill Haak Adels, *The Wisdom of the Saints* (New York: Oxford University Press, 1987), p. 81.

Chapter 15

1. From the *Rite of Penance*, International Committee on English in the Liturgy, Inc., 1974.
2. From *Pastoral Care of the Sick: Rites of Anointing and Viaticum*, International Committee on English in the Liturgy, Inc., 1982.

Chapter 17

1. Anthony De Mello, *One Minute Wisdom* (Garden City, New York: Doubleday & Company, Inc., 1986), p. 4.

Chapter 18

1. Adapted from Charles Arcodia, *Stories for Sharing* (Newtown, NSW, Australia: E.J. Dwyer, 1992), p. 7.
2. Quoted in Ronda DeSola Chervin, *Quotable Saints* (Ann Arbor, MI: Servant Publications, 1992), p. 120.

Chapter 22

1. Adapted from Charles Arcodia, *Stories for Sharing* (Newtown, NSW, Australia: E. J. Dwyer, 1991), p. 71.

ABOUT THE AUTHOR

Michael Francis Pennock is a theology teacher at St. Ignatius High School in Cleveland. He is the author of several books for teenagers and adults, including the *Friendship in the Lord* series and *What We Really Want to Know*. He and his wife, Carol, have four children, Scott, Jennifer, Amy, and Christopher. They live in North Olmsted, Ohio.